S0-BRQ-912

EFFECTIVE SUCCESSION PLANNING

ENSURING LEADERSHIP CONTINUITY AND BUILDING TALENT FROM WITHIN

WILLIAM J. ROTHWELL

American Management Association

New York • Atlanta • Boston • Chicago • Kansas City • San Francisco • Washington, D.C.
Brussels • Mexico City • Tokyo • Toronto

This book is available at a special
discount when ordered in bulk quantities.
For information, contact Special Sales Department,
AMACOM, a division of American Management Association,
135 West 50th Street, New York, NY 10020.

This publication is designed to provide accurate and authoritative information in regard to the subject matter covered. It is sold with the understanding that the publisher is not engaged in rendering legal, accounting, or other professional service. If legal advice or other expert assistance is required, the services of a competent professional person should be sought.

Library of Congress Cataloging-in-Publication Data

Rothwell, William J., 1951–
    Effective succession planning : ensuring leadership continuity and building talent from within / William J. Rothwell.
        p.   cm.
    Includes bibliographical references (p.   ) and index.
    ISBN 0-8144-0206-2
    1. Leadership.   2. Chief executive officers—United States—Succession.   3. Executive ability.   4. Organizational effectiveness.   I. Title.
HD57.7.R689   1994
658.4'092—dc20   *94-27808*
                                                              CIP

© 1994 AMACOM, a division of
American Management Association, New York
All rights reserved.
Printed in the United States of America.

This publication may not be reproduced,
stored in a retrieval system,
or transmitted in whole or in part,
in any form or by any means, electronic,
mechanical, photocopying, recording, or otherwise,
without the prior written permission of AMACOM,
a division of American Management Association,
135 West 50th Street, New York, NY 10020.

Printing number

10 9 8 7 6 5 4 3 2

To my wife,
Marcelina,
and to my daughter,
Candice.
Without their patience and support,
this book would never have been written.

Contents

Part II
Laying the Foundation for a Succession Planning Program   63

Part III
Assessing the Present and the Future   141

List of Exhibits

Preface

The world faces a crisis of leadership. Indeed, as Warren Bennis and Burt Nanus point out, "a chronic crisis of governance—that is, the pervasive incapacity of organizations to cope with the expectations of their constituents—is now an overwhelming factor worldwide."[1] Evidence can be found in many settings: Citizens are losing faith in their elected officials to address problems at the national, regional, and local levels; many among the religious are losing faith in church leaders, because of those high-profile leaders who have been stricken with sensationalized scandals; and, consumers are losing faith in business leaders to act responsible and ethical.

A crisis of governance is also widespread inside organizations. Employees wonder whether they can hold on to their jobs when downsizing has become more the norm than the exception. Employee loyalty is an often cited casualty of this crisis. Employee morale, influenced by the perception that top managers cannot effectively cope with the external challenges confronting their organizations, has suffered.

Concern is not restricted to hourly production workers. Executives, middle managers, and supervisors wonder about their futures following buyouts, mergers, acquisitions, and consolidations. According to an article in *Business Week,* "Turnover at the top is hitting levels without precedent. . . . The jobs of chief executive and chief operating officer *will never be as secure as they once were.*"[2] The middle management ranks have been slashed since the recession of 1990, intensifying concern among surviving middle managers about their futures and among supervisors about their potential for promotion from within. Management employees at all levels also wonder how their employment prospects will be affected by business process reengineering, total quality, diversity, high-quality customer service, self-directed work teams, and other issues that demand pioneering approaches. Some managers experience a *squashed-tomato effect* in which they are crushed between threefold pressures: top management's desire to increase employee involvement and empowerment; their subordinates' desires to increase their autonomy; and competitive challenges to do more with less.[3]

Amid these pressures, it is more necessary than ever for organizations to plan for leadership continuity and employee advancement at all levels. But that is easier said than done. It is not consistent with either long-standing tradition, which favors short-term succession planning, or the current trend favoring slimmed-down staffing, which creates a shallow talent pool from which to choose future leaders.

In previous decades, labor in the United States was plentiful and easily taken for granted. Managers had the leisure to groom employees for advancement over long time spans and to overstaff as insurance against turnover in key positions. That was as true for management as for non-management employees. Most jobs did not require extensive prequalification. Seniority, as measured by time with an organization or in an industry, was sufficient to ensure advancement. Succession planning activities properly focused on leaders astride the peak of tall organizational hierarchies, because organizations were controlled from the top down and were thus heavily dependent on the knowledge, skills, and attitudes of top management leaders.

But times have changed. Few organizations have the luxury to overstaff in the face of fierce competition from abroad and economic restructuring efforts sweeping industries. Middle management, the traditional training ground for top-level talent, has been dramatically eroded in absolute numbers and demoralized in attitude. The results of a survey conducted by consultants at the Hay Group revealed that "for the first time in the history of our surveys, fewer than half the middle managers took a favorable view about their opportunities for advancement."[4]

At the same time, products, markets, and management activities have grown more complex. Many jobs now require extensive prequalification, both inside and outside organizations. A track record of demonstrated and successful performance, more than mere seniority, has become a key consideration as fewer employees compete for diminishing advancement opportunities. As employee empowerment has broadened the ranks of decision makers, leadership has become decentralized rather than concentrated in the hands of a few at the top.

For these reasons, organizations must take proactive steps to plan for future talent needs at all levels and implement programs designed to ensure that the right leaders are available for the right jobs in the right places and at the right times to meet organizational requirements. Much is at stake in this process: "The continuity of the organization over time requires a succession of persons to fill key positions."[5] There are important social implications as well. As management guru Peter Drucker explains:

> The question of tomorrow's management is, above all, a concern of our society. Let me put it bluntly—we have reached a point where we simply will not be able to tolerate as a country, as a society, as a government, the danger that any *one of our major companies will decline or collapse because it has not made adequate provisions for management succession.* [Emphasis added.][6]

Recent research adds weight to the argument favoring succession planning. First, it has been shown that firms in which the CEO has a specific successor in mind are more profitable than those in which no specific successor has been identified. A possible reason is that selecting a successor "could be viewed as a favorable general signal about the presence and development of high-quality top management."[7] In other words, superior-performing CEOs view succession planning and leadership continuity as top priorities. Succession planning has also been credited with driving a plant turnaround by linking the organization's continuous improvement philosophy to individual development.[8]

But ensuring leadership continuity can be daunting. The rules, procedures, and techniques used in the past appear to be growing increasingly outmoded and inappropriate. It is time to revisit, rethink, and even reengineer succession planning. That is especially true because, in the words of one observer of the contemporary management scene, "below many a corporation's top two or three positions, succession planning [*for leadership talent*] is often an informal, haphazard exercise where longevity, luck, and being in the proverbial right place at the right time determines lines of succession."[9] A haphazard approach to succession planning bodes ill for organizations in which leadership talent is diffused—and correspondingly important—at all hierarchical levels.

The Purpose of This Book

Succession planning and leadership development figure prominently on the agenda of many top managers. Indeed, one study of Fortune 500 companies in the United States revealed that these issues ranked third in importance to corporate presidents—trailing only financial condition and profitability but ahead of such other important corporate objectives as productivity, innovation, marketing, worker performance, and public responsibility.[10] Yet, despite that senior management interest, the task often falls to human resource management (HRM) and human resource development (HRD) professionals to spearhead and coordinate efforts to establish and operate planned succession programs and avert succession crises.

In that way, they fill an important, proactive role increasingly desired of them by top managers, and they ensure that succession planning issues are not lost in the shuffle of daily crises.

But succession planning is rarely, if ever, treated in undergraduate or graduate college degree programs—even in those specifically tailored to preparing HRM and HRD professionals. For this reason, HRM and HRD professionals often need assistance when they coordinate, establish, operate, or evaluate succession planning programs. This book is intended to provide that help. It offers practical, how-to-do-it advice on succession planning. The book's scope is deliberately broad. It encompasses more than management succession planning, which is the most frequently discussed topic by writers and consultants on succession planning. Stated succinctly, the purpose of this book is to reassess succession planning and offer a fresh but practical approach to ensuring leadership continuity in key positions and building leadership talent from within.

Succession planning should support strategic planning and provide an essential starting point for management and employee development programs. Without it, organizations will have difficulty maintaining leadership continuity—or identifying appropriate leaders when a change in business strategy is necessary. While most large corporations operate succession planning programs, small and medium-size businesses also need them. In fact, inadequate succession plans are a common cause of small business failure when founding entrepreneurs fade from the scene and leave no one to continue their legacy.[11]

Whatever an organization's size or your job responsibilities, then, this book should provide useful information on establishing, managing, operating, and evaluating succession planning programs.

Sources of Information

As I began writing this book I decided to explore state-of-the-art succession planning practices. As in an earlier and related book,[12] I consulted several major sources of information:

1. *A tailor-made survey.* In October 1993 I surveyed 350 HRD professionals about succession planning practices in their organizations. Selected survey results, which were compiled in February 1994, are published in this book.
2. *Phone surveys and informal benchmarking.* I spoke by phone with vendors of succession planning software and discussed succession planning with HRD professionals in major corporations.
3. *Other surveys.* I researched other surveys that have been conducted

on succession planning in recent years and, giving proper credit when due, I summarize key findings of those surveys at appropriate points in the book.

4. *A literature search.* I conducted an exhaustive literature review on succession planning—with special emphasis on what has been written on the subject over the last five years. I also looked for case study descriptions of what real organizations have been doing.

5. *Firsthand experience.* Before entering the academic world, I was responsible for a comprehensive management development (MD) program in a major corporation. As part of carrying out that role I coordinated management succession planning. My experiences are reflected in this book.

The aim of these sources is to ensure that *Effective Succession Planning* will provide a comprehensive and up-to-date treatment of typical *and* best-in-class succession planning practices in organizations of various sizes and types operating in different industries.

The Scheme of This Book

Effective Succession Planning is written for those wishing to establish, revitalize, or review a succession planning program within their organizations. It is intended to meet the needs of HRM and HRD executives, managers, and professionals. It also contains useful information for chief executive officers, chief operating officers, general managers, university faculty members who do consulting in this area, management development specialists who are looking for a detailed treatment of the subject as a foundation for their efforts, succession planning program coordinators, and others bearing major responsibilities for developing management, professional, technical, sales, or other employees.

The book is composed of four parts. Part I sets the stage. Chapter 1 opens with several ministudies, brief fictional case studies illustrating typical—and a few rivetingly atypical—problems in succession planning (SP). The chapter also defines SP, distinguishes it from replacement planning, emphasizes its importance, explains why organizations sponsor SP programs, describes different approaches to SP, and defines management and leadership.

Chapter 2 opens with a detailed case study description of an exemplary SP program in a well-known corporation. The chapter draws conclusions from the case about the characteristics of effective succession planning programs, pinpoints common problems with such programs, offers advice for solving those problems, summarizes important trends affecting succession planning, lists key requirements for an effective succession planning program, and provides a simple "seven-pointed-star model" to guide succession planning. (The model introduced in Chapter 2 is the organizing scheme for Chapters 3 through 10).

Part II consists of Chapters 3 through 5. It lays the foundation for an effective succession planning program.

Chapter 3 describes how to make the case for change, often a necessary first step before any change effort can be launched. The chapter reviews such important steps in this process as assessing current succession planning practices, demonstrating business need, determining program requirements, linking succession planning to strategic planning and human resource planning, benchmarking succession planning practices in other organizations, creating a vision for systematic succession planning, clarifying the values to guide the succession planning program, and securing management commitment.

Building on the previous chapter, Chapter 4 explains how to clarify roles in a succession planning program, how to formulate the program's mission and its policy and procedure statements, and how to identify target groups and set program priorities.

Chapter 5 rounds out Part II. It offers advice on preparing a program action plan, communicating the action plan, conducting succession planning meetings, designing and delivering training to support succession planning, and counseling managers about succession planning problems in their areas of responsibility.

Part III is composed of Chapters 6 and 7. It focuses on assessing present work requirements in key positions, present individual performance, future work requirements, and future individual potential. Crucial to an effective succession planning program, these activities are the basis for subsequent individual development planning.

Chapter 6 examines the present situation. It addresses the following questions:

- Where are the key leadership positions in the organization?
- What are the work requirements in key positions?
- How is individual performance appraised?
- How is information about work requirements and individual performance monitored?

Chapter 7 examines the future. Related to Chapter 6, it focuses on these questions:

- What key positions are likely to emerge in the future?
- What will be the work requirements for those positions?

- What is individual potential assessment, and how can it be carried out?
- How can 360 degree feedback be used?

Part IV consists of Chapters 8, 9, and 10. Chapters in this part suggest action strategies for closing the "developmental gap" between present and future work requirements in key positions and between individual work experience, performance, and potential.

Chapter 8 offers advice for testing the organization's overall bench strength, explains why an internal promotion policy is important, defines the term *individual development plan* (IDP), describes how to prepare and use an IDP to guide individual development, and reviews important methods to support internal development.

Chapter 9 moves beyond the traditional approach to succession planning, which Chapter 8 emphasized. It offers alternatives to internal development as the means by which to meet replacement needs. The basic idea of the chapter is that a work need underlies any replacement need. There are, of course, other ways to meet work needs than by replacing a key position incumbent. The chapter provides a decision model to distinguish those situations when replacing a key position incumbent is warranted from those when it is not.

Chapter 10 is about evaluation, and it examines possible answers to three simple questions: What is evaluation? What should be evaluated in succession planning? And how should a succession planning program be evaluated?

An Epilogue concludes the book by addressing special issues in succession planning. More specifically, it examines how to:

- Accelerate the development of high potentials through HiPo programs.
- Avoid critical turnover after downsizing.
- Build diversity and multiculturalism into succession planning.
- Adapt succession planning to team environments.

The Epilogue concludes with three predictions about the future of succession planning.

William J. Rothwell
University Park, Pennsylvania

Acknowledgments

Writing a book resembles taking a long journey. Researching, drafting, and repeatedly revising a book requires more time, effort, patience, and self-discipline than most authors care to admit, and more dedication than many would-be authors are willing to offer.

Yet no book is written in isolation. Completing such a journey requires any author to take directions, that is, advice, from many people along the way.

This is my opportunity to thank those who have helped me. I would therefore like to extend my sincere appreciation to my graduate research assistant, Helen Markus, for helping me track down both common and arcane studies on succession planning. I would also like to thank the following people, listed in alphabetical order, for their help in reviewing drafts of this manuscript at various stages of completion and offering their valuable insights on ways to improve it:

- Joseph Benkowski, Technical Training Manager, Miller Brewing Company, Milwaukee, Wisconsin.

- David Dubois, a Principal Associate in the Rockville, Maryland–based consulting firm Strategic Performance Improvement Associates; 1994 Chairperson of the American Society for Training and Development's National Publishing Review Committee; and author of the highly regarded *Competency-Based Performance Improvement* (HRD Press, 1993).

- William Lowthert, Manager of Nuclear Training, Pennsylvania Power and Light, Berwick, Pennsylvania.

- P. Wayne Reagan, Chairman of Delphi Systems, Kansas City, Missouri, a vendor of succession planning software and consulting services.

These individuals provided me with valuable advice, information, and encouragement, although I bear ultimate responsibility for any defects in the final product. Now at the end of my journey, I owe them a debt of gratitude for their help along the way.

Finally, I would like to thank Adrienne Hickey and other staff members at AMACOM, who offered numerous useful ideas on the project while also demonstrating enormous patience with me.

Part I

Background Information About Succession Planning

This part introduces succession planning (SP) with several problematic ministudies—brief fictional case studies—that allow you to assess how well positioned your organization is to handle common succession problems. Part I also does the following:

- Defines SP.
- Distinguishes SP from replacement planning.
- Emphasizes the importance of SP.
- Explains the reasons that organizations establish and operate systematic SP programs.
- Describes approaches to SP.
- Defines management and leadership.
- Provides a case study description of a traditional approach to SP.
- Reviews strengths and weaknesses of the traditional approach.
- Offers advice on handling the weaknesses of the traditional approach.
- Summarizes important trends affecting the environment in which SP is operated.
- Explains the need for a new approach to SP and provides a "seven-pointed-star model" for systematic succession planning to guide such an approach.

1

What Is Succession Planning?

How is your organization handling succession planning? The following fictional—but quite possible—ministudies should help you come up with a reliable answer.

Five Ministudies: Can You Solve These Succession Problems?

Read the following ministudies and then decide how *your* organization would solve the problem presented in each. If you can offer an effective solution to all the ministudies, then your organization may already have an effective succession planning program in place; otherwise, there may be an urgent need to devote more attention to succession planning.

1. An airplane crashes in the desert, and no one aboard survives. Among the victims are the top managers of Acme Engineering, a successful consulting firm. When Acme's vice president of human resources receives the news, she gasps, turns pale, looks blankly at her secretary, and voices the first question that enters her mind:

"Now who's in charge?"

2. Georgina Myers, supervisor of a key assembly line, has just called in sick after two years of perfect attendance. She personally handles all purchasing and production scheduling in the small plant and oversees the assembly line as well. The production manager, Mary Rawlings, does not know how the plant will function without this key employee, but she is sure that production will be lost today because Georgina has no trained backup.

3. Marietta Diaz is convinced that she was not promoted to supervisor because of racial and sexual discrimination. Her manager, Wilson Smith, assures her that the decision to promote Gordon Hague rather than Marietta was based strictly on individual merit and supervisory job requirements. As Smith explains to her, "You just don't have the skills and

experience to do the work. Gordon already has those skills." But Marietta remains troubled. How, she wonders, could Gordon have acquired those skills in his previous nonsupervisory job?

4. Morton Wile is about to retire as CEO of Multiplex Systems. For several years he has been grooming L. Carson Adams to be his successor and has long believed that Adams would make an excellent CEO. Adams has served as executive vice president and chief operating officer, and his performance has been exemplary in those positions.

But, as his retirement date approaches, Wile is beginning to receive questions about his handpicked successor. Several division vice presidents and members of the board of directors have asked him privately how wise it is to allow Adams to take over, since (it is whispered) he has long had a high-profile extramarital affair with his secretary and is rumored to be an alcoholic. How, they wonder, can he be chosen to assume the top leadership position while he carries such personal burdens?

Wile is reluctant to talk to Adams about these matters. But he is sufficiently troubled to think about hiring an executive search firm to find a CEO candidate from outside the company.

5. Linda Childress is general manager of a large consumer products plant in the Midwest. She has helped her plant weather three storms in recent years. The first was a corporate-sponsored voluntary early-retirement program, which began eight years ago. In that program Linda lost her most experienced workers. Among its effects in the plant: costly work redistribution, retraining, retooling, and automation.

The second storm was a layoff that occurred five years ago. It was driven by fierce foreign competition in consumer products manufacture. The layoff cost Linda fully one fourth of her most recently hired workers and many middle managers, professionals, and technical employees. It also led to a net loss of protected labor groups in the plant's workforce to a level well below what it had taken the company ten years of ambitious efforts to achieve. Other consequences: increasingly aggressive union action in the plant; isolated incidents of violence against management personnel by disgruntled workers; growing evidence of theft, pilferage, and employee sabotage; and skyrocketing absenteeism and turnover rates.

The third storm swept the plant on the heels of the layoff. Just three years ago corporate headquarters announced a companywide Total Quality Management (TQM) program. Its aims: to improve product quality and customer service, build worker involvement and empowerment, reduce scrap rates, and meet competition from abroad.

While the goals were laudable, the TQM program was greeted with skepticism because it was introduced so soon after the layoff. Many employees—and supervisors—voiced the opinion that "corporate headquarters is using TQM to clean up the mess *they* created by chopping heads first and asking questions about work reallocation later." However, since job security is an issue of paramount importance to everyone at this plant, the external consultant sent by corporate headquarters to introduce TQM received grudging cooperation.

But the TQM initiative has created side effects of its own. One is that executives, middle managers, and supervisors are uncertain about their new roles in TQM and the results expected of them. Another is that employees, pressured to do better work with fewer resources, are complaining bitterly that compensation practices do not reflect their increased responsibilities, efforts, or productivity.

Against this backdrop, Linda has noticed that it is becoming more difficult to find backups for hourly workers and ensure leadership continuity in the plant's middle- and top-management ranks. Although the company has long conducted an annual "succession planning" ritual in which standardized forms, supplied by corporate headquarters, are sent out to managers by the plant's human resources department, Linda cannot remember when the forms were actually used during a talent search. The major reason, Linda believes, is that managers and employees have rarely followed through on the individual development plans (IDPs) established to prepare people for advancement opportunities.

Defining Succession Planning And Succession Planning Programs

As these ministudies illustrate, organizations have to plan for talent that will assume key leadership positions or backup positions on a temporary or permanent basis.

Among the first writers to recognize that universal organizational need was Henri Fayol (1841–1925). Fayol's classic fourteen points of management, first enunciated early in the twentieth century and still widely regarded today, indicate that management has a responsibility to ensure the "stability of tenure of personnel."[1] If that need is ignored, Fayol believed, key positions would end up being filled by ill-prepared people.

Succession planning (SP) is the process that helps ensure the stability of tenure of personnel. It is perhaps best understood as *any effort designed to ensure the continued effective performance of an organization, division, department, or work group by making provision for the development and replacement of key people over time.* It has also been defined as:

> a means of identifying critical management positions, starting at the levels of project manager and supervisor and extending up to the

highest position in the organization. Succession planning also describes management positions to provide maximum flexibility in lateral management moves and to ensure that as individuals achieve greater seniority, their management skills will broaden and become more generalized in relation to total organizational objectives rather than to purely departmental objectives.[2]

A *succession planning program* (SPP) is a *deliberate and systematic effort by an organization to ensure leadership continuity in key positions and encourage individual advancement.* Systematic "succession planning occurs when an organization adapts specific procedures to insure the identification, development, and long-term retention of talented individuals."[3]

Succession planning need not be limited solely to management positions or management employees. Indeed, an SPP may also address the needs for critical backups in any job category—including key people in the professional, technical, sales, clerical, and production ranks. The need to extend the definition of succession planning beyond management is becoming more important as organizations take active steps to build high-performance and high-involvement work environments in which decision making is decentralized and leadership is diffused throughout an empowered workforce.

One aim of succession planning is to match the organization's available (present) talent to its needed (future) talent. Another is to help the organization meet the strategic and operational challenges facing it by having the right leaders at the right places at the right times to do the right things. In these senses succession planning should be regarded as a fundamental tool for organizational learning because SP should ensure that the lessons of organizational experience—what is sometimes called institutional memory—will be preserved and combined with reflection on that experience to achieve continuous improvement in work results (what is sometimes called double-loop learning).[4]

Distinguishing Succession Planning From Replacement Planning

Succession planning should not be confused with *replacement planning,* though they are compatible and often overlap. The obvious need for some form of replacement planning is frequently a driving force behind efforts that eventually turn into succession planning programs, as ministudy 1 at the opening of this chapter dramatically emphasizes.

In its simplest form, replacement planning is a form of risk management. In that respect it resembles other organizational efforts to manage risk. Examples include storing computerized records in several locations to reduce the chance they will be lost during a fire or segregating accounting duties to reduce the chance of embezzlement. The chief aim of replacement planning is to reduce the chances of catastrophic effects stemming from the immediate and unplanned loss of key job incumbents.

However, succession planning goes beyond replacement planning. SP is proactive and attempts to ensure the continuity of leadership by building talent from within the organization through planned leadership development activities. It should be regarded as one tool for implementing strategic plans.

The Importance of Succession Planning

Many requirements must be satisfied if organizations are to survive in a fiercely competitive and dynamic environment. One key requirement is that replacements must be available to assume critically important leadership positions as they become vacant. Indeed, "succession planning, like a relay race, has to do with passing on responsibility. . . . Drop the baton and you lose the race."[5]

Numerous surveys over the years have emphasized the importance of succession planning. Chief executives consistently cite the issue as one of their chief concerns. According to one article, leadership succession has also surfaced as an issue of major concern to corporate boards:

> A survey by Korn/Ferry International of corporate board member policies and practices asked chairpersons to assess the importance of issues facing their companies in the next five years. Those typically seen as trendsetters—the billion-dollar companies—rated *management succession as the third most important issue,* on the heels of financial results and strategic planning [emphasis added]. According to Lester Korn, CEO of the search firm, boards are beginning to realize that they have "the same obligations to protect the human resource asset base for the shareholders as they do to protect the balance sheet of the corporation."[6]

There are several reasons why both CEOs and corporate boards are so interested in succession planning.

First, top managers are aware that the continued survival of the organization depends on having the right people in the right places at the right times. Strategic success is, in large measure, a function of having the right leadership. Leaving leadership development to chance and hoping that qualified successors can be found inside or outside the organization on short notice when needed may have worked at one time. But that approach will not work now. Some effort must be made to ensure that the organization is *systematically* identifying and preparing high-potential candidates for key positions.

Second, as downsizing has led to reductions in the middle-management ranks—a traditional training ground and source of top-management talent—there are simply fewer people available to advance to the top ranks from within. That means that great care must be taken to identify promising candidates early and to actively cultivate their development. Individuals who are *both* high performers on their present jobs and high potentials for future leadership positions should not be taken for granted. The reason: Slimmed-down organizations have reduced their absolute numbers. Worse yet, members of this group are differentially affected by downsizing. The reason: As work is redistributed after a downsizing, high performers end up shouldering more of the burden to get the work out while (in most cases) the rewards they receive are held constant. They are thus more likely to become dissatisfied and leave the organization than their less productive peers. To avoid that problem—which can be disastrous for the future leadership continuity of the organization—top managers must take active steps to reward them and advance them in a manner commensurate with their increased contributions.

Third, when succession planning is left informal and thus unplanned, job incumbents tend to identify and groom successors who are remarkably like themselves in appearance, background, and values. They establish a "bureaucratic kinship system" that is based on "homosocial reproduction."[7] As Rosabeth Moss Kanter explains:

> Because of the *situation* in which managers function, because of the position of managers in the corporate structure, social similarity tends to become extremely important to them. The structure sets in motion forces leading to the replication of managers as the same kind of social individuals. And the men who manage reproduce themselves in kind.[8]

As a consequence, white males tend to pick other white males as successors. That practice, of course, perpetuates such problems as the so-called glass ceiling and subtle forms of employment discrimination. To avoid these problems and promote diversity and multiculturalism in the workplace, systematic efforts must be made to identify and groom the best successors for key positions—not just those who resemble the present key job incumbents.

Succession planning is important for other reasons as well. Indeed, it "forms the basis for (1) communicating career paths to each individual; (2) establishing development and training plans; (3) establishing career paths and individual job moves; (4) communicating upward and laterally concerning the management organization; and, (5) creating a more comprehensive human resources planning system."[9]

Reasons for a Succession Planning Program

Why should an organization support a systematic succession planning program? To answer that question, I designed a written survey instrument and mailed it to 350 randomly selected members of the American Society for Training and Development (ASTD) in October 1993. By November 1993 I had received 64 completed surveys for a response rate of 18 percent—a respectable response, considering that the survey was nearly twenty pages long. Of the respondents, 30 (47 percent) indicated that their organizations are presently operating a systematic succession planning program; the remaining 34 respondents (53 percent) reported that their organizations are not operating a systematic succession planning program. Exhibit 1-1 presents demographic information about the respondents' industries; Exhibit 1-2 charts the sizes of the respondents' organizations; Exhibit 1-3 presents information about the respondents' job titles; and, Exhibit 1-4 summarizes the respondents' perceptions about the chief reasons why their organizations operate systematic succession planning programs. The reasons listed on Exhibit 1-4 are more fully detailed as follows:

1. *To identify "replacement needs" as a means of targeting necessary training, employee education, and employee development.* This was, in the survey respondents' view, the main reason why organizations sponsor systematic succession planning. In other words, succession planning becomes a driving force to identify justifiable employee training, education, and development needs and to focus organizational efforts to develop leaders. Training helps employees meet their current job responsibilities; employee education prepares them to advance to future responsibilities; employee development can be a tool for individual enlightenment or organizational learning.

2. *To provide increased opportunities for "high-potential" workers.* My survey respondents indicated that this is the second most important reason to sponsor systematic succession planning. Although definitions of *high potentials* (HiPos) may differ, HiPos are usually regarded as those employees who have the potential for future advancement. Hence, a very important reason for succession planning is to identify appropriate ways to accelerate HiPo development.

Exhibit 1-1. Demographic information about respondents to a 1993 survey on succession planning: industries.

Industry*	Organizations with Succession Planning Programs (total respondents N = 29)		Organizations without Succession Planning Programs (total respondents N = 32)	
	Frequency	Percentage	Frequency	Percentage
• Manufacturing	15	52%	15	47%
• Transportation/ communication/ electric/gas	3	10	2	6
• Retail trade	3	10	2	6
• Finance/insurance/ real estate	4	14	5	16
• Health care	1	3	2	6
• Government/ armed forces	0	0	0	0
• Other services	2	7	4	13
• Other industries	3	10	1	3

*Not all respondents chose to answer this question.
**Other services and industries included food service, wholesale/distribution, engineering/construction, food/restaurant, agriculture, one not-for-profit foundation, and an investor-owned public water supplies utility.
SOURCE: William J. Rothwell, "Results of a 1993 Survey on Succession Planning Practices," unpublished, The Pennsylvania State University, 1994.

3. *To increase the talent pool of promotable employees.* Respondents in organizations sponsoring systematic succession planning cite the above as the third most important reason for such planning. Succession planning formalizes the process of preparing people to fill key positions in the future. Of course, the term *talent pool* may mean a group of individuals—rather than one identifiable successor—from which possible successors for key positions may be selected.

4. *To contribute to implementing the organization's strategic business plans.* Succession planning should not be conducted in a vacuum; rather, it should be linked to, and supportive of, organizational strategic plans, human resource plans, human resource development plans, and other organizational planning activities. Perhaps for this reason my survey respondents indicated that the fourth most important reason to sponsor systematic succession planning is to "contribute to implementing the organization's strategic plan."

Strategic planning is the process by which organizations choose how

(text continues on page 14)

Exhibit 1-2. Demographic information about respondents to a 1993 survey on succession planning: size.

Number of Employees*	Organizations with Succession Planning Programs (total respondents N = 30)		Organizations without Succession Planning Programs (total respondents N = 33)	
	Frequency	*Percentage*	*Frequency*	*Percentage*
0–99	1	3%	1	3%
100–249	1	3	1	3
250–499	0	0	0	0
500–1,999	7	23	8	24
2,000–4,999	4	13	9	27
5,000 or more	17	57	8	24

*Not all respondents chose to answer this question.
SOURCE: William J. Rothwell, "Results of a 1993 Survey on Succession Planning Practices," unpublished, The Pennsylvania State University, 1994.

Exhibit 1-3. Job titles of survey respondents.

Respondent Job Title*	Organizations with Succession Planning Program (total respondents N = 24)		Organizations without Succession Planning Program (total respondents N = 31)	
	Frequency	*Percentage*	*Frequency*	*Percentage*
• Trainer	2	8%	5	16%
• Personnel manager	2	8	3	10
• Trainer with some personnel management duties	3	13	4	13
• Personnel manager with training duties	7	29	4	13
• Personnel manager without training duties	0	0	0	0
• Other	10	42	15	48

*Not all respondents chose to answer this question.
SOURCE: William J. Rothwell, "Results of a 1993 Survey on Succession Planning Practices," unpublished, The Pennsylvania State University, 1994.

Exhibit 1-4. Reasons for succession planning programs.

	Degree of Importance					Ranked by Mean
	Not Important				Very Important	
	1	2	3	4	5	
1. Identify "replacement needs" as a means of targeting necessary training, employee education, and employee development (N = 29).	0	0	3 (9%)	8 (24%)	18 (62%)	1
2. Provide increased opportunities for high-potential workers (N = 30).	0	1 (3%)	3 (10%)	11 (37%)	15 (50%)	2
3. Increase the talent pool of promotable employees (N = 29).	1 (3%)	2 (6%)	4 (12%)	7 (21%)	15 (52%)	3
4. Contribute to implementing the organization's strategic business plans (N = 29).	1 (3%)	1 (3%)	4 (14%)	14 (48%)	9 (31%)	4
5. Help individuals realize their career plans within the organization (N = 29).	0	3 (10%)	4 (14%)	16 (55%)	6 (21%)	5

Statement						
6. Encourage the advancement of diverse groups—such as minorities or women—in future jobs within the organization (N = 29).	1 (3%)	2 (6%)	7 (24%)	12 (41%)	7 (24%)	6
7. Improve employees' ability to respond to changing environmental demands (N = 29).	1 (4%)	4 (16%)	11 (44%)	7 (28%)	4 (16%)	7
8. Improve employee morale (N = 29).	2 (7%)	6 (21%)	11 (38%)	9 (31%)	1 (3%)	8
9. Cope with effects of downsizing (N = 29).	6 (21%)	8 (28%)	6 (21%)	6 (21%)	3 (10%)	9
10. Cope with the effects of voluntary separation programs, such as early retirement offers and employee buyouts (N = 29).	11 (38%)	9 (31%)	3 (10%)	3 (10%)	3 (10%)	10
11. Reduce head count to essential workers only (N = 29).	14 (48%)	12 (41%)	1 (3%)	1 (3%)	1 (3%)	11
12. Decide which workers can be terminated without damage to the organization (N = 29).	20 (69%)	8 (28%)	1 (3%)	0	0	12

SOURCE: William J. Rothwell, "Results of a 1993 Survey on Succession Planning Practices," unpublished, The Pennsylvania State University, 1994.

they will survive and compete. It involves formulating and implementing a long-term plan by which the organization can take maximum advantage of its internal organizational strengths and external environmental opportunities while minimizing the effects of internal organizational weaknesses and external environmental threats.

In order to implement a strategic plan, organizations require the right people in the right places at the right times. Without them, strategic plans cannot be realized. Hence, leadership identification and succession is critical to the successful implementation of organizational strategy. Particularly at top-management levels, as Thomas Gilmore explains, "performance criteria are rarely cut and dried. They often flow from a strategic plan which the chief executive is responsible for developing and carrying out."[10] At least five approaches may be used to integrate strategic plans and succession plans:[11]

a. *The top-down approach.* Corporate strategy drives succession planning. Leaders identified through a systematic succession planning process support the successful implementation of strategy.

b. *The market-driven approach.* Succession planning is governed by marketplace needs and requirements. As necessary talent is required to deal with competitive pressures, it is sought out.

c. *The career planning approach.* Succession planning is tied to strategic plans through individual career planning processes. In consultation with their organization superiors and others, individuals examine their own career goals in light of the organization's strategy and make decisions about how they can best contribute to emerging organizational needs while also improving their own chances for eventual advancement.

d. *The futuring approach.* Succession planning becomes a vehicle for anticipating talent needs stemming from corporate strategy. It is viewed as a way to scan external environmental conditions and match the organization's internal talent to the demands created by those conditions.

e. *The rifle approach.* Succession planning is focused on solving specific, identifiable problems confronting the organization—such as higher than expected turnover in some organizational levels or job categories.

Consider what role succession planning should play in supporting the strategic plans of *your* organization. In doing that, realize that "there is no one universal approach that works well across all companies; rather, effective companies match their succession strategies to their business strategies."[12]

Related to strategic planning is human resource planning (HRP), which is "the process of analyzing an organization's human resource needs under changing conditions and developing the activities necessary to satisfy these needs."[13] HRP is comprehensive in scope, examining an organization's workforce and work requirements. One result of HRP should be a long-term plan to guide an organization's personnel policies, programs, and procedures.[14]

Few authorities dispute the growing importance of HRP. As Manzini and Gridley note:

> The need for people with increasingly specialized skills, higher managerial competencies, and commitment to new levels of excellence, with professional qualifications in disciplines that did not exist a few decades ago—at costs commensurate with their contribution to organizational objectives—is and will continue to be the overriding 'business' concern of the organization."[15]

Succession planning is integrally related to HRP, though SP is usually more focused on leadership needs and leadership skills. Many techniques and approaches that have evolved for use in HRP may also be applied to SP.

Succession planning may also be integrated with human resource development (HRD), which is perhaps best understood as "the integrated use of training and development, organization development, and career development to improve individual, group, and organizational effectiveness."[16] HRD is thus linked to *planned* learning activities sponsored by organizations. HRD planning (HRDP) is "the process of changing an organization, stakeholders outside it, groups inside it, and people employed by it through planned learning so they possess the knowledge and skills needed in the future."[17]

Succession planning should focus on identifying and developing critically important leadership talent. Moreover, SP may rely on means other than planned learning or promotion-from-within to meet talent requirements. For instance, critical succession needs may be met by external recruitment, internal transfer, or other means. However, SP should be a consideration in HRDP, though the results of one survey revealed that (at least with management personnel) succession planning is a driving force behind developmental activities in fewer than 39 percent of responding firms.[18]

5. *To help individuals realize their career plans within the organization.* Organizations invest substantially in the training of their employees. Employee performance may improve with experience as individuals advance

along a learning curve in which they master organization-specific and job-specific knowledge. When individuals leave an organization, their loss to the organization can be measured.[19] If they remain with one employer to realize their career plans, then the employer benefits from their experience. In this sense, then, succession planning can serve as a tool by which individuals can be prepared for realizing their career plans within the organization. That reason was cited by survey respondents as the fifth most important for organizations to sponsor systematic succession planning.

6. *To encourage the advancement of diverse groups.* The workforce in the United States is becoming more diverse, reflecting the nation's population. At present, the United States is home to people of many ancestral groups: 58 million German, 39 million Irish, 33 million English, 24 million African, 15 million Italian, 12 million Mexican, 10 million French, 9 million Poles, 9 million Native Americans, and 6 million Dutch.[20] English is spoken by 198.6 million, Spanish by 17.3 million, and all other languages by 8.4 million.[21] Of recent immigrants to the United States, 22 percent have come from Mexico, 8 percent from Vietnam, 6.3 percent from the Philippines, 4.5 percent from the former Soviet Union, 4.3 percent from the Dominican Republic, 4 percent from China, 3.8 percent from India, 2.7 percent from El Salvador, 2.6 percent from Poland, and 2.1 percent from the United Kingdom.[22]

Unfortunately, not all workers have historically been treated equally or equitably. Discrimination, while prohibited by federal and state laws, still occurs. Indeed, the realization of that prompted U.S. Supreme Court Justice Thurgood Marshall to explain that as a black in America in 1991, he did not feel free.[23] While reactions to that view may vary, there is increasing recognition of a need to promote *multiculturalism,* which:

> involves increasing the consciousness and appreciation of differences associated with the heritage, characteristics, and values of many different groups, as well as respecting the uniqueness of each individual. In this approach, diversity has a broad meaning that encompasses sex and ethnic groups along with groups based on such attributes as nationality, professional discipline, or cognitive style.[24]

Perhaps as an indication of increasing recognition that organizations have a responsibility to pursue diversity at all levels, respondents to my survey indicated that "encouraging the advancement of diverse groups" is the sixth most important reason for organizations to sponsor systematic succession planning. Many organizations build in to their succession planning programs special ways to accelerate the development of legally protected labor classes and diverse groups.

7. *To improve employees' ability to respond to changing environmental demands.* "One role of the leader," writes Thomas Gilmore, "is to shield the organization from ambiguity and uncertainty so that people can do their work."[25] Organizations sponsor succession planning as one means by which to prepare people to respond to—or even anticipate—changing environmental demands. People groomed for key positions transform the ambiguity and uncertainty of changing external environmental demands to vision and direction.

8. *To improve employee morale.* Succession planning can be a means by which to improve employee morale by encouraging promotions from within. Indeed, promotions from within "permit an organization to utilize the skills and abilities of individuals more effectively, and the opportunity to gain a promotion can serve as an incentive."[26] The promoted employee's example heartens others. Moreover, particularly during times of forced layoffs, promotions from within and "inplacement" (movements from within of individuals otherwise slated for layoff) can boost morale and can help offset the negative effects of what Warren Boroson and Linda Burgess call "survivors' syndrome."[27]

9. *To cope with the effects of downsizing.* Most of the respondents to my survey work in organizations that have undergone radical workforce restructuring in recent years (see Exhibit 1-5). Downsizing has been—and continues to be—a fact of life in corporate America. Since 1988, America's largest employers have slashed over 1.8 million jobs from their payrolls. Middle managers and professionals have been particularly affected—many, of course, by the loss of their jobs. But downsizing often adversely affects the survivors as well. Although jobs may be eliminated, work duties and responsibilities that go with those jobs remain. As a consequence, there is often a need to identify those who can perform activities even when nobody is assigned special responsibility for them. Succession planning can be one tool for that purpose.

10. *To cope with the effects of voluntary separation programs.* Voluntary separation is closely related to layoffs and is often a preliminary step to it. In a voluntary separation, employees are offered incentives to leave the organization, such as prorated pay by years of service or years added to retirement. Like a layoff, a voluntary separation requires work to be reallocated as productive employees leave the organization. That requires some effort to identify "successors." Hence, succession planning can be valuable in identifying how—and to whom—work should be reallocated after restructuring.

Exhibit 1-5. Workforce reductions among survey respondents.

Question: In the last five years, has your organization experienced [*check as many below as apply*]:

	Organizations with Formal Succession Programs (N = 30)	Organizations without Formal Succession Programs (N = 33)
Reduction by attrition	20 (67%)	20 (61%)
A reduction in force	17 (57%)	24 (73%)
A hiring freeze	17 (57%)	19 (58%)
A layoff	15 (50%)	17 (52%)
An early retirement offer	10 (33%)	13 (39%)

Other: Reengineering
Other: Redeployment to subsidiaries
Other: An increase in staff (almost 300%)
Other: Partnerships/joint ventures with partner receiving employees
Other: Position elimination

SOURCE: William J. Rothwell, "Results of a 1993 Survey on Succession Planning Practices," unpublished, The Pennsylvania State University, 1994.

11. *To reduce head count to essential workers only.* In an age of fierce competition, processes must be reengineered to decrease costs, reduce cycle time, and increase quality and output. Processes must be continually reexamined in light of results required, and not be taken for granted because they have always been performed. In such environments, "companies don't need people to fill a slot, because the slot will only be roughly defined. Companies need people who can figure out what the job takes and do it, people who can create the slot that fits them. Moreover, the slot will keep changing."[28] Head count will also change to keep pace with shifting requirements.

12. *To decide which workers can be terminated without damage to the organization.* When making hiring decisions, employers have long considered an individual's potential for long-term advancement as well as his or her suitability for filling an immediate job vacancy. Perhaps the same concerns are associated with an organization's policy with respect to termination. This would explain why linking termination of employees to organizational damage control was cited by survey respondents as the twelfth most important reason for organizations to sponsor succession planning.

Approaches to Succession Planning

There are numerous approaches to succession planning. They may be distinguished by *direction, timing, planning, scope, degree of dissemination,* and *amount of individual discretion.*

Direction

Who should make the final decisions in succession planning? The answer to that question has to do with *direction.*

A *top-down approach* to succession planning is directed from the highest levels. The corporate board of directors, CEO, and other top managers oversee program operations—with or without the assistance of a part-time or full-time succession planning coordinator, a management development (MD) specialist, or a human resource generalist assigned to help with the program. The highest-level leaders make decisions about how competence and performance will be assessed for present positions, how future competence and potential will be identified, and what developmental activities, if any, will be conducted with a view toward preparing individuals for advancement and building the organization's bench strength of leadership talent.

In contrast, a *bottom-up approach* to succession planning is directed from the lowest levels. Employees and their immediate supervisors actively participate in all activities pertaining to succession planning. They are also on the lookout for promising people to assume leadership positions. Decisions about succession planning are closely tied to individual career planning programs, which help individuals assess their present strengths, weaknesses, and future potential. Top managers receive and act on decisions made at lower levels.

A *combination approach* attempts to integrate top-down and bottom-up approaches. Top managers are actively involved in establishing succession planning policies and procedures. They remain actively involved in the succession planning program. Employees and their immediate supervisors are also actively involved in every step of the process. Some effort is made to integrate succession planning and individual career planning.

Timing

How much time is devoted to succession planning issues, and when is that time devoted to it? The answer to that question has to do with *timing.*

Succession planning may be conducted *fitfully, periodically,* or *continuously.* When handled fitfully, systematic succession planning does not exist because no effort is made to plan for succession. The result is that every vacancy becomes a crisis.

When handled periodically, succession planning is carried out on a fixed schedule—usually on an annual basis. Often it distinctly resembles an employee performance appraisal program, which is typically part of the succession planning effort. Managers complete a series of forms that may include performance appraisals, individual potential assessments, individual development plans (IDPs), and a replacement chart for their areas of responsibility. This information is then turned over to the human resources department and/or to an individual assigned responsibility for succession planning.

When handled continuously, succession planning requires ongoing decision making, information gathering, and action taking. Less attention is devoted to forms than to results and developmental activities. Employees at all levels are expected to contribute to the continuous improvement of themselves and others in the organization through mentoring, networking, sponsorship, training, education, development, and other means.

Planning

How much planning is conducted for succession? The answer to that question has to do with the *planning* component of a succession planning program.

Succession planning may be a *systematic* effort that is deliberately planned and is driven by a written, organization wide statement of purpose and a policy. On the other hand, it may be an *unsystematic* effort that is left unplanned and informal. An unsystematic effort is driven by the idiosyncrasies of individual managers rather than a deliberate plan and strategy for preparing individuals for advancement and for ensuring leadership continuity.

Scope

How many—and what kinds—of people in the organization are covered by succession plans? The answer to that question has to do with program *scope*.

Succession planning may range from the *specialized* to the *generalized*. A specialized program targets leadership continuity in selected job categories, job levels, functions, or locations. Often, such programs grow out of crises—such as excessive turnover in selected areas of the organization. On the other hand, a generalized program aims to prepare individuals for advancement in all job categories, job levels, functions, and locations.

It is often a starting point for identifying individualized training, education, and development needs and for helping individuals meet their career goals.

Degree of Dissemination

How many people participate in succession planning processes? The answer to that question has to do with the program's *degree of dissemination*. It is a philosophical issue that stems from, and influences, the organization's culture.

The degree of dissemination may range from *closed* to *open*. A *closed succession planning program* is treated as top secret. Managers assess the individual potential of their employees without the input of those affected by the assessment process. Decisions about whom to develop, and how to develop them, is limited to a need-to-know basis only. Individual career goals may, or may not, influence these decisions. Top managers are the sole owners of the succession planning program and permit little or no communication about it. Secrecy is justified on two counts: (1) Succession issues are proprietary to the organization and may reveal important information about its strategic plan that should be kept out of the hands of competitors; and (2) decision makers worry that employees who are aware of their status in succession plans may develop unrealistic expectations or may "hold themselves hostage" for higher pay raises or faster promotions. To avoid these problems, decision makers keep confidential the succession planning process and its outcomes.

On the other hand, an *open succession planning program* is treated with candor. Work requirements, competencies, and success factors at all levels are identified and communicated. The succession planning process, and its possible outcomes, are described to all who ask. Individuals are told how they are regarded. However, decision makers do not promise high performers with high potential that they are guaranteed advancement; rather, they send the message that "you must continue to perform in an exemplary way in your current job *and* take active steps to prepare yourself for the future in order to benefit from it. While no promises will be made, preparing yourself for the future will usually help you qualify for advancement better than not preparing yourself."

Amount of Individual Discretion

How much say do individuals have in assessing their current job performance and their future advancement potential? The answer to that question has to do with the *amount of individual discretion* in a succession planning program.

There was a time in business in the United States when it was assumed that everyone wanted to advance to higher levels of responsibility or that everyone was willing to relocate geographically whenever asked to do so. Such assumptions are no longer safe to make: Not everyone is willing to make the sacrifices that go with increased responsibility; not everyone is willing to relocate, especially not those faced with the complexities of dual-career families or elderly parents requiring care.

Mandated succession planning ignores individual career goals. Decision makers identify the best candidates for jobs, regardless of individual preferences. Whenever a vacancy occurs, internal candidates are approached first. While given right of refusal, they may also be subjected to pressure to accept a job change for the good of the organization.

Verified succession planning appreciates the importance of the individual in succession planning. Decision makers identify desirable candidates for each job and then verify their interest in it by conducting career planning interviews or discussions. When a vacancy occurs, internal candidates are approached—but decision makers are already aware of individual preferences, career goals, and interests. No pressure is exerted on the individual; rather, decision makers seek a balance in meeting organizational succession needs and individual career goals.

Ensuring Leadership Continuity in Organizations

There is more than one way to ensure leadership continuity and thereby fill critically important positions. These may be generally classified as *traditional* and *nontraditional*. Each can have important implications for succession planning. Hence, each warrants brief review.

Traditional Approaches

In 1968, M. Haire noted that people can make only six types of job movements in any organization: in *(entry)*, out *(termination)*, up *(promotion)*, down *(demotion)*, across *(lateral transfer)*, or progress in place *(development in the current position)*.[29] Any one—or all—of these traditional approaches can, of course, be used as a means to meet succession needs for key positions.

Moving people into an organization (entry) is associated with recruitment and selection. In short, "hiring off the street" is one way to find successors for key positions. However, people hired from outside represent a gamble: They have little stake in the organization's status quo, though they may have valuable knowledge in which the organization is otherwise deficient. They may generate conflict when trying to put new ideas into action. That conflict may be destructive or constructive.

Employers in a 1991 survey reported significant difficulty in recruiting qualified workers to fill jobs: 21.5 percent of the employers reported having difficulty filling all positions; 24.8 percent reported difficulty 75 percent of the time; 24.2 percent reported having difficulty 50 percent of the time; 19.8 percent reported having trouble 25 percent of the time; and, only 9.7 percent of employers reported never having difficulty.[30]

Despite these problems, hiring from outside is increasing, because many firms consider it the best way to go. In fact, "just a decade ago, outside succession was still considered the last resort. According to James Kennedy, editor and publisher of *Executive Recruiter News,* employers now use search firms to fill roughly 30 percent of top level positions. In 1979, that figure stood at a mere 15 percent."[31]

But top managers may be reluctant to hire more than a certain percentage of outsiders for key positions because they do represent a gamble. Their track records are difficult to verify, and their ability to work harmoniously in a new corporate culture may be difficult to assess. If they fail, outsiders may be difficult to terminate both because managers can be reluctant to "fire" people and because wrongful discharge litigation is an issue of growing concern.

Moving people out of an organization *(termination)* is associated with layoffs, downsizings, reductions in force, firings, and employee buyouts. It is generally viewed negatively, continuing to carry a social stigma for those "let go" and a public relations concern for organizations that regularly terminate individuals with or without cause. Yet, if properly used, termination can be an effective tool for removing less than effective performers from their positions, thereby opening up opportunities for promising high-potential employees with proven track records.

Moving people up in an organization *(promotion)* is associated with upward mobility, advancement, and increased responsibility. Succession planning has long been linked with this approach more than with any other. Indeed, replacement charts are common tools of succession planning in many organizations, and they usually imply an upward progression from within the organization—and often within the same division, department, or work unit. Job posting programs can also be paired with replacement charting so as to communicate vacancies and provide a means by which to permit movement across functions, departments, and locations.

Promotion from within does have distinct advantages: It sustains (or improves) employee morale and it smooths transitions by ensuring that key positions are filled by those whose personalities, philosophies, and skills are already known to others in the organization. At present, nearly three fourths of all management talent in the United States is promoted from within.[32]

However, experts advise limiting the percentage of positions filled through internal promotion. One reason is that it tends to reinforce the existing culture. Another reason is that it can end up perpetuating the racial, sexual, and ethnic composition already present in the leadership ranks.[33]

There are other problems with strict promotion-from-within approaches to succession planning. First, exemplary job performance in one position is no guarantee of success in a higher-level position. Requirements at different organizational levels are not identical—and that is particularly true in management.[34] Effective promotion-from-within requires planning and rarely occurs by luck.

Moving people down in an organization *(demotion)*, like terminating them, is commonly viewed negatively. Yet it, too, can be an effective source for leadership talent on some occasions. For instance, when an organizational unit is being disbanded, effective performers from that unit may fill vacancies in other parts of the organization. Individuals may even accept demotions voluntarily if they believe that such moves will increase their job security or improve their long-term career prospects.

Moving people across an organization *(lateral transfer)* is becoming more common in the wake of recent downsizing efforts. (It is sometimes linked to what has come to be called *inplacement*.)[35] That, too, can be a valuable means by which to cross-fertilize the organization, giving new perspectives to old functions or activities. Job rotations, either temporary or permanent moves from one position to others as a means of relieving industrial ennui or building individual skills, is a unique form of transfer that can also be used in succession planning.[36]

Finally, progress in place *(development in the current position)* represents a middle ground between lateral transfer and upward mobility. It has become more common in recent years as opportunities for advancement have diminished. Progress in place is based on the central premise that no job—no matter how broad or complex—fully taps individual potential. As a result, individuals can be developed for the future while remaining where they are, doing what they have always done, and shouldering new duties or assignments. Stagnation is thus avoided by "loading" the job horizontally or vertically (*horizontal loading* means adding job responsibilities similar to what the individual has already done; *vertical loading* means offering new job responsibilities that challenge the individual to learn more.) As many as eighty-eight methods may be used to develop individuals where they are.[37]

Related to progress in place is the notion of *dual career ladders* in which individuals may advance along two different career tracks: a *management track* (in which advancement is linked to increasing responsibility for people), and a *technical track* (in which advancement is linked to increasingly sophisticated responsibility within a given function or area of expertise). The organization may establish special rewards, incentives, and compensation programs to encourage advancement along dual career tracks.[38]

Nontraditional Approaches

Experienced managers know that there is more than one way to fill a critical position. Job movements, described in the previous section, represent a traditional approach. They are commonly associated with succession planning. Alternatives to that, which I shall call nontraditional approaches, are probably being increasingly used as managers in slimmed-down organizations struggle to meet succession planning challenges while finding themselves restricted in the external hiring and internal promoting that they may do.[39]

One nontraditional approach might be called *organizational redesign*. When a vacancy occurs in a key position, decision makers do not automatically "move someone into that place"; rather, they break up the work duties and reallocate them across the remaining key positions or people. The desired effect is to reduce head count while holding results constant. It also develops the remaining key people by giving them exposure to a new function, activity, or responsibility. However, if rewards do not match the growing workload, exemplary performers who have been asked to do more may grow disenchanted. There is also a limit to how much can be loaded on people before they are incapable of performing effectively.

A second nontraditional approach is *process redesign*. Decision makers do not automatically assume that a key position needs to be replaced when it becomes vacant; rather, they review that function from top to bottom, determining whether it is necessary at all—and if it can be done in new ways that require fewer people.

A third nontraditional approach is *outsourcing*. Rather than assume that all key positions need to be performed internally, decision makers periodically reassess whether activities can be more cost-effectively handled externally. If head count can be reduced through outsourcing, the organization can decrease succession demands.

A fourth nontraditional approach involves *trading personnel temporarily with other organizations*. This approach builds on the idea that organizations can temporarily trade resources for their mutual benefit. Excess capacity in one organization is thus tapped temporarily by others. An advantage of this approach is that high performers or high potentials who are not immediately needed by one organization can be pooled for use by others, who usually offset their salaries and benefits. A disadvantage is that lending organizations risk losing these talented workers completely if they are spirited away by those having greater need of their services and greater ability to reward and advance them.

A fifth nontraditional approach involves establishing *talent pools*.[40] Instead of identifying *one* likely successor for each critical position, the organization sets out to develop *many* people for *many* positions. That is accomplished by mandated job rotations so that high potentials gain exposure to many organizational areas and are capable of making multifaceted contributions. While that sounds fine in theory, there are practical difficulties with using that approach. One is that productivity can decline as new leaders play musical chairs and learn the ropes in new organizational settings.

A sixth nontraditional approach is to establish *two-in-the-box* arrangements. Motorola has long used this approach. "Since most Motorola businesses are run by a general manager and an assistant general manager, the assistant slot is used to move executives from one business to another for a few years so they can gain a variety of experiences."[41] A form of overstaffing that would not be appealing to some organizations, this approach permits individual development through job rotations while preserving leadership continuity. It is akin to forming an executive team in which traditional functional senior executives are replaced by a cohesive team that collectively makes operating decisions, effectively functioning in the place of a chief operating officer.[42]

A seventh nontraditional approach is to establish *competitive skill inventories* of high-potential workers *outside the organization*. Rather than develop organizational talent over time, an organization identifies predictable sources of high-potential workers and recruits them on short notice as needed. A disadvantage of this approach is that it can engender counterattacks by organizations that have been "robbed" of talent.

Of course, there are other nontraditional ways by which to meet successor needs in key positions. Here is a quick review of a few of them:

▪ *Temping*. The organization makes it a practice to hire individuals from outside on a short-term basis to fill in during a search for a successor. The temps become candidates for consideration. If they do not work out, however, the arrangement can be severed on short notice.

▪ *Job sharing*. An experienced employee in a key position temporarily shares the job with another in order to provide on-the-job training, or to assess how well the candidate can perform.

▪ *Part-time employment*. Prospective candidates for key positions are brought in on a part-time basis. They are carefully assessed before employment offers are made.

- *Consulting.* Prospective candidates for key positions are brought in as consultants on projects related to the position duties. Their performance is carefully assessed before employment offers are made.

- *Overtime.* Prospective candidates from within the organization are asked to work in other capacities in addition to their current jobs. This represents overtime work. The employer then assesses how well the individuals can perform in the key positions, making allowances for the unusual pressure under which the individuals are functioning.

- *Job rotation.* Prospective candidates for key positions are developed from within by moving, for an extended time, into another job or rotating in a series of preparatory jobs.

- *Use of retirees.* The organization looks to retired individuals with proven track records to return to critical positions temporarily—or permanently.

The important point about succession planning is that numerous approaches may be used to satisfy immediate requirements. However, a continuing and systematic program is necessary to ensure that talent is being prepared inside the organization.

Defining Management and Leadership

As I bring this chapter to a close, it seems fitting to offer definitions of management and leadership.

By definition, *management* is a function of position. It has to do with creating an environment in which other people can perform and develop. Management employees are commissioned by organizations and are rarely chosen directly by those with whom they work.

On the other hand, *leadership* may be understood—in one sense, at least—as the ability to exercise influence over others. Leadership can be exhibited both by those who enjoy the authority of management positions and by those who don't. Natural leaders emerge as part of any group's formation.

Much has been written about leadership recently.[43] Despite years of research, however, leadership remains a mystery. But it is probably safe to say that leadership is essentially a function of (1) the individual, (2) the followers, (3) the situation, and (4) the timing.

1. *Individuals* who exert leadership are able to influence others by persuading them, teaching them, coercing them, or rewarding them. Leadership is thus about the ability to exercise power and exert influence. Leaders are willing to exert power, are self-confident about their own abilities, and are motivated to influence others. At the same time, others find them credible and persuasive.

2. *Followers* are also essential to leadership. No leader can influence others unless the followers are willing to be influenced. To be influenced, followers must be convinced that the leader has an idea or offers a path that will result in conditions better than those existing at present.

3. *The situation* includes both the environment in which leaders must function and the activities they are to conduct and/or the results they are charged to accomplish. Leaders can only flourish when they have keen insight about their culture, both national and corporate, and about the people over whom they are to exert influence.

4. *Timing* is the final variable that affects leadership. To exert influence, leaders must find that a window of opportunity exists in which others are experiencing a crisis or are searching for an alternative course of action. Since adults are highly motivated to learn—and thus be influenced—when they are grappling first hand with a problem, the appropriate timing for leadership is often during or immediately following a crisis.

Summary

After opening with five pertinent fictional ministudies to illustrate the importance of succession planning, the chapter defined SP as *any effort designed to ensure the continued effective performance of an organization, division, department, or work group by making provision for the development and replacement of key people over time.* A succession planning program was defined as a *deliberate and systematic effort by an organization to ensure leadership continuity in key positions and encourage individual advancement.* Succession planning is proactive and should not be confused with more limited-scope and reactive replacement planning, which is a form of risk management.

Succession planning is important for several reasons: (1) The continued survival of the organization depends on having the right people in the right places at the right times; (2) as a result of recent economic restructuring efforts in organizations, there are simply fewer people available to advance to the top ranks from within; (3) succession planning is needed to encourage diversity and multiculturalism in organizations; and (4) succession forms the basis for communicating information about career paths, establishing development and training plans, establishing career paths and individual job moves, communicating upward and laterally, and creating a more comprehensive human resources planning system.

Organizations sponsor systematic succession planning programs for various reasons. The three most important, based on my 1993 survey, are to:

1. Identify "replacement needs" as a means of targeting necessary training, employee education, and employee development.
2. Provide increased opportunities for "high-potential" workers.
3. Increase the talent pool of promotable employees.

Approaches to succession planning may be distinguished by *direction, timing, planning, scope, degree of dissemination,* and *amount of individual discretion.* Succession needs may be met through *traditional* and *nontraditional* approaches. SP should be linked to, and supportive of, strategic plans, human resources plans, human resources development plans, and other organizational plans.

Finally, I defined management as a function of position, but I defined leadership as the ability to exert influence over others.

2

The Need for a New Approach

What are the characteristics of a state-of-the-art succession planning program? Read over the following case study carefully to see how succession planning is handled by a well-known corporation. As you read, make a list to answer this question: *What characteristics of the succession planning program at Kmart have most contributed to its effectiveness?* When you finish your list, compare it to the list provided in the discussion following the case study.

CASE STUDY: KMART

"When this department was organized in April 1988, our CEO, Joe Antonini, told me that one of my key responsibilities was to have replacements in line for him and all the officers of the company," says David Vine, senior vice president for executive resources at Kmart.* [Vine himself is now a former Kmart officer. Since this interview, he has retired and been succeeded by Frederic M. Comins, Jr., vice president for executive resources at the time of the interview, in which Comins also participated.]

"The first thing I did was to interview some thirty of our officers here," Vine recalls. "I also went to all our regional offices and our subsidiaries to get to know all our people better.

"In addition, I visited some nonretailing companies, such as IBM and General Motors, which are known to have very good, formal, succession planning programs."

Annually, each corporate officer must submit his future business plan to the executive resources department as it relates to human resources and to the company's growth strategies. "We give them a chart," says Vine. "They must list their successors in rank order and

*The source of this case study is Jay L. Johnson, "How Kmart Plans for Executive Succession," *Discount Merchandiser* 32:5 (1992), pp. 108–110. The article is reprinted here by permission of *Discount Merchandiser.*

say when they think these people will be ready. And we ask everyone who reports directly to an officer to do the same thing. Then, we meet with these people and discuss their recommended successors in detail."

Succession planning extends to all levels of the company. "While the formal succession planning meetings are certainly our main source of information, there are other sources," says Comins. "We have a total organization of some 350,000 people. Hopefully, there are many who are promotable, who will advance to the next level of responsibility and higher."

Training Fast and Early

"Competition is keen today," Comins continues. "To be good you have to have the best people, and you have to train them early in their careers."

"Years ago," Vine points out, "our people stayed in the stores twenty to twenty-five years, and were then promoted to buyer jobs or higher. Today, the object is to identify our own promising people early and move them fast.

"We specifically ask our officers when they want to retire. Today, it's rare for a person to work until sixty-five years of age. Some leave at fifty-five. They are obligated to tell us their retirement plans. It's line management's responsibility."

"One of our principal missions is to strengthen the bench—provide for high-quality succession management," Comins adds. "Each executive has an obligation to prepare people to assume more responsibilities. Annually, we look at the organization through the succession planning process. At other times through related processes, we see how deep the bench is, where there are voids.

"It is every senior person's responsibility, whether an officer or not, to let us know when they see someone with extraordinary talent. We survey the whole field, reaching out as far as assistant store managers. When told of extraordinary talent, we try to validate that person's exceptional potential. First, we examine their present job performance. Then we interview them in a highly structured format, testing their cognitive abilities, their interpersonal strengths and weaknesses, and their job-related strengths and weaknesses. We call it a '360' because of the 360 degrees in a circle, within which we strive through a variety of tested tools to get as complete a picture of the person as possible."

Once individuals are designated, Comins reports, "We set up specific, developmental programs for them to speed up their growth."

"The programs extend all the way from the executive vice presidential level to the assistant store manager level," says Vine. "Generally, they are assistant store managers who have been with Kmart for at least two years. They are assigned to this office for eighteen months with specific jobs. Not only do they have contact with the officers and other various people in the main office, they have to produce. We may move people horizontally to broaden them in other areas, to give them breadth of experience. We may assign them to special task forces or to committees with special assignments. These people we have identified from time to time sit in on executive committee meetings as observers. We want them to be familiar with all areas of the company—to know what's going on.

"Every month, they must also visit some of our out-of-town stores, and write reports on what they find in them and those of our competitors. These reports are sent directly to our CEO, with copies to this department."

"Fantastic" Meetings

"Every quarter, they meet with Joe Antonini and us to say what they have accomplished over the last three months, and what are their goals for the next three months.

"These quarterly meetings with Antonini are absolutely fantastic. He challenges them with specific questions, and they love it. They tell him what they've been doing. He may feel that they could improve in a certain area. He may challenge them, giving them something he wants them to work on, either individually or as a group by the next time they meet.

"You cannot imagine the number of times a week that we talk to Antonini by phone or in his office. We work with him regularly to make sure we keep everything in perspective—to maintain a vision based on today's realities and the future. Right now, we have charts mapping out our direction for five years down the road."

Since mid-1990, when Comins joined this department, there have also been round-table discussions that Comins inaugurated. Each month, a company officer makes a presentation to the group. Prior to these meetings, members of the group are asked to submit questions to the particular officer. "They ask some very good questions," Comins reports, "specific to the job/function and maybe how it relates to other areas—finances or information systems, for example. These are very inquisitive people, asking very intelligent questions. The sessions last two or two-and-a-half hours. Occasionally, these special trainees put someone on the spot, causing an executive to think quickly on his feet.

It's very exciting. They are not afraid to ask anything. The common thread is to constantly broaden their horizons."

What qualities are being sought for high-level positions? How will Kmart recognize the individual and individuals that will someday lead the company? "There are thousands of promotable people in a company this size," Comins acknowledges. "But there aren't thousands with the potential to necessarily be an officer of the company, or lead Kmart. We are looking for qualities that surpass what it takes to get just to the next job."

Antonini Recognized

Before the days of the executive resources department, what gauges were used to spot outstanding talent? "In talking to people in the past," Vine recalls, "I would say they recognized Joe Antonini as being very creative, very innovative. He was always a risk taker both as a store manager, and as a district manager. He was not afraid to try something new. Those qualities were noticed. Most important, he made money for the store he managed and for the district he was in charge of. That said a lot.

"But someone may be an outstanding store manager for twenty or thirty years and advance no further. Our whole assessment process is designed to pick people with senior executive potential. We look for creative individuals, people with initiative, people who are willing to make decisions, to take risks. They should have a high energy level, be self-confident, and be able to sell their ideas. No matter how good they are at producing a profit, today they must have excellent human relations skills. If they are going to be leaders, they have to have goals, have to know how to get there, and must have others who want to go in the same direction. Today they can't use force or threats, because management style is different. We are looking for leaders."

In the executive succession process, there may be a tendency on the part of the present executive to pick a successor with less potential than himself. Addressing that possibility, Comins says, "I don't think people feel threatened anymore. I think people at the highest levels understand that it is their responsibility to identify and develop talent. I don't think they view it as a threat in this organization.

"Joe Antonini has made a major impact on the whole thought process within the organization. Probably, we now embrace change more than ever before."

Another tool to ensure successful executive advancement is a formal mentor program. "People I've talked to in the past tell me that most of them had a mentor, not formally designated," recalls Vine.

"We've thought long and hard about the mentor program. We try to match up people who will hit it off, where the protégé will learn from the mentor. Number one, we pick someone from a different functional area, not the person's boss. It's somebody they can go to and feel comfortable with, and somebody who can give the protégé understanding of another part of the company."

"It doesn't just help the protégé," Comins adds. "It helps the mentor as well. It's a nonthreatening relationship because the mentor is not his boss, nor his boss's boss. The mentor has no input in the protégé's performance appraisal. Assuming the relationship takes hold, it can be very intimate, like that of a coach or adviser. Obviously, it's up to both people to make the relationship work. When we match them up, we always say, '49 percent of this is the company's obligation, but 51 percent is your own.' They have to make things happen. They are in charge of their destiny. We are here to maximize their potential.

"These various programs are all designed to broaden the perspective of someone who someday will have a key role in leading the organization. It's like the story of three blind men who touch an elephant at different points: the trunk, a leg, and the tail, and define the elephant by only what they feel.

"Joe Antonini understands the entire elephant. And the people who will run major functions of this company, or one of its subsidiaries, will have to know they are dealing with an elephant.

"Kmart is not just a discount retail company. This is a world-class corporation with a global impact that happens to be in retailing."

Reviewing the Case: Characteristics of an Effective Succession Planning Program

What characteristics of the succession planning program at Kmart have most contributed to its effectiveness? Compare your answers to that question with the list of characteristics appearing below. (The list is in no particular order of importance.)

1. *Top management participation and support.* Kmart's CEO Joe Antonini personally participates in the succession planning program and thereby demonstrates strong personal support for it. His involvement motivates participants and ensures that other members of the top management team devote time and effort to the succession planning program. With Antonini's personal attention—which goes beyond simple support—succession planning receives far more attention than it otherwise would.

2. *A needs-driven program with external benchmarking.* The Kmart program began with top-level discussions about the specific business needs

that the program would be designed to serve. The individual asked to coordinate the program also made benchmarking visits to organizations that have well-deserved reputations for effective succession planning practices. That helped tailor the Kmart succession planning program to the unique company culture while simultaneously taking advantage of state-of-the-art approaches that could be usefully adapted from organizations with more mature programs.

3. *Focusing of attention.* As the case illustrates, Kmart is not content to allow succession planning to occur serendipitously; rather, a systematic effort is focused on accelerating the development of high-potential employees who have verified advancement potential.

4. *Dedicated responsibility.* If a goal deserves attention, someone must be held responsible for achieving it. At Kmart, a special corporate officer is charged with high-level responsibility for coordinating succession planning. That ensures that the issue is given full-time attention by someone with close access to the top-management team.

5. *Extension of succession planning to all levels.* Kmart is not content to restrict succession planning to the top rungs of the corporate ladder but extends it to all levels. Note that the greatest emphasis is placed at the *lowest* management levels, where the most positions and people exist.

6. *A systematic approach.* The case emphasizes that a regular, annual process is in place to focus attention on succession planning in every part of the organization. Each senior officer participates, forwarding completed forms to a central office. Those forms are, in turn, used to identify high-potential employees and operate a planned developmental program that is specifically geared to them.

7. *A comparison of present performance and future potential.* Management succession at Kmart is not a function of personal favoritism or seniority; rather, the organization has a means by which to compare present job performance and future potential. The organization also makes use of "360-degree feedback" to identify individual developmental needs for top-level talent. Individuals thought to possess special potential participate in structured interviews and other means by which to validate that potential.

8. *Clarification of high-level replacement needs.* At Kmart, the organization makes the effort to determine the retirement plans of key job incumbents. (In this book the term *key job incumbent* refers to an individual presently occupying a key leadership position.) In that way, the organization is better able to identify developmental time spans for each key position.

9. *Obligation of executives to identify and prepare successors.* Kmart emphasizes this obligation on the part of each executive.

10. *Establishment and maintenance of specific developmental programs.* At Kmart, employees thought to have high potential participate in a planned developmental program.

Programs of this kind are often used in large corporations and may extend over many years.[1] Such programs may be viewed in three stages, which are based on the level of participants' experience with the organization. In stage 1, there is a relatively large pool of prospective high potentials. They range from little experience through eight years with the organization. They are taught general management skills. Only 6 percent of those in stage 1 make it to stage 2, where they participate in tailor-made developmental experiences, intensive on-the-job development, and specialized courses, and occupy important positions. Only 6 percent of those in stage 2 progress to stage 3, where they occupy important positions and are carefully groomed for senior positions.

11. *On-the-job development of high potentials.* Kmart does not emphasize classroom training or off-the-job development to the exclusion of action learning or learning from experience. For this reason, high-potential employees are expected to produce while participating in the developmental program.

12. *Establishment of familiarity with who, what, when, where, why, and how.* Kmart is so enormous that it requires developmental experiences just to help individuals familiarize themselves with the corporate environment. That is a key emphasis of the developmental program. As a result, participants become much more knowledgeable about the corporate culture— who does what, when they do it, where business-related activities are performed, why they are worth doing, and how they are accomplished. In this way, the internal development program emphasizes knowledge, skills, and abilities unique to Kmart and essential to success in performing at higher organizational levels.

13. *Encouragement of critical questioning.* Top managers who address high-potential employees find that they are occasionally confronted with questions about "the way we have always done it." Critical questioning encourages creative thinking by top managers as well as by high-potential employees. It thus becomes a tool for business process reengineering.

14. *Emphasis on the qualities necessary to surpass movement to the next higher-level job.* Kmart's exemplary succession planning program emphasizes more than merely preparing individuals to move from one box on the organization chart to the next higher-level box. It is, instead, geared to building competencies leading to advancement beyond the next job. It is thus long-term and strategic in scope.

15. *Emphasis on formal mentoring.* Mentoring and coaching have been the subject of growing attention in recent years as management writers

have recognized that individual development is more heavily influenced by the on-the-job work environment than by off-the-job training, education, or development experiences.[2] (Indeed, as much as 90 percent of an individual's development occurs on the job.[3])

A mentor or coach provides advice about dealing with challenges presented by the work environment—including interpersonal problems and political issues. "Mentoring occurs when a talented junior person forms an attachment to a sensitive and intuitive senior person who understands and has the ability to communicate with the individual."[4] Mentors are thus teachers. They are not in positions of authority over their protégés. Nor do they necessarily serve as special advocates and cheerleaders for their protégés as sponsors do, although they can serve in those roles too.

Mentors are typically chosen by the protégé. Hence, most mentoring occurs informally. Kmart has a formal mentoring program in which an effort is made to match up promising junior employees with more experienced, more savvy senior employees.

16. *Other characteristics.* On your list, you may have identified other characteristics of an effective succession planning program. In reality, of course, there are no "right" or "wrong" characteristics. Indeed, as James McElwain puts it, although there is no foolproof formula for success, there are a number of essentials to a good succession process:

- A systematic approach to identifying succession candidates
- Cross-divisional sharing of people and information
- Leadership that rewards managers for promoting rather than hoarding their best employees
- Career paths that move not just up a specialized ladder but across the company
- Frequent opportunities for employees to accept new challenges
- Recognition that employees have a stake in the company and share in its successes.[5]

In my 1993 survey of succession planning practices, I asked the respondents to indicate the characteristics of effective succession planning programs. The survey results are presented in Exhibit 2-1. I have created a questionnaire, shown in Exhibit 2-2, which you can use to assess the succession planning program in your organization.

Identifying and Solving Problems with the Traditional Approach to Succession Planning

The Kmart case summarizes an excellent, state-of-the-art approach to succession planning in a large corporation. However, not all organizations

(text continues on page 48)

Exhibit 2-1. Characteristics of effective succession planning programs.

Question: It is possible that effective succession planning programs share certain common characteristics across organizations. Review possible characteristics listed in column 1. Then, in column 2, check (✓) Yes or No to indicate whether your organization's succession planning program has that characteristic. Finally, in column 3, circle a code to indicate how important you believe the characteristic to be for an effective succession planning program. Use the following scale:

1 = Not at all important
2 = Not very important
3 = Somewhat important
4 = Important
5 = Very important

For the succession planning program, has your organization:	Does your organization's succession planning program have this characteristic?		How important do you believe this characteristic to be for an effective succession planning program?					Mean	Importance Ranked by Mean
	Yes	No	Not Important				Very Important		
			1	2	3	4	5		
1. Established a means to appraise individual performance?	29 (97%)	1 (3%)	1 (3%)	0	0	10 (33%)	19 (63%)	4.53	1
	N = 30					N = 30			

Item									Mean	No.
2. Established a means to compare individual skills to the requirements of a future position?	22 (73%)	8 (27%) N = 30	0	1 (3%)	3 (10%) N = 29	6 (21%)	19 (66%)		4.48	2
3. Established a way to review organizational talent at least annually?	25 (83%)	5 (17%) N = 30	1 (4%)	0	1 (4%) N = 28	10 (36%)	16 (57%)		4.43	3
4. Established a way to plan for meeting succession planning needs through individual development plans?	19 (63%)	11 (37%) N = 30	1 (3%)	1 (3%)	0 N = 29	11 (38%)	16 (55%)		4.38	4
5. Fixed responsibility for organizational oversight of the program?	24 (83%)	5 (17%) N = 29	0	2 (7%)	3 (10%) N = 29	9 (31%)	15 (52%)		4.28	5

(continues)

Exhibit 2-1 *(continued).*

For the succession planning program, has your organization:	Does your organization's succession planning program have this characteristic?		How important do you believe this characteristic to be for an effective succession planning program?						Importance Ranked by Mean
			Not Important			*Very Important*			
	Yes	*No*	*1*	*2*	*3*	*4*	*5*	*Mean*	
6. Established a means to track development activities to prepare successors for eventual advancement?	15 (52%)	14 (48%)	0	1 (4%)	2 (7%)	16 (57%)	9 (32%)	4.18	6
	N = 29				N = 28				
7. Established a means to evaluate the results of the succession planning program?	8 (28%)	21 (72%)	0	2 (8%)	4 (16%)	7 (28%)	12 (48%)	4.16	7

Item			N						Mean	Rank
8. Established a program action plan?	24 (83%)	5 (17%)	N = 29	0	2 (7%)	4 (15%) N = 27	11 (41%)	10 (37%)	4.07	8
9. Established a way to forecast future talent needs?	14 (47%)	16 (53%)	N = 30	0	2 (7%)	1 (4%) N = 27	17 (65%)	7 (26%)	4.07	8
10. Devised means to keep records for individuals who are designated as successors?	25 (86%)	4 (14%)	N = 29	1 (3%)	2 (7%)	3 (10%) N = 29	12 (41%)	11 (38%)	4.03	9
11. Tied the succession planning program to organizational strategic plans?	20 (69%)	9 (31%)	N = 29	1 (3%)	3 (10%)	2 (7%) N = 28	7 (24%)	15 (52%)	4.00	10
12. Tied the succession planning program to individual career plans?	24 (83%)	5 (17%)	N = 29	3 (10%)	0	5 (17%) N = 28	14 (48%)	6 (21%)	3.86	11
13. Established a means to clarify present position responsibilities?	20 (69%)	9 (31%)	N = 29	0	3 (10%)	6 (21%) N = 29	12 (41%)	8 (28%)	3.86	11

Tie (8, 8)

Tie (11, 11)

(continues)

Exhibit 2-1 (*continued*).

| For the succession planning program, has your organization: | Does your organization's succession planning program have this characteristic? | | How important do you believe this characteristic to be for an effective succession planning program? | | | | | | Importance Ranked by Mean |
	Yes	No	Not Important 1	2	3	Very Important 4	5	Mean	
14. Established a schedule of program events based on the action plan?	21 (72%)	8 (28%) N = 29	0	3 (11%)	5 (18%) N = 28	14 (50%)	6 (21%)	3.82	12
15. Tied the succession planning program to training programs?	24 (83%)	5 (17%) N = 29	0	2 (7%)	8 (29%) N = 28	11 (39%)	7 (5%)	3.82	13
16. Prepared written program goals to indicate what results the succession planning program should achieve?	18 (62%)	11 (38%) N = 29	0	2 (8%)	10 (36%) N = 26	5 (19%)	9 (35%)	3.81	14

Question			N						N	Mean	
17. Articulated a written philosophy about the program?	18 (62%)	11 (38%)	N = 29	2 (7%)	3 (11%)	6 (21%)	11 (39%)	6 (21%)	N = 28	3.79	15
18. Prepared a written program purpose statement?	23 (77%)	7 (23%)	N = 30	1 (4%)	2 (8%)	7 (27%)	8 (31%)	8 (31%)	N = 26	3.77	16
19. Established a means to clarify future position responsibilities?	15 (52%)	14 (48%)	N = 29	2 (7%)	3 (11%)	2 (7%)	18 (64%)	3 (11%)	N = 28	3.61	17
20. Fixed responsibility of each participant in the program?	14 (50%)	14 (50%)	N = 28	3 (11%)	2 (7%)	5 (19%)	10 (37%)	7 (26%)	N = 27	3.59	18
21. Created workshops to train individuals about career planning?	10 (34%)	19 (66%)	N = 29	1 (4%)	4 (15%)	5 (19%)	12 (46%)	4 (15%)	N = 26	3.54	19
22. Established a written policy statement to guide the program?	15 (52%)	14 (48%)	N = 29	2 (7%)	4 (15%)	7 (26%)	10 (37%)	4 (15%)	N = 27	3.37	20
23. Identified what groups are to be served by the program, in priority order?	16 (55%)	13 (45%)	N = 28	4 (15%)	1 (4%)	8 (30%)	10 (37%)	4 (15%)	N = 27	3.33	21

(continues)

Exhibit 2-1 (*continued*).

For the succession planning program, has your organization:	Does your organization's succession planning program have this characteristic?		How important do you believe this characteristic to be for an effective succession planning program?					Mean	Importance Ranked by Mean
	Yes	No	Not Important				Very Important		
			1	2	3	4	5		
24. Developed a means to budget for a succession planning program?	9 (31%)	20 (69%) N = 29	3 (12%)	6 (23%)	3 (12%) N = 26	11 (42%)	3 (12%)	3.19	22
25. Created workshops to train management employees about the succession planning program?	10 (34%)	19 (66%) N = 29	2 (8%)	9 (35%)	5 (19%) N = 26	4 (15%)	6 (23%)	3.12	23

26. Established *measurable* objectives for program operation (such as number of positions replaced per year)?	8 (28%)	21 (72%) N = 29	3 (12%)	5 (19%)	8 (31%) N = 26	8 (31%)	2 (8%)	3.04	24
27. Established incentives/ rewards for managers with identified successors?	0	29 (100%) N = 29	8 (31%)	7 (27%)	5 (19%) N = 26	2 (8%)	4 (15%)	2.50	25
28. Established incentives/ rewards for identified successors in the succession planning program?	0	29 (100%) N = 29	9 (35%)	7 (27%)	6 (23%) N = 26	4 (15%)	0	2.19	26

SOURCE: William J. Rothwell, "Results of a 1993 Survey on Succession Planning Practices," unpublished, The Pennsylvania State University, 1994.

Exhibit 2-2. Assessment questionnaire for effective succession planning.

Directions: Complete the following assessment questionnaire to determine how well your organization is presently conducting succession planning. Read each item in the questionnaire. Circle **Y** for *yes,* **N/A** for *not applicable,* or **N** for *no* opposite each item. Spend about fifteen minutes; when you finish, score and interpret the results using the instructions appearing at the end of the questionnaire. Then share your completed questionnaire with others in your organization. Use the questionnaire as a starting point to determine the need for a more systematic approach to succession planning in your organization.

In your organization, would you say that succession planning:	*Circle your response below:*		
1. Enjoys top management participation, involvement, and support?	Y	N/A	N
2. Is geared to meeting the unique needs of the organization?	Y	N/A	N
3. Has been benchmarked with best-in-class organizations?	Y	N/A	N
4. Is a major focus of top-management attention?	Y	N/A	N
5. Is the dedicated responsibility of at least one high-level management employee?	Y	N/A	N
6. Is extended to all levels rather than restricted to top positions only?	Y	N/A	N
7. Is carried out systematically?	Y	N/A	N
8. Is heavily influenced by a comparison of present performance and future potential?	Y	N/A	N
9. Is influenced by identification of high-level replacement needs?	Y	N/A	N
10. Has sensitized each executive to an obligation to identify and prepare successors?	Y	N/A	N
11. Has prompted the organization to establish and conduct specific developmental programs that are designed to accelerate the development of high-potential employees?	Y	N/A	N
12. Is guided by a philosophy that high-potential employees should be developed while working rather than primarily through off-the-job experiences?	Y	N/A	N
13. Has prompted the organization to focus developmental programs on increasing the familiarity of high-potential employees with who does what, when they do it, where they do it, why they do it, and how they do it?	Y	N/A	N

In your organization, would you say that succession planning:	*Circle your response below:*		
14. Has prompted the organization to focus developmental programs on critical questioning of "the way things have always been done"?	Y	N/A	N
15. Emphasizes qualities to surpass movement to the next higher level job?	Y	N/A	N
16. Has prompted your organization to examine, and perhaps use, formal mentoring?	Y	N/A	N
17. Is conducted systematically rather than anecdotally?	Y	N/A	N
18. Encourages the cross-divisional sharing of people and information?	Y	N/A	N
19. Is reinforced by a leadership that actively rewards managers for promoting (rather than holding on to) their best employees?	Y	N/A	N
20. Is supported by career paths that move not just up a specialized ladder but across the company?	Y	N/A	N
21. Is supported by frequent opportunities for employees to accept new challenges?	Y	N/A	N
22. Is driven, in part, by recognition that employees have a stake in the organization and share in its successes?	Y	N/A	N
23. Has prompted an explicit policy favoring promotion from within?	Y	N/A	N
Total	___	___	___

Scoring and Interpreting the Assessment Questionnaire Give your organization 1 point for each **Y** and a 0 for each **N** or **N/A** listed above. Total the points from the **Y** column and place the sum in the space next to the word **total**. Then interpret your score in the following way:

20 or more points	=	Succession planning appears to be handled in an exemplary manner in your organization.
18–20	=	The succession planning efforts of your organization could stand improvement. However, succession planning is being handled effectively for the most part.
14–17	=	Succession planning is a problem in your organization. It deserves more attention.
14 or less	=	Your organization is handling succession planning in a crisis mode. It is very likely that successors for critically important positions have not been identified and are not systematically developed. Immediate corrective action is desirable.

handle succession planning so effectively. Indeed, two experts speaking at the 1988 American Management Association Human Resources Conference indicated that succession planning is being woefully ignored by a majority of companies in the United States.[6] A 1992 survey of management development (MD) practices revealed that large corporations use succession planning needs in planning MD practices significantly less often than they do strategic plans and individual development plans.[7]

Many problems bedevil the traditional approach to succession planning. Exhibit 2-3 summarizes the chief difficulties of using succession planning that were described by the respondents to my 1993 survey on succession planning practices.

Exhibit 2-3. Chief difficulties with succession planning programs.

Question: What are the chief difficulties that your organization has experienced with a succession planning program? **N = 30 respondents**

[*What follows are direct quotations from survey respondents.*]
"To keep the plan updated."
"Follow-up of planned actions and activities."
"Inaction after the discussions."
"Time/acceptance and support of current supervisor."
"With very few openings per year, it's difficult to give everyone the opportunities to develop in new and different areas. Tough also to set objective measures for the success of the program. We've still got lots of work to do on the 'development' side of the program."
"No action plans/poor inventory methods/poorly identified candidates."
"Resources required to monitor and make effective."
"The charge that it creates an 'elite' that, once identified, gets all the development opportunities."
"Sticking with the plan when the actual openings occur."
"No active development plans established."
"Predicting the future—fewer development opportunities in flat organization."
"Writing the policy/plan."
"Acceptance and implementation the easiest."

Question: What are the chief difficulties that your organization has experienced with a succession planning program? **N = 30 respondents**

"Scheduling due to other high priorities; communication from the top."

"Sharing of succession planning data/follow-through on individual development."

"Support from some business unit HR managers."

"Managers struggle in making the step from HR planning to the creation of effective employee developmental plans. Those that do so, however, then falter in carrying them out. Need more effective means of identification of talent across functional/organizational lines—will consider multifunctional teams to conduct HR planning and use of competencies at various levels."

"Getting participation from very small, remote areas."

"Having people promoted who were not discussed at annual meeting."

"Resistance to formalized procedure."

"Not holding executives accountable for staying with or implementing their plan when needed."

"Few openings; therefore, little opportunity to move people forward."

"Organizational restructure has changed targeted positions and development strategies."

"Data requirements."

"Despite the presentations we make, not enough awareness on executives' part of the overall process."

"Executives and managers don't think in long-range terms, focus too much on near term, are not familiar with how to work 'nontechnical' leadership/organizational/people issues, are not familiar with ASD [assessment, selection, development] technology."

"We don't take it seriously—we complete the paperwork, don't stress leadership skills needed and opportunistically develop people. Program is not 'diverse.'"

"Resistance in planning ahead and taking the time required to identify gaps in performance and in the organization."

SOURCE: William J. Rothwell, "Results of a 1993 Survey on Succession Planning Practices," unpublished, The Pennsylvania State University, 1994.

Seven Common Problems Affecting Succession Planning Programs

1. *Lack of support.* HR managers find that a major disadvantage in establishing a company succession plan is lack of support from top management. Indeed, "the attitude of too many corporation executives is 'why bother?'"[8] If top managers lack a sense of urgency, no succession planning program can be effective.

If top managers are unwilling to support a systematic approach to succession planning, it cannot succeed. If that is the case, the best strategy is to try to win over one or more credible *idea champions.* Especially promising for those roles are well-respected top managers who have recently—

and, if possible, personally—experienced the work-related problems that stem from having no successor prepared to assume a critically important position when a vacancy occurs.

2. *Corporate politics.* A second problem with succession planning is that it can be affected by corporate politics. Instead of promoting employees with the most potential or the best track record, top managers—or, indeed, any level of management employee—may "use the corporate ladder to promote friends and allies, while punishing enemies, regardless of talent or qualifications."[9] If allowed to operate unchecked, corporate politics can supplant performance and potential as an advancement criterion.

To solve this problem, decision makers must insist on formal ways to identify work requirements and assess performance and potential rather than permit subjective judgments to prevail. (Methods of conducting formal assessments will be described in later chapters of this book.) Informal judgments are notoriously prone to problems. Among them: *recency bias* (performance or potential is assessed with a heavier-than-desirable emphasis on recent and singular successes or failures); *pigeon-holing* or *stereotyping* (supervisors develop impressions of individuals that are difficult to change); *the halo or horn effect* (supervisors are overly influenced in their judgments of individuals by singular events); *the pygmalion effect* (supervisors see what they expect to see); and *discrimination* (treating people differently solely on the basis of sex, race, age, or other factors unrelated to job performance). Left unchecked, informal judgments may also lead supervisors to pick and groom successors like themselves.

3. *Quick-fix attitudes.* A third problem with the traditional approach to succession planning is that it can encourage quick-fix attitudes. Effectiveness is sacrificed to expediency. That can have far-ranging consequences, because ill-chosen leaders can prompt higher-than-normal turnover among their followers, create employee morale problems, and even bankrupt an otherwise sound business. Leadership *does* matter, and leaders cannot be cultivated quickly or easily.[10] Excellent leaders can be cultivated only over time.

4. *Low visibility.* Top-level executives do not always see the direct benefits of succession planning. The farther they are removed from daily operations—and numerous direct reports—the less valuable succession planning can seem to be to them. As Ann Atkinson, vice president of training, management and organization development for Days Inn of America, has said, "Between now and the end of the century, HR managers will propose—and implement—several succession plans for their companies. The plans will constantly be reviewed and replaced because someone in authority at the company will decide no benefits are being reaped."[11]

To solve this problem, succession planning *must* be made a high-visibility issue. Further, it must enjoy the active support—and direct participation—of management employees *at all levels*. Without that active support and direct participation, top managers will have no ownership stake in succession planning.

5. *The rapid pace of organizational change.* Traditional succession planning once worked well enough in stable environments and organizations. In those settings, vacancies could be predicted, candidates could be trained for targeted jobs, and a homogeneous workforce led to easy transitions and assured continuity.

But the rapid pace of organizational change has raised serious questions about the value of the traditional, fill-in-the-box-on-the-organization-chart approach to replacement-oriented succession planning. Indeed, one management consultant, asking whether succession planning is worth the effort, arrived at this conclusion: "The simple answer is no. Predicting succession (over, say, a three-to-five-year time frame) in an era of constant change is fast becoming an impossibility."[12]

To solve this problem, decision makers need to look beyond a simple technological solution, such as the use of succession planning software for personal computers designed to accelerate the organization's ability to keep pace with staffing needs and changes. That can help, but more dramatic solutions are also needed. Possible examples: Focus on work requirements, competencies, and success factors so as to maximize the value of developmental activities; increase the use of job rotations to prompt management employees to become more flexible; use action learning and real-time education to equip management employees with the flexibility they need to cope with rapid change; establish team-based management so that key work requirements develop, and are spread across, different individuals; and, move beyond a focus on "filling boxes on an organization chart" to "meeting work requirements through innovative means."[13]

6. *Too much paperwork.* Top managers in most organizations have a low tolerance for paperwork. A colleague of mine jokes that top managers in his organization "won't respond to a one-page survey or read beyond the first page of a memo." One reason for this is that top managers are often overburdened with paperwork, since they receive it from so many quarters. Technology, which was once blessed as a solution to information overload, now seems to be contributing to it; and managers now find themselves coping with burgeoning messages from electronic mail, faxes, and other sources.

Hence, one problem with the traditional approach to succession planning is that it may require substantial paperwork to:

- Assess present work requirements.
- Appraise current individual performance.

- Assess future work requirements.
- Assess individual potential for advancement.
- Prepare replacement charts.
- Identify future career paths.
- Identify key positions requiring replacements.
- Establish individual development plans (IDPs) to help individuals narrow the gap between their present work requirements/ performance and future work requirements/potential.

While full-time MD specialists or part-time HR generalists can provide assistance in record keeping, they can seldom supply the details for every person, position, and requirement in the organization.

Perhaps the best approach is to minimize the amount of paperwork required for succession planning. But that is difficult to do. Whenever possible, however, succession planning coordinators, management development professionals, or human resource professionals should supply information that is readily available from sources other than the immediate organizational superiors of employees participating in succession planning efforts. That way, the superiors can focus their attention on identifying the talent needed to implement business strategy, identifying critical positions and high-potential talent, and formulating and following through on individualized developmental planning.

7. *Too many meetings.* The traditional approach to succession planning can create resistance not only due to the massive paperwork it can generate, but also to the numerous and time-consuming meetings it can require. For instance, to carry out succession planning, management employees may need to participate in:

- *Kickoff meetings.* Such meetings, conducted by the CEO, are intended to reinforce the importance of the succession planning effort.
- *Organizational, divisional, functional or other meetings.* These meetings may focus on succession planning for each job category, organizational level, function, or location.
- *Work requirements meetings.* If the organization makes it a policy to base succession on identifiable work requirements, competencies, success factors, or some other "objective criteria," then management employees will usually be involved in meetings to identify them.
- *Employee performance appraisal meetings.* In most organizations, management employees appraise the performance of their immediate subordinates as a part of the succession planning program.

- *Career path meetings.* If the organization attempts to identify predictable, desirable, or historical relationships between jobs, then management employees may be asked to participate in meetings to further that effort.
- *Career planning meetings.* If the organization tries to discover individual career goals and interests as a means to do a "reality check" on possible successors, then management employees may have to meet with each employee covered in the succession plan.
- *Potential assessment meetings.* Assessing individual potential is future-oriented and may require meetings different from those required for performance appraisal.
- *Development meetings.* Planning for individual development, as a means of narrowing the gap between what individuals know or do presently and what they must know or do to qualify for advancement, may require time-consuming individual meetings.
- *Training, education, and developmental meetings.* Realization of succession plans may call for time-consuming meetings centered around training, education, and development.

While consolidating meetings can be done to save some time, each meeting listed above serves an important purpose. Attending meetings can require a significant time commitment from management employees at all levels.

Trends Affecting Succession Planning

The most important trends affecting succession planning are the same as those dramatically affecting management. However, the relative importance of these trends may differ by industry, organization size, and other factors. A 1993 survey of top managers revealed that their top priorities include quality improvement, employee education and skill building, productivity improvement, employee empowerment, and production process changes.[14] In a similar vein, recent research has revealed that the following trends are the most important ones affecting management:

- Increased expectations for more participation from all levels of the workforce
- Increased use of flatter and more flexible organization designs
- An increased need for worker commitment
- An organizationwide change in emphasis from loyalty to merit
- Increased diversity of the workforce
- The globalization of business[15]

Increased Expectations for More Workforce Participation

Employee involvement and empowerment are among the most prominent business trends in recent years, although existing research evidence
suggests that 10 percent or fewer of U.S. businesses have attempted to
implement "high-involvement management."[16] However, much has been
written on the topic, and many business leaders have accepted the notion
that today's workers, to be motivated effectively, must (at least) participate
in decisions affecting them.

On a practical level, that means succession planning must be designed
to allow workers to be involved in—and thus committed to—their own
development. Indeed, what is known about employee involvement suggests that employees will not support succession planning unless they have
a say in decisions affecting them. That view is, of course, at odds with
the thinking in organizations in which succession plans are handled in
utmost secrecy.

Increased Use of Flatter, More Flexible Organization Designs

Organizations have been restructuring and reengineering to cut costs, increase profitability and competitiveness, and improve communication by
reducing the number of management layers between frontline workers
and top-level decision makers.

Downsizing is one way that restructuring has been carried out. Its
effects have been dramatic: "According to data from the U.S. Bureau of
Labor Statistics and *Fortune,* the total number of regular employees of Fortune 500 companies fell from more than 16 million in 1979 to approximately 12 million in 1991."[17] That means about 4 million people have lost
their jobs in the wake of downsizing.

Use of flexible staffing approaches is another way that restructuring
has been carried out. Businesses are substituting *contingent* (part-time or
temporary) workers for *long-term* (once called permanent) employees to
hold down soaring employee benefit costs and secure better control over
staffing as workloads fluctuate. Employers wish to avoid emotionally de-
pressing—and sometimes violent—firings or layoffs whenever possible.

Downsizing and flexible staffing have created a work environment
in which there are fewer, and dwindling, opportunities for advancement.
Organizations have shorter career ladders. Employees also feel less secure
about it:

> According to a recent Gallup Poll, only 35 percent of employees are
> satisfied with their job security. This figure represents a 10 percent

reduction in the satisfaction level since 1989. Indeed, a Roper Poll indicated that morale and job satisfaction in American workplaces are at their lowest points since the Roper organization began tracking employee attitudes two decades ago.[18]

As a consequence, employees feel that they should receive immediate rewards for exemplary performance. They cannot depend on being around to reap long-term rewards, such as advancement. That makes employees—and organizations—less likely to encourage succession planning. Immediate gratification and short-term thinking are rewarded most.

An Increased Need for Worker Commitment And A Change in Emphasis from Loyalty to Merit

"To further complicate the relationship between employee and employer, downsizing, and the increasingly competitive nature of business, compels organizations to be more dependent on their employees to perform well," writes Charlene Marmer Solomon in a 1992 article in *Personnel Journal*. Companies expect more of employees, adds Solomon. "At a time when companies have fewer financial resources to entice workers, businesses need to attract and retain top talent."[19]

Employees are thus expected to do more with less and to demonstrate loyalty and commitment in the process. The problem is, fewer organizations than ever before can hold out the enticement of advancement that may be associated with seniority. Workers want to know "what's in it for me?" in everything they do. "Keeping a steady paycheck" is not a satisfactory answer for most employees. Commitment is earned both by employer and employee. As Solomon explains, "It's safe to say that the definition of loyalty and the expectation of commitment between employer and employee are in transition."[20] It seems to be moving toward a view that employment relationships will continue only so long as they benefit *both* employee and employer.

As a result of changing views toward loyalty, employers must find ways to develop people as quickly and as cost-effectively as possible. Long developmental periods benefit neither the individual nor the organization, since neither can be dependent on a continuing relationship.

Increased Diversity of the Workforce

Perhaps no other trend in the United States has greater implications for changing succession planning, and other approaches to human resources management, than workforce diversity. Among the most important trends:

 • Population and labor force growth will slow dramatically. Between 1990 and 2000, labor force growth is expected to be only 22 percent—less than at any time since the Great Depression of the 1930s.[21] Younger workers will be in comparative short supply. One result: Organizations may face stiffer competition in finding and keeping younger workers, those who have traditionally begun work in entry-level positions.

 • By the year 2000, approximately 50 percent of the workforce will be women, and 61 percent of the women will be at work. Women will compose about three fifths of the new entrants into the labor force between 1990 and 2000.[22] As a result, women's issues regarding succession planning—such as concern over the so-called glass ceiling in which women are unable to advance beyond a certain level on the corporate hierarchy[23]—will grow as an issue of pressing concern. It is already closely monitored, and many women are quite aware that less than 1/2 of 1 percent of the highest-paid officers and directors of the 799 largest publicly held corporations are women.[24]

 • Minorities and immigrants will increase as relative percentages of the U.S. labor force. For example, nonwhites will compose "29 percent of the net additions to the workforce between 1990 and 2000 and will be more than 15 percent of the workforce in the year 2000."[25] At the same time, approximately 600,000 new immigrants are entering the workforce each year, despite more restrictive immigration laws, and are dramatically altering the face of economies in the South and West, where they are most heavily concentrated.[26] Succession planning practices will have to be sensitive to the new face of the U.S. workforce, encouraging practices that will build sensitivity to—and tap the productivity potential of—an increasingly diverse workforce.

Each trend described above will result in a U.S. workforce that is more diverse. No longer will it be easy, effective, or desirable to choose successors who closely resemble the individuals they are being groomed to replace.

The Globalization of Business

Globalization is likely to remain the byword of the future. As the world becomes more interconnected electronically through various media, managers must learn to be more adept at managing across borders, cultures, and time. As Peter Drucker puts it, in the increasingly interdependent and interconnected global economy, "Management has emerged as the decisive factor of production. It is management on which competitive position has to be based."[27] As Drucker notes, world business may be increasingly intertwined, but competitive successes in the global marketplace depend on the ability of leadership talent in each national culture to do the most efficient and effective job of managing information, capital, people, and land.

That makes succession planning a critical issue in coping with the future. To deal effectively in a global marketplace, managers must appreciate cultural differences and be equipped to handle them. That means international assignments and foreign languages will become increasingly important for business leaders in the United States. Many multinational corporations are already giving their high-potential managers exposure to international assignments early in their careers so "they observe, learn and run diverse operations."[28]

Key Requirements for a New Approach To Succession Planning

Succession planning needs to be reengineered if it is to be effective in meeting the needs of today's organizations. The traditional approach to succession planning must be reexamined because, in many settings, the fundamental assumptions on which it is based are no longer valid. Few organizations today are static, few workers can depend on long tenure with their employers, and few employers are willing to invest large sums in employee development when job security and employee loyalty are uncertain. Moreover, the trends described earlier in this chapter imply additional changes that should be made to adapt succession planning to present trends and future challenges—such as gearing it to permit more participation, adapting it to flatter and more flexible organization designs, making it compatible with a change in emphasis from loyalty to merit, ensuring that it encourages increasing diversity and that it facilitates business globalization.

But what are the key requirements that a new approach to succession planning must meet if it is to work effectively now and in the future? They are summarized below and emphasize what decision makers should do:

1. *Think beyond merely replacing key positions or people.* Organizational structures can sometimes be refitted more easily than individuals can be replaced. Explore innovative ways to tap individual talents while achieving the same or better work results.

2. *Think long-term but act short-term* in order to counteract the erosion of job security and employee loyalty. The long-term must be carried out in the short-term.

3. *Integrate learning and working.* Considering the uncertainty of to-day's organizational environments, successors must be prepared for the future while performing productively in the present. That makes *action learning,* in which planned developmental activities are directly tied to work performance, the most promising training, education, and development effort for potential successors.

4. *Think outside as well as inside organizational boundaries and explore innovative succession planning approaches.* Increasingly, organizations must look to new models to achieve the same results. Among other recent trends is a move toward looking beyond organizational boundaries to identify resources that can be tapped temporarily or permanently as needs arise. Partnerships may be temporary or permanent, and they make many organizations simultaneously collaborators and competitors.

A new approach to succession planning must take this trend into account. Decision makers must discard the notion that successors must always be promoted from within and from among those with the longest tenure. More innovative approaches must at least be considered.

Key Steps in a New Approach to Succession Planning

How should systematic succession planning be carried out in organizational settings? While the answer to this question may vary by national culture, organizational culture, and top-management values, one way is to follow a "seven-pointed-star model" for systematic succession planning. That model is illustrated in Exhibit 2-4. The steps in the model, summarized below, provide the structure on which Chapters 3 through 10 of this book are based.

1. *Make the commitment to systematic succession planning, and establish a succession planning program.* To some extent, this first step represents a leap of faith in the value of planned over unplanned approaches to succession planning. The organization's decision makers should:

- Assess current problems and practices.
- Assess and demonstrate the need for the program.
- Determine the organization's exact succession planning program requirements.

Exhibit 2-4. The seven-pointed-star model for systematic succession planning.

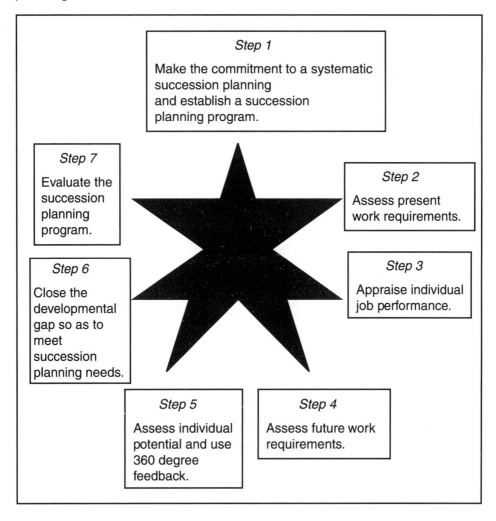

- Link the succession planning program directly to organizational and human resource strategic plans.
- Benchmark succession planning practices in other organizations.
- Clarify the roles of different groups in the program.
- Formulate a program mission statement.
- Write a policy and procedures to guide the program.
- Identify target groups to be served by the program.
- Establish program priorities.
- Prepare an action plan to guide the program.

- Communicate the action plan.
- Conduct succession planning meetings to unveil the program and review progress continuously.
- Train those involved in the program.
- Counsel managers about succession planning problems in their areas of responsibility.

2. *Assess present work requirements.* Only by assessing the present work requirements in key positions can decision makers prepare individuals for advancement in a way that is solidly grounded on work requirements. In this step, decision makers should clarify where key leadership positions exist in the organization and should apply one or more approaches to determining work requirements.

3. *Appraise individual performance.* How well are individuals presently performing their jobs? The answer to this question is critical because most succession planning programs assume that people must be performing well in their present jobs in order to qualify for advancement. As part of this step, the organization should also begin establishing an inventory of talent so that it is clear what human assets are available.

4. *Assess future work requirements.* What will be the work requirements in key leadership positions in the future? By attempting to assess future work requirements, decision makers may help prepare future leaders to cope with changing requirements.

5. *Assess future individual potential and use 360-degree feedback.* How well are individuals prepared for advancement? What talents do they possess, and how well do those talents match up to future work requirements? To answer these questions, the organization should establish a process to assess future individual potential. That future-oriented process should not be confused with past- or present-oriented employee performance appraisal.

6. *Close the developmental gap.* How can the organization meet succession planning needs by developing people internally or by using other means? The organization should establish a continuing program to cultivate future leaders internally. Decision makers should also explore alternatives to traditional promotion-from-within methods of meeting succession needs.

7. *Evaluate the succession planning program.* Improving the succession planning program depends on subjecting it to evaluation to assess how well it is working. Evaluation is the final step of the model. The results of evaluation should, in turn, be fed back to step 1 and used to make program refinements.

Summary

This chapter opened with a case study to illustrate an exemplary approach to succession planning and provide a list of characteristics that are found in exemplary succession planning programs. The chapter summarized typical problems afflicting succession planning programs and suggested possible solutions to them. Recent trends affecting succession planning programs were also reviewed, and a seven-pointed star model for systematic succession planning was supplied.

Part II

Laying the Foundation For A Succession Planning Program

The chapters in this part examine the process for laying the foundation for a systematic succession planning program in an organization by

- Assessing current problems and practices
- Demonstrating the need
- Determining organizational requirements
- Linking succession planning activities to organizational and human resource strategy
- Benchmarking succession planning practices in other organizations
- Creating a vision for systematic succession planning
- Clarifying the values that will be used to guide the succession planning program
- Obtaining and building management commitment to systematic succession planning
- Clarifying roles of various groups in the program
- Developing a written program mission statement, policy, and philosophy
- Identifying target groups to be served
- Establishing initial program priorities
- Preparing a program action plan
- Communicating the action plan
- Conducting succession planning meetings
- Training management and employees for program-related roles
- Counseling managers to deal with succession planning issues uniquely affecting them and their work areas

3
Making the Case for Change

For many years, introducing and consolidating change has been a center-piece of debate among managers and writers about management. Many believe that the essence of management's job is to be an instrument for progressive change—or, at least, to create an environment suitable for progressive change.

Establishing a systematic succession planning program in an organization that has never had one is a major change effort. It requires a quantum leap from the status quo, what some call *transformational change*. Success depends on demonstrating, at the outset, a need for change. The only exception is the rare case in which decision makers have already reached a consensus to depart radically from past practice.

To make the case for change in succession planning it will usually be necessary to:

- Assess current problems and practices.
- Demonstrate the need.
- Determine organizational requirements.
- Link succession planning activities to organizational and human resource strategy.
- Benchmark succession planning practices in other organizations.
- Create a vision for systematic succession planning.
- Clarify the values that will be used to guide the succession planning program.
- Obtain and build management commitment to systematic succession planning.

These issues are the focus of this chapter. They may seem to be monumental issues—and sometimes they are—but addressing them is essential to laying a solid foundation on which to build a systematic succession planning program.

Assessing Current Problems and Practices

Information about current problems and practices is needed before it is possible to build a convincing case for change. Planning for the future requires information about the past and present.

Current Problems

Crisis is a common impetus for change. As problems arise and are noticed, people naturally search for solutions. As the magnitude and severity of the problems increase, the search for a solution intensifies.

The same principles apply to succession planning. If the organization has experienced no crises in finding qualified successors, maintaining leadership continuity, or facilitating individual advancement, then few decision makers will feel an urgent need to direct attention to these issues. On the other hand, succession planning is likely to attract increasing attention when any or all of the following problems surface:

- Key positions are filled only after long delays.
- Key positions can be filled only by hiring from outside.
- Key positions have few people "ready now" to assume them (that is called *weak bench strength*).
- Vacancies in key positions cannot be filled by those who inspire confidence in their abilities.
- Key positions are subject to frequent or unexpected turnover.
- Replacements for key positions are frequently unsuccessful in performing some or all of their new duties.
- High performers or high-potential employees are leaving the organization in droves.
- Individuals routinely leave the organization to advance themselves professionally or to achieve their career goals.
- Decision makers complain about weak bench strength.
- Employees complain that decisions about whom to advance are not based on who is best qualified but rather on caprice, nepotism, expediency, or personal favoritism.
- Employees and decision makers complain that decisions about whom to promote into key positions are adversely affected by discrimination.

To build a case for a systematic approach to succession planning, ask decision makers how often they face these problems. In addition, focus attention on identifying the most important problems the organization is facing and review how those problems influence (or are influenced by) existing succession planning practices. If possible, document actual succession problems that have been experienced in the past—including horror stories (anecdotes about major problem situations) or war stories (anecdotes about negative experiences). Although anecdotes do not necessarily reflect existing conditions accurately, they can be powerfully persuasive and can help convince decision makers that a problem warrants investigation. Use them to focus attention on the organization's present succession planning practices—and, when appropriate, the need to change them from informal to systematic.

In my 1993 survey, I asked the respondents whose organizations use succession planning to indicate whether it has become more important over the last few years. Their answers are revealing, indicating that many current problems have emerged that necessitate increased attention to succession planning (see Exhibit 3-1).

Current Practices

In large organizations using an informal approach to succession planning, nobody is aware of the methods being used *within* the organization. In those settings succession planning is handled idiosyncratically—or not at all—by each manager. As a consequence, nobody is aware of the organization's existing practices.

A good place to start, then, is to find out what practices are currently being used in the organization. Exemplary, albeit isolated, approaches may already be in use, and they may serve as excellent starting points on which to begin a systematic approach. They enjoy the advantage of a track record because they have already been tried out in the organization and probably have one or more managers who support them.

To emphasize this point, I am aware of one Fortune 500 corporation that uses an informal approach to succession planning. Managers establish their own succession planning approaches as they feel they are warranted. Those activities vary dramatically. Most managers make no effort to conduct succession planning. As vacancies occur, replacements are frantically sought. Filling key positions is a crisis-oriented activity. (That is true in many organizations that do not use systematic succession planning programs, as respondents to my 1993 survey of such organizations revealed. See Exhibit 3-2.)

But even in this organization one major operating division has established a practice of circulating a confidential memo each year to department managers to request their nominations for their own replacements. No attempt is made to verify that the candidates possess the requisite knowledge and skills suitable for advancement, to verify that the candi-

Exhibit 3-1. The importance of succession planning.

Question: Has succession planning become *more important* to your organization over the last few years? If the answer is *yes,* briefly tell why; if *no,* briefly tell why.

[*What follows are direct quotations from survey respondents.*]

"Yes, to allocate resources for the future."

"Yes, for restructuring and executive retirements."

"Yes, fewer available candidates; cost-effective."

"Yes, our turnover is 5% with few opportunities. We need to make sure that when possible, we're promoting the best available."

"Yes, we've found ourselves in the terrible position of not having candidates for key positions."

"Yes, due to increased interface with parent company and expansion."

"Yes, due to downsizing."

"Yes, flatter organization requires broader skills."

"Yes, to replace president/CEO in the short- /long-term unscheduled event."

"Yes, it's important to corporation's strategic and business planning."

"Yes, due to reorganization/increase in industry competition."

"Yes, 'bench strength.'"

"Yes, it provides adaptability to change and promotes diversity; it enables us to do more with less."

"Yes, fewer opportunities for advancement means the need to identify, develop, and promote the 'finest.'"

"Yes, to identify needed skills of internal employees."

"Yes, we are running so 'lean' we must have people getting the right development—they need to be effective in their current and future job[s]."

"Yes, to provide broader talent pool."

"Yes, it allows fewer people to carry out more complex roles in a flatter organization."

"Yes, due to hiring restrictions."

"Yes, due to increased competition, technical sophistication, and EEO/AA issues."

"Yes, due to retirements of key executives and lack of general management talent."

"Yes, due to aging work force."

SOURCE: William J. Rothwell, "Results of a 1993 Survey on Succession Planning Practices," unpublished, The Pennsylvania State University, 1994.

Exhibit 3-2. Making decisions about successors (in organizations without systematic succession planning).

Question: How are decisions made about successors for positions in your organization? **N = 34** (Circle as many responses below as apply.)

	Number of Respondents
"We usually wait until positions are vacant and then scurry around madly to find successors."	20
"Whenever a position opens up, we rely on expediency to identify someone to fill it, hoping for the best."	15
"We secretly prepare successors."	10

Other (*please specify briefly*):
- Training and development program.
- Job posting.
- Usually scurry a long, long time.
- CEO.
- Fill from in-house first then advertise for qualified applicants.
- Use information from our manpower audit system.
- Committee decides to fill from within or recruit from outside.
- Promote.

SOURCE: William J. Rothwell, "Results of a 1993 Survey on Succession Planning Practices," unpublished, The Pennsylvania State University, 1994.

dates are willing to accept new assignments, to ensure their availability, if needed, or to prepare them for advancement. However, the practice of circulating a memo is an excellent place to start a systematic approach to succession planning. It can be a focal point to direct attention to the issue, and to the need to adopt a systematic approach.

Use three approaches to assess the current status of succession planning in the organization: (1) Talk to others informally; (2) send out an electronic mail question; or (3) conduct a written survey.

1. *Talk to others informally.* Ask key decision makers how they are handling succession planning practices. Begin by talking to the chairman, or chief executive officer, and the vice president of human resources; they are likely to be more aware of the processes than others. Then discuss the matter with other top managers. Pose questions like the following:

- How is the organization presently handling succession planning? What is being done at the highest levels? at the lower levels? in different divisions? in different locales?
- In your opinion, what should the organization be doing about succession planning, and why do you believe so?

- What predictable losses of key personnel are anticipated in your area of responsibility? For example, how many pending retirements are you aware of? Will pending promotions lead to a *domino effect* in which a vacancy in one key position, filled by a promotion from within, will set off a chain reaction that leads to a series of vacancies in other positions?
- What people or positions are absolutely critical to the continued successful operation of your division, function, department, or location? How would you handle the sudden and unexpected loss of a key person? several key people?
- Have you experienced the loss of a key person in the last year or two? What were the consequences of that loss? How did you handle the situation? If you had to do it again, would you handle it the same way? If so, why? If not, why not?
- What regular efforts, if any, do you make to identify possible replacements for key people or positions in your part of the organization? (For example, do you discuss this issue as part of performance appraisals? during business planning activities? in other ways?)
- What efforts, if any, do you make to identify individuals with the potential to advance beyond their current positions?
- How do you prepare individuals to advance when you perceive they have potential? What systematic efforts are made to train, educate, or develop them for future positions?
- What strongly held beliefs do you have about succession planning? For instance, do you believe the organization should inform possible successors of their status (and thereby risk creating a *crown prince problem*)? Or should it conceal that information (and risk losing high-potential employees who are tapped for better advancement prospects elsewhere)?
- How do you believe the organization should handle *plateaued workers*, who will advance no farther, and *blocked workers*, who are unable to advance beyond their current positions because they are blocked by plateaued workers above them?

When you finish interviewing decision makers, prepare a summary of the results about succession planning practices in the organization. Cite individual names only if given explicit permission to do so. Include a summary of current information on effective succession planning practices obtained externally (from sources such as this book) and then ask if more attention should be devoted to the topic. The reactions you receive should provide valuable clues about how much interest and support exists among key decision makers to explore a systematic approach to succession planning.

2. *Send out an electronic mail question.* A top manager in a large corporation focused attention on systematic succession planning merely by sending out an E-mail message to his peers. He posed this question: "Assume that you lost a key department manager on short notice through death or disability. (You can choose any department you wish.) Who is "ready" to assume that position? Name *anyone*." The question provoked a flurry of responses. By merely posing it he served an important role as a *change champion*. He drew attention to weak bench strength in the organization's supervisory ranks.

Try the same approach in your organization, or find just one top manager who will pose a similar question to colleagues by E-mail. That will certainly draw attention to the issue. It may also open debate or create an impetus for change.

3. *Conduct a written survey.* A written survey may be used as an alternative to informal discussions. Unlike informal discussions, however, a written survey is a high-profile effort. Many people will probably see it.

For that reason, be sure to follow the organization's protocol for authorizing a written survey. That may mean discussing it, prior to distribution, with the CEO, the vice president of human resources, or others they suggest. Ask for their approval to conduct the survey, and solicit their input for questions of interest to them. In some organizations they may also wish to attach their own cover letters to the survey, which is desirable because it demonstrates their awareness and support—and should also increase the response rate.

Use the questionnaire appearing in Exhibit 3-3 as a starting point, if you wish. It may save you time in developing one that is tailor-made to meet your organization's needs.

Once the questionnaire has been completed, feed the results back to the decision makers. In that way they can read for themselves what their peers have to say about the organization's current approach to succession planning. That can help them focus on specific problems to be solved and achieve a consensus for taking action.

However, conducting surveys is not without risks. Surveys may, for instance, surface opposition to a systematic succession planning program. That will make it more difficult to make the case in the future.

Demonstrating the Need

Few decision makers are willing to invest time, money, or effort in any activity from which they believe few benefits will be derived. It is thus essential to tie succession planning issues directly to pressing organizational problems and to the organization's core mission.

Exhibit 3-3. A questionnaire for assessing the status of succession planning in an organization.

[*Cover Memo*]

To: Top managers of [*name of corporation*]

From: —————————————————

Subject: Questionnaire on Succession Planning Practices

Date: ___ /___ /9___

Succession planning may be understood as *any effort designed to ensure the continuation of an organization by making provision for the replacement of key positions and people over time.* It may be *systematic* or *informal.* In systematic succession planning, an organization's managers attempt to prepare successors for key positions; in informal succession planning, no effort is made to prepare successors, and, as vacancies occur in key positions, managers respond to the crises at that time.

Please take a few minutes to respond to the questions appearing below. When you are finished, return the completed survey to [*name*] by [*date*] at [*location*]. Should you have questions, feel free to call me at [*phone number*].

Thank you for your cooperation!

The Questionnaire

Directions: Please take a few minutes to write down your responses to each question appearing below. This questionnaire is intended to be anonymous, though you are free to sign your name if you wish. You will receive a confidential report that summarizes the key responses and recommends action steps.

---

1. In your opinion, how well is this organization presently conducting *succession planning?* Circle your response in the left column. Next to your answer, briefly explain why you feel as you do.

   Very well
   Adequately
   Inadequately
   Very poorly

2. Should this organization establish/improve its approaches to succession planning? **Yes   No**

3. In your area of responsibility, which of the following have you established? Circle your response in the center column below.

Question	Response	Your Comments
a. A systematic means for identifying possible replacement needs stemming from retirement or other predictable losses of people?	Yes No	
b. A systematic approach to performance appraisal so as to clarify each individual's *current performance?*	Yes No	
c. A systematic approach to identifying individuals who have the potential to advance one or more levels beyond their current positions?	Yes No	
d. A systematic approach by which to accelerate the development of individuals who have the potential to advance one or more levels beyond their current positions?	Yes No	
e. A means by which to keep track of possible replacement by key position?	Yes No	

Please return the completed questionnaire to [*name*] by [*date*] at [*location*]. Should you have questions, feel free to call me at [*phone number*]. You will receive a summary of the anonymous survey results by [*date*].

THANK YOU FOR YOUR COOPERATION!

But exactly how is that done?

The answer to that question may vary across organizations. Each organization is unique; each organization has its own culture, history, and leadership group. But there are several possible ways by which to demonstrate the need for a systematic succession planning program. They are described below.

Hitchhiking on Crises

You can demonstrate need by hitchhiking on a crisis. As key positions become vacant or key people depart unexpectedly, seize that opportunity to poll decision makers informally. Begin by summarizing the recent crisis.

Contrast what happened with what could have happened if a systematic approach to succession planning had been used. Describe the impact of poorly planned succession planning on customers and employees, if you can. Then describe possible future conditions, especially future staffing needs that might result from recent downsizing, early retirement offers, or employee buyouts. Ask decision makers whether they believe it is time to explore a systematic approach to meeting succession needs. Then be ready to offer a concrete proposal for the next steps to take.

Seizing Opportunities

Need can also be demonstrated by detecting and seizing latent opportunities. In one organization, for example, the human resources department studied top managers' ages and projected retirement dates. The results were astonishing: All were due to retire within five years, and no replacements had been identified or developed. In that case, the HR department detected a brewing crisis and helped avert it. The organization subsequently established a systematic succession planning program that enjoyed strong support—and great success.

Any major strategic change will normally create opportunities. For instance, when AT&T was deregulated, decision makers realized that the organization's future success (and even survival) depended on identifying and developing new leaders who could thrive in a highly competitive, market-driven environment. That raised questions about the developmental needs of successors who had been nurtured during a period of regulation. It also prompted developmental activities to increase the market-oriented skills of future leaders.

Use the worksheet appearing in Exhibit 3-4 to focus your attention on ways to demonstrate the need for succession planning by hitchhiking on crises and seizing opportunities.

Showing the "Bottom-Line" Value

Demonstrating the need for a systematic succession planning program by what might be called "showing the bottom-line value" can be tough to do. As Jac Fitz-Enz writes:

> One of the difficulties in trying to measure the work of planners is that their output is primarily a plan of the future. By definition, we will not know for one, three, or perhaps five years how accurate their predictions were. In addition no one is capable of predicting future events, and therefore it is not fair to blame the planner for unforeseeable events. It is impossible to measure the value of a long-term plan in the

Exhibit 3-4. A worksheet for demonstrating the need for succession planning.

Directions: How can the need for a systematic succession planning program be demonstrated in an organization? Use the questions below to help you organize your thinking. Answer each question in the space appearing below it. Then compare your responses to those of others in the organization.

---

1. What *crises,* if any, have occurred in placing high-potential individuals or filling key positions in recent years? Describe the situations and how the organization coped with them. Then describe what happened (the outcomes) of those strategies.
   Make a list:

2. What opportunities, if any, have you noticed that may affect the knowledge, skills and abilities that will be needed by management employees in the future? (In particular, list strategic changes and then draw conclusions about their implications for knowledge, skills, and abilities.) Describe how those strategic changes are likely to affect the knowledge, skills, and abilities needed by management employees in the future.
   Make a list of strategic changes:

---

short term. Planners thus often feel frustrated because they cannot prove their worth with concrete evidence.[1]

Those involved in succession planning may feel that they face exactly the same frustrations to which Fitz-Enz alludes.

However, he has suggested ways to measure each of the following:

- How many positions need to be filled?
- How long does it take to fill positions?
- How many positions were filled over a given time span?

Succession planning may thus be measured by the number of key positions to be filled, the length of time required to fill them, and the number of key positions filled over a given time span. Of course, these measures are not directly tied to such bottom-line results for an organization as return on equity, return on investment, or cost-benefit analysis. But they are good places to start.

As Fitz-Enz rightly points out, the central questions to consider when quantifying program results are these:

- What factors are really important to the stakeholders?
- What action can influence results?[2]

Meaningful, quantifiable results can be obtained only by focusing attention directly on answering these questions. Decision makers must be asked what *they* believe to be the most important variables and actions that can be taken by the organization. This information, then, becomes the basis for establishing the financial benefits of a succession planning program.

When measuring succession planning results, decision makers may choose to focus on such issues as these:

- *How long does it take to fill key positions?* Measure the average elapsed days per position vacancy.
- *What percentage of key positions are* actually *filled from within?* Divide the number of key positions filled from within by the total number of key positions.
- *What percentage of key positions are capable of being filled from within?* Divide the number of high-potential workers available by the number of expected key position vacancies annually.
- *What is the percentage of successful replacements to all replacements?* Divide the number of retained replacements in key positions by all replacements made to key positions.

Of course, issues of importance to top managers, and appropriate measures of bottom-line results, will vary across organizations. The point is that these issues must be identified before appropriate criteria and bottom-line measures can be assigned.

Another way to view the bottom-line measure of a succession planning program is to compare the expenses of operating the program to the benefits accruing from it. That may be difficult to do, but it is not impossible.

As a first step, identify direct and indirect program expenses. Direct expenses result solely from operating a succession planning program. An example might be the salary of a full- or part-time succession planning coordinator. Indirect expenses result only partially from program operations. They may include partial salary expenses for managers involved in developing future leaders or the cost of materials to develop high potentials.

As a second step, identify direct and indirect program benefits. (This can be tricky, but the key to success is involving decision makers so that they accept and have ownership in the program benefits that are claimed.) Direct benefits are quantifiable and financially oriented. They might include savings in the fees of search firms. Indirect benefits might include the goodwill of having immediate successors prepared to step in, temporarily or permanently, whenever vacancies occur in key positions.

As a third step, compare the costs and benefits. Will the organization gain financially if a systematic approach to succession planning is adopted? In what ways? How can the relative effectiveness of the program be related directly to the organization's pressing business issues and core mission?

For additional information on cost-benefit analysis, review what has been written about evaluating the bottom-line value of training programs.[3] Modify those approaches to clarify costs and benefits of a systematic succession planning program.

Of course, apart from hitchhiking on crises, seizing opportunities, and showing the cost-benefit ratio for program operations, other ways might be used to demonstrate the need for a systematic approach to succession planning. Consider: How has the need been successfully demonstrated for other new programs in the organization? Can similar approaches be used to demonstrate a need for a systematic succession planning program?

Determining Organizational Requirements

All organizations do not share identical requirements for succession planning programs. Differences exist due to the organization's industry, size, stage of maturity, management values, internally available expertise, cost, time, and other considerations. Numerous surveys confirm that these and other issues can affect the appropriate design of succession planning programs.[4]

However, top-management goals are probably key considerations. What do they believe to be essential for a succession planning program? The most important questions on which to focus attention might include the following:

- How eager are top managers and other decision makers to systematize the organization's succession planning process(es)?
- How much time and attention are decision makers willing to devote to assessing key position requirements? identifying leadership competencies? identifying success factors for advancement in the organization? appraising individual performance? preparing and implementing individual development plans (IDPs) to ensure the efficient preparation of individuals for advancement into key positions?
- How stable is the current organizational structure? work processes? Can either or both be reliably used to plan for leadership continuity or replacements?
- How willing are decision makers to devote resources to cultivating talent from within?
- How much do decision makers prefer to fill key position vacancies from inside rather than from outside the organization?
- How willing are decision makers to use innovative alternatives to simple replacements from within?

Begin determining the essential requirements of an effective succession planning program by interviewing top managers. Pose the questions appearing above. Add others as pertinent to the organization. (As a starting point, use the interview guide appearing in Exhibit 3-5 for this purpose.) Then prepare and circulate a written proposal for a succession planning program that conforms to the consensus opinions of key decision makers.

Exhibit 3-5. An interview guide for determining the requirements for a succession planning program.

Directions: Use this interview guide to help you formulate the requirements for a systematic succession planning program for your organization. Arrange to meet the top managers and pose the following questions. Record notes in the spaces below. Then use the results of the interview as the basis for preparing a proposal for a systematic succession planning program. [*You may add questions if you wish.*]

---

1. What are your thoughts about how to approach succession planning in this organization *in a planned way?*

2. How should *key positions* be defined in this organization?

3. How should the work requirements of key positions be clarified?

4. How should current job performance be assessed?

5. How stable is the current organization structure? Will it be adequate to use as the basis for identifying key positions requiring successors in the future?

6. How should the qualifications or requirements for each key position be determined in the future?

7. How should individuals who have the potential to meet the qualifications for key positions be identified?

(continues)

Exhibit 3-5 (*continued*).

---

8. In your opinion, what are the essential resources that must be provided by the organization in order to accelerate the development of high-potential employees?

9. How should the development and progress of high-potential employees be tracked?

10. What other thoughts do you have about the essential requirements for an effective succession planning program in this organization? Why do you believe they are essential?

Linking Succession Planning Activities to Organizational And Human Resources Strategies

Succession planning should be linked to organizational and human resources strategy. However, achieving those linkages can be difficult.

Linking Organizational Strategy and Succession Planning

Organizational strategy refers to the way that the business chooses to compete. Important steps in the process include:

1. Determining the organization's purpose, goals, and objectives
2. Scanning the external environment to identify future threats and opportunities

3. Appraising the organization's present strengths and weaknesses
4. Examining the range of strategies
5. Choosing a strategy that is likely to seize maximum advantage from future opportunities by building on organizational strengths
6. Implementing strategy, particularly through changes in structure, policy, leadership, and rewards
7. Evaluating strategy periodically to assess how well it is helping the organization to achieve its strategic goals and objectives

Achieving effective linkage between organizational strategy and succession planning is difficult for three major reasons: (1) While effective strategy implementation depends on having the right people in the right places at the right times, it is not always clear *who* the right people are, *where* the right places are, and *when* those people will be needed. (2) Strategy is frequently expressed in a way that does not lend itself easily to developing action plans for succession planning. For instance, decision makers may focus attention on "increasing market share" or "increasing return-on-investment" without describing what kind of leadership will be needed to achieve those ambitious goals. (3) Organizational strategy *as practiced* may differ from organizational strategy *as theorized*,[5] which complicates the process of matching leadership to strategy. That can happen when daily decisions do not match written organizational strategy.

To overcome these problems, decision makers must take active steps to build the consideration of succession planning issues into the formulation of strategic plans. During the review of organizational strengths and weaknesses, for instance, decision makers should consider the organization's leadership talent. What kind of expertise is presently available? During strategic choice and implementation, decision makers should also consider whether the organization has the right talent to "make it happen." Who possesses the knowledge and skills that will contribute most effectively to making the strategy a reality? How can individuals be developed to help them acquire that knowledge and those skills? How can the organization establish an action plan to *manage* the human assets as effectively as the financial assets? Only by answering these questions—and taking active steps to narrow the gap between available and necessary talent—can the organization link its strategy and its succession planning.

Linking Human Resources Strategy and Succession Planning

Human resources strategy is the means that the organization chooses to make the most effective use of its HR programs and activities to satisfy organizational needs. Important steps in this process parallel those in organizational strategy making:

1. Determining the purpose, goals, and objectives of the HR function
2. Scanning the external environment to identify future threats and opportunities affecting HR inside and outside the organization
3. Appraising the organization's present HR strengths and weaknesses
4. Examining the range of HR strategies available
5. Choosing an HR strategy that is likely to support the organizational strategy
6. Implementing HR strategy through changes in such programs as training, selection, compensation, benefits, and labor relations
7. Evaluating HR strategy periodically for how well it supports organizational strategy

Unfortunately, efforts to integrate HR strategy and organizational strategy have met with only mixed success. As Golden and Ramanujam write, "The lack of integration between human resource management (HRM) and strategic business planning (SBP) processes is increasingly acknowledged as a major source of implementation failures. It is often alleged that companies develop strategic plans based on extensive marketing and financial data but neglect the human resource requirements necessary to successfully implement them."[6] Numerous theories have been developed over the years to identify ways to link organizational and HR strategy.[7] However, little evidence exists to show that great strides have been made in doing that.[8]

To link HR planning and succession planning, decision makers should examine how well HR policies and practices help (or hinder) leadership continuity, individual advancement, and the cultivation of internal talent. More specifically:

- How does the organization conduct recruitment, selection, and placement? How much consideration is given during this process to long-term retention and development of prospective or new employees?
- How does the organization conduct training, education, and development? How much (relative) attention is given to the long-term cultivation of employee talent as opposed to focusing attention on training individuals to meet immediate job requirements?
- How well do existing compensation and benefit practices support internal placement? transfers? promotions? Do implicit *disincentives* exist to dissuade employees from wanting to accept promotions or assume leadership roles?
- How do existing labor relations agreements affect the organization's promotion, rotation, transfer, and other employment practices?

To integrate HR strategy and succession planning, examine existing HR program efforts such as selection, training, compensation, and benefits against succession planning needs. Identify HR practices that could encourage or that presently discourage effective succession planning. Then take active steps to ensure that HR practices facilitate, and do not impede, long-term efforts to groom leadership talent from within.

Benchmarking Succession Planning Practices In Other Organizations

Discussions with top managers and other key decision makers in an organization should yield valuable information about the needs that a succession planning program should meet. But that information can be supplemented by benchmarking succession planning practices in other organizations. Moreover, the results of benchmarking may intensify the interests of key decision makers in succession planning because it may demonstrate that other organizations are using better, or more effective, methods. As Robert C. Camp explains: "Only the approach of establishing operating targets and productivity programs based on industry best practices leads to superior performance. That process, being used increasingly in U. S. business, is known as *benchmarking*."[9] Benchmarking has also surfaced in recent years as a powerful tool for improving organizational work processes and is frequently associated with total quality management. Its primary value is to provide fresh perspectives, and points for comparison, from other organizations. It can thereby accelerate the process of introducing a state-of-the-art program by comparing existing practices in one organization to the best practices already in use elsewhere.

Although there are various ways by which to conduct benchmarking, Camp suggests that it should be carried out in the following way:

1. Identify what to benchmark.
2. Identify comparative organizations.
3. Determine a data collection method, and collect data.
4. Determine the current performance "gap."
5. Project future performance levels.
6. Communicate benchmark findings and gain acceptance for them.
7. Establish functional goals based on the results of the benchmarking study.
8. Develop action plans based on the results of the benchmarking study.

9. Take action and monitor progress.
10. Recalibrate benchmarks.[10]

Typically, then, benchmarking begins when decision makers make a commitment. They clarify their objectives and draft questions to which they seek answers. Comparative organizations, often but not always in the same industry, are chosen. A suitable data collection method is selected, and written questionnaires and interview guides are frequently used for data collection. Site visits (field trips) are arranged to one or more organizations identified as being "best in class."

Benchmarking should not be pursued as a fishing expedition; rather, it should be guided by specific objectives and questions. Participants should start out with some familiarity with the process—such as succession planning practices. (That may mean that they have to be briefed before participating in a site visit.) Several key decision makers should go on the site visits so they can compare practices in other organizations with their own. That is an excellent way, too, to win over skeptics and demonstrate that "the way we have always done it here" may not be the best approach.

Most Fortune 500 companies are well-known for their effective succession planning practices. Blue-chip companies such as Motorola, Xerox, IBM, AT&T, General Electric, Coca-Cola, and General Motors, among others, are perhaps best known for conducting effective succession planning. They may rightly be considered best-in-class companies. Appropriate contacts at these organizations should be contacted through such professional societies as the Human Resource Planning Society (41 East 42 Street, Suite 1509, New York, N.Y. 10017), the American Management Association (135 W. 50th Street, New York, N.Y. 10020), the American Society for Training and Development (1640 King Street, Alexandria, Va. 22313), or the Society for Human Resource Management (606 N. Washington Street, Alexandria, Va. 22314).

Always develop questions *before* making a site visit (see the list of possible questions in Exhibit 3-6). Then contact representatives from two or three of those organizations and ask if they are willing to host benchmarking visits to their locations. If so, send them the questions ahead of the visit so that they have time to prepare their responses. Sometimes they may wish to see the questions in advance before they commit to a visit.

It may be difficult to arrange benchmarking visits on succession planning. Some organizations consider the process sensitive to their operations—and revealing about their corporate strategies. Consequently, one approach is to seek access to organizations where you or others in your organization have personal contacts. If necessary, begin with local organizations that have successfully established succession planning. Identify

(text continues on page 88)

Exhibit 3-6. An interview guide for benchmarking succession planning practices.

Directions: Use this interview guide to help you prepare and share questions in advance of a benchmarking visit to an organization known for its effective succession planning practices. Pose the following questions and record notes in the spaces below. Use the results in formulating a proposal for establishing or improving succession planning in your organization. [*Add questions as appropriate for your organization.*]

---

1. What mission statement has been established to guide succession planning in your organization?

2. What goals and objectives have been established for succession planning in your organization?

3. What policy and philosophy statement has been *written* to guide succession planning in your organization? Would it be possible to obtain a copy?

4. How does your organization define *key positions?* What positions, if any, are given special attention in your succession planning program? Why are they given that attention?

5. How does your organization identify, describe, or clarify the requirements of key positions? (For example, has your organization

(continues)

Exhibit 3-6 (*continued*).

---

made an effort to identify job responsibilities, competencies, or success factors by level?)

6. How does your organization assess current *job performance* for succession planning purposes? (Do you use the organization's existing performance appraisal system—or something else?)

7. Does your organization use replacement charts based on the current organization chart? (If not, why not?)

8. How does your organization determine the qualifications or requirements for each future key position?

9. How does your organization attempt to integrate succession planning with organizational strategy? with human resources strategy?

10. How does your organization identify successors for key positions?

11. How does your organization identify high-potential employees, those who are capable of advancing two or more levels beyond their current placement?

12. How does your organization establish individual development plans (IDPs) to accelerate the development of high-potential employees?

13. What special programs, if any, has your organization established to accelerate the development of high potentials?

14. What special computer software, if any, does your organization use to support its succession planning program?

15. How does your organization evaluate the succession planning program?

16. What special problems has your organization encountered with succession planning? How have those been solved?

them by talking to your peers in local chapters of the American Society for Training and Development (ASTD), the Society for Human Resource Management (SHRM), or other professional societies.

Obtaining and Building Management Commitment To Systematic Succession Planning

Securing management commitment to systematic succession planning may not occur rapidly. Skeptics are difficult to convince in short order. It will take time and proof of tangible evidence of success to win them over.

Opinions about Succession Planning

My 1993 survey of succession planning practices revealed sharp disparities in opinions about systematic succession planning programs. Examine Exhibit 3-7; then consider how you would answer those questions about top management opinions in *your* organization. Turn then to Exhibit 3-8 and consider how you would characterize your own opinions about systematic succession planning.

Creating a Vision for Systematic Succession Planning

A *vision* is a credible and realistic view of a future, desirable state. *Visioning* is the process of creating that view.[11]

Visioning for systematic succession planning is thus a process of crystallizing a new view about how an organization can meet its succession needs. Use the worksheet appearing in Exhibit 3-9 to facilitate visioning for systematic succession planning among key stakeholders in your organization.

Clarifying the Values to Guide the Succession Planning Program

"A *value*," write Dave Francis and Mike Woodcock, "is a belief in action. It is a choice about what is good or bad, important or unimportant. Values shape behavior."[12] Values are worthy of attention precisely because they do shape behavior.

Organizations embody values in their corporate cultures, and values are the underpinning of management decisions. While frequently unexamined and inarticulated as embodied in cultures or in decisions, values

Exhibit 3-7. Opinions of top managers about succession planning.

Question: How would you summarize the opinions of top managers in your organization about a succession planning program?

	Organizations with Planned Succession Programs N = 30	Organizations without Planned Succession Programs N = 34
1. They believe a succession planning program is worthwhile and that a formal program is better than an informal program.	18	5
2. They believe that a succession planning program is worthwhile but are not aware of how to manage it efficiently and effectively.	12	10
3. They don't believe succession planning is worth the time required for it.	2	8
4. I don't know what they think about a succession planning program.	1	8
5. They have no clue why such a program might be worthwhile.	1	7
6. Other (*please describe briefly*):		

• They do not like bureaucracy and worry that a plan might add that and take away flexibity.
• Control of selection for executive roles is extremely centralized. Our CEO drives these decisions with the executive staff inputting to the decision.
• Every opening is used as an opportunity to redefine, restructure, or reduce. This happens frequently at the level that reports to vice presidents. Also, our HR function is leery of establishing a program, like succession planning, that builds in or creates expectations that may not be fulfilled.

SOURCE: William J. Rothwell, "Results of a 1993 Survey on Succession Planning Practices," unpublished, The Pennsylvania State University, 1994.

Exhibit 3-8. Opinions of human resources professionals about succession planning.

Question: How would you summarize *your* opinions about a succession planning program?

	Organizations with Planned Succession Programs N = 30	Organizations without Planned Succession Programs N = 34
1. Succession planning is critically important to this organization at this time.	17	15
2. I believe a succession planning program is important.	10	13
3. I believe a succession planning program is worthwhile, but other programs are more important for this organization right now.	3	9
4. I don't believe such a program is important.	0	0
5. I believe that other methods work better in identifying and preparing possible successors.	0	0
6. Other (*please describe briefly.*)		

- Important and good when linked to integrated development systems.
- Career planning.
- Our informal system seems to work satisfactorily.

SOURCE: William J. Rothwell, "Results of a 1993 Survey on Succession Planning Practices," unpublished, The Pennsylvania State University, 1994.

are central to understanding corporate cultures and to changing them. *Values clarification* is the process of articulating values.

There are two kinds of values: terminal and enabling. *Terminal values* are the results or outcomes that are sought; *enabling values* are exhibited in pursuit of terminal values. Happiness, as Aristotle pointed out in his famous ancient work *The Nicomachean Ethics*, is a terminal value; honesty is an enabling value.

As the case is made for establishing a systematic succession planning

Exhibit 3-9. A worksheet for clarifying a vision to guide succession planning.

Directions: Use this worksheet to help you carry out a visioning exercise on systematic succession planning. In the space below, describe *how you envision a systematic succession planning program will work in this organization.* Feel free to be creative and to exercise your imagination. What we want is your description of "how this process should work in the future if it were functioning ideally." The results of this exercise will be compiled and used to distill an essential vision to guide the startup of this program.

---

program, stakeholders should be directed to examine their values to ensure that the program's mission is guided by the values prized by, manifested in, or desired by the organizational culture. For instance, stakeholders should consider the extent to which they prize the following values:

- Customer service
- Social responsibility
- Social justice
- Quality
- Productivity
- Efficiency
- Effectiveness
- Employee empowerment
- Employee involvement
- Employee development and growth

Moreover, stakeholders may examine the values implicit in each reason for sponsoring a systematic succession planning program (see the reasons listed in Exhibit 1-4).

When making the case for a systematic succession planning program, the succession planning coordinator or a change champion may wish to clarify corporate values—if they have not previously been clarified—and/or help stakeholders determine how those values should be related to, and guide, a succession planning program. The worksheet appearing in Exhibit 3-10 may be helpful for this purpose. Use it when appropriate in a meeting with top managers, with a succession planning committee, or with other key stakeholders.

Understanding How to Secure Management Commitment

Diane Dormant's ABCD model is a helpful tool for understanding how to secure management commitment. ABCD is an abbreviation based on the first letter of several key words. Her model suggests that large-scale organizational change, such as the introduction of a systematic succession planning program, can be understood by examining *adopters* (who is affected by the change?), *blackbox* (what is the change process?), *change agent* (who is making the change?), and *domain* (what is the change context?).[13]

The most valuable feature of Dormant's model is her view that different strategies are appropriate at different stages in the introduction of a change. The change agent should thus take actions to facilitate change that are keyed to the adopter's stage in accepting an innovation.

Dormant believes that adopters progress through five identifiable stages in accepting an innovation:[14]

Exhibit 3-10. A worksheet for clarifying the values to guide systematic succession planning.

Directions: Use this worksheet to help you clarify the underlying values of the organization and to identify how systematic succession planning should be related to those values. In the left column, list what you believe to be the organization's "core values." To clarify them, answer these questions:

1. What characteristics are most highly prized in this organization?
2. What characteristics must an individual exhibit to be promoted or to advance in this organization?

Then, in the right column, describe how you believe a systematic succession planning program should support or be related to these core values. To clarify that issue, answer these questions in the space opposite to each value listed in the left column:

1. How should the systematic succession planning program relate to the value?
2. What activities of systematic succession planning would help support (or change) this value?

When you finish, be prepared to discuss your worksheet with others in the organization.

Core Values	How a Systematic Succession Planning Program Should Support the Core Values
1.	
2.	
3.	
4.	
5.	
6.	

1. *Awareness.* During this first stage, adopters have little information about the innovation. They are passive and are generally unwilling to seek information. To deal with the awareness stage, change agents should advertise the innovation, making efforts to attract attention to it and provide positive information about it.

2. *Self-concern.* In this second stage, adopters are more active. They express concern about how they will be individually affected by a change and pose questions about the consequences of an innovation. Change agents should deal with this stage by enacting the role of counselor—answering questions and providing relevant information.

3. *Mental tryout.* Adopters remain active in the third stage and ask pointed questions related to their own applications of an innovation. Change agents should enact the role of demonstrators, providing relevant examples and demonstrating to adopters how they may apply an innovation to their unique situations.

4. *Hands-on trial.* In this fourth stage, adopters are interested in learning how to apply an innovation to their own situations. Their opinions about the innovation are being formed from personal experience. Change agents should provide them with training and detailed feedback about how well they are applying the innovation. Testimonials of success will be persuasive during this stage, helping to shape the conclusions reached by the adopters about an innovation.

5. *Adoption.* By the fifth and final stage, which Dormant calls adoption, adopters have integrated the innovation into their work and are interested in specific problem solving that is related to their own applications. Change agents should provide personal support, help adopters find the resources they need to perform effectively, and provide rewards for successful implementation.

Applying these stages to the process of obtaining and building management support for systematic succession planning should be apparent. The appropriate strategies that change agents should use depend on the stage of acceptance. See Exhibit 3-11.

An important point to bear in mind is that a succession planning program will be effective only when it enjoys support from its stakeholders. Indeed, the stakeholders must perform succession planning for it to work. The results of a 1987 survey revealed that "much of the actual work of succession planning *is* done by line managers." Seventy-eight percent of the respondents said that overall responsibility for the process resides with the human resources function. However, all the respondents agreed that "the CEO, President and/or Board of Directors participates in the process of reviewing succession and development plans."[15] Hence, obtaining and

Exhibit 3-11. Actions to build management commitment to succession planning.

Stage of Acceptance	Appropriate Actions
Awareness	1. Advertise succession planning to management employees. 2. Provide general information about succession planning.
Self-concern	1. Answer questions. 2. Provide relevant information.
Mental tryout	1. Provide relevant examples of applications of succession planning policy/practices to specific functions or activities within the organization. 2. Demonstrate how succession planning may be used in each organizational area.
Hands-on trial	1. Offer training on succession planning. 2. Meet with top managers individually to discuss succession planning in their areas. 3. Collect and disseminate testimonials of success.
Adoption	1. Provide personal support to top managers on applications of systematic succession planning. 2. Help program users perform effectively through individualized feedback and counseling. 3. Identify appropriate rewards for succession planning.

building management commitment to systematic succession planning is essential to the success of an effective program.

Summary

When preparing to introduce a systematic succession planning program, begin by assessing the organization's current succession planning problems and practices, demonstrating the business need for succession planning, determining the organization's unique succession planning requirements, linking the succession planning program to the organization's strategic plans and human resource plans, benchmarking succession planning processes in other organizations, and obtaining and building management commitment.

This chapter has reviewed these steps and thereby demonstrated ways by which to make the case for change.

The next chapter begins where this chapter ends. It emphasizes the importance of clarifying roles in the succession planning program, developing a program mission statement and related policies and procedures, identifying target groups, setting program priorities, establishing program credibility, preparing a program action plan, communicating the action plan, training management and employees for their roles, and conducting program kickoff meetings and briefing sessions.

4

Starting Up a Systematic Succession Planning Program

An organization should be ready to start up a systematic succession planning program once the case has been persuasively made that one is needed. Start-up usually involves taking such action as clarifying roles in the succession planning program, formulating a program mission statement, writing a program policy, clarifying program procedures, identifying groups targeted for program action, and setting program priorities. This chapter focuses on these issues.

Clarifying Program Roles

What are roles? How can roles in a succession planning program be clarified so that organizational members know what they should do to support the effort? This section answers these questions.

Understanding Roles

A *role* is an expected pattern of behaviors and is usually linked to a job in the organization. Although most organizations outline responsibilities in job descriptions, few job descriptions are sufficiently detailed to clarify how job incumbents should carry out their duties or interact with others. However, roles do permit such clarification. Indeed, "a role may include attitudes and values as well as specific kinds of behavior. It is what an individual must do in order to validate his or her occupancy of a particular position."[1]

Role theory occupies a central place in writings about management and organizations. Internalizing a role has often been compared to the communication process (see Exhibit 4-1). *Role senders* (role incumbents) bring to their roles expectations about what they should do, how they

Exhibit 4-1. A model for conceptualizing role theory.

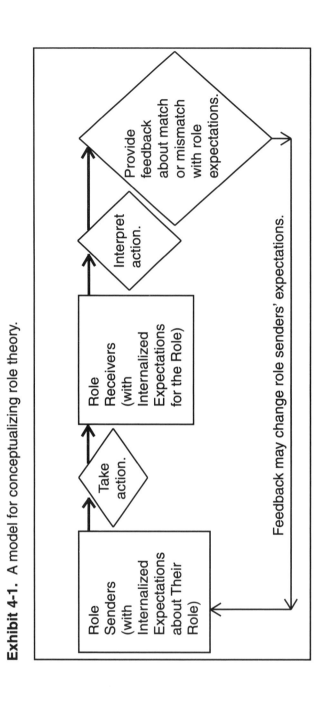

should do it, and how they should interact with others. Their expectations are influenced by their previous education, experience, values, and background. They are also influenced by what they are told about the role during the recruitment, training, and selection process. *Role receivers*—others in the organization with whom role senders interact—observe these behaviors and draw conclusions from them based on their own expectations. They provide feedback to indicate whether the behavior matches what they expect. That feedback, in turn, may affect the role senders' expectations and behaviors.

To complicate matters, individuals enact more than one role in organizations. For instance, they may serve as superiors, colleagues, and subordinates. They may also enact roles outside the organization, such as spouse, parent, child, citizen, churchgoer, or professional. Each role may carry its own culturally bound expectations for behavior.

Multiple roles can lead to *role conflict*. For example, supervisors may be expected by their employers to act in the best interests of the organization. That means they must occasionally make hard-nosed business decisions. On the other hand, supervisors may also be expected to represent the interests and concerns of their subordinates to the employer. To cite another example: Human resource managers may perceive their own role to be facilitative and that they should provide advice to operating managers when they must reach decisions about HR issues. But operating managers may expect them to act forcefully and proactively on their own, spearheading new initiatives and taking steps to avert future HR problems that may arise in the organization. In both examples, conflicting expectations may lead role incumbents to experience stress and frustration.

Effective performance is influenced by congruence in role expectations. Role senders can achieve desired results only when they know what they are expected to do *and* when role receivers make their expectations clear.

Applying Role Theory to Succession Planning

As role theory indicates, performance is influenced by shared role expectations. As one step in establishing systematic succession planning, clarify program roles so that individuals throughout the organization are aware of what they are expected to do and how they are expected to behave.

At the outset, direct attention to the roles to be enacted by three important groups: (1) management employees, (2) program facilitators, and (3) program participants. These roles may overlap. In each case, however, it is important to surface what group members already believe about their roles in succession planning, feed that information back to them, provide information about alternative roles, and seek consensus on desirable roles.

Think of the roles of management employees as ranging along one continuum from active to passive and along another continuum from supporter to opponent. (See the grid in Exhibit 4-2 to help conceptualize those roles.) Management employees who take an active role believe that succession planning should occupy much of their time. They feel that they should be defining present work requirements, planning for future work requirements, appraising individual performance, assessing individual potential, planning for individual development, and participating in developmental activities. On the other hand, management employees who take a passive role believe that issues other than succession planning should occupy their time. A supporter sees systematic succession planning as a valuable activity; an opponent has reservations about it.

Think of facilitators' roles as ranging along a continuum from directive to nondirective. Facilitators who take a directive role indicate what they expect from those participating in a systematic succession planning program. They then attempt to enforce that by providing briefings, training, or written directions to help others understand what they are supposed to do. Operating managers and top managers who are assigned responsibilities as succession planning coordinators may adopt that role—particularly during the start-up phase when many may be confused about what to do.

On the other hand, facilitators who take a nondirective role attempt to identify what various stakeholders want from the program and what behaviors the stakeholders believe to be associated with those desired program results. They collect information from stakeholders, feed it back to them, and help them establish their own roles and action plans. Much time may be spent one-on-one to help managers and employees at different levels understand what their roles should be.

Participant roles range along one continuum from aware to unaware and along another continuum from organizationally focused to personally/individually focused. Participants are defined as those tapped by the organization to be involved in the succession planning process. They are usually designated to be developed for one or more future positions. They may be aware or unaware that they have been thus designated by the organization as a possible successor. They may be focused on satisfying their personal needs in the future (an individual focus) or on satisfying the organization's needs (an organizational focus).

To clarify roles, ask managers, facilitators, and participants to answer the following questions:

1. What they are presently doing to help the organization meet its future succession needs.

Exhibit 4-2. Management roles in succession planning: a grid.

Level of Support

		Supporter	Opponent
L E V E L **O F** **E F F O R T**	**A C T I V E**	• Champions succession planning efforts vigorously. • Views management's role as one geared to developing and motivating people.	• Opposes succession planning vigorously. • Views management's role as one geared to making profits— even when that means demotivating people.
	P A S S I V E	• Expresses general support for succession planning, with reservations about some approaches. • Wishes more "study" and "analysis" would be conducted.	• Prefers to devote time to other activities.

   2. What they think they should do to help the organization establish a systematic succession planning program to meet its future succession needs.

   3. What in their opinion should be the role(s) of managers and employees in supporting an effective succession planning program in the organization.

Pose these questions in meetings or circulate written surveys as appropriate. If neither approach will work due to a desire to keep a succession planning program "secret," then ask top managers these questions and ask how roles to support succession planning may be clarified throughout the organization.

Formulating a Mission Statement

Why is an organization undertaking a systematic succession planning program? What outcomes do stakeholders desire from it? These questions should be answered during the program start-up phase in order to achieve agreement among stakeholders about the program's purpose and desired results.

The lack of a mission statement has been called the Achilles heel of succession planning programs. As Walter R. Mahler and Stephen J. Drotter point out, these programs have too often been established without careful thought being given to purpose or desired outcomes. "Company after company," they write, "rushed into program mechanics. Time went by and disillusionment set in. The programs did not live up to their promises."[2] The reason for that, they believe, is that program mission was never adequately clarified at the outset.

What Is a Mission Statement?

A mission, or purpose, statement describes the purpose of a program, or the reason for its existence. (In this context, *mission* and *purpose* may be regarded as synonymous.)

Formulating a mission statement is a first step in organizational planning. Writers on organizational strategy suggest that formulating organizational mission should precede formulating strategy. An organizational mission statement answers such questions as these:

- Why is the organization in business?
- What results is it trying to achieve?
- What market does it serve?
- What products or services does it offer?

Mission statements may also be formulated for organizational functions (such as operations, finance, marketing, or personnel), divisions, locations, or activities. At levels below the organization, mission statements for functions, divisions, locations or activities should answer such questions as these:

- Why does the function, division, location or activity exist?
- How does it contribute to achieving the organization's mission? strategic plans?
- What outcomes or results are expected from it?

Mission statements may also provide philosophical statements (what do we believe?), product or service descriptions (what is to be made or sold?), customer descriptions (whose needs are to be served?), and rationale (why is the mission worth performing?).

What Questions about Succession Planning Should Be Answered by a Mission Statement?

Like any organizational effort, a succession planning program should have a mission statement to explain why it exists, what outcomes are desired from it, why those outcomes are valuable, what products or services will be offered, who will be served by the program, and other issues of importance.

However, mission statements for succession planning programs will vary across organizations. After all, not all programs are designed to serve the same purpose, achieve the same results, or offer the same products or services. So what specific issues should be addressed in a mission statement for a succession planning program?

One way to begin to answer that question is to focus attention on issues of particular importance to the organization. With this process, decision makers will formulate the program's mission. Such issues may include:

1. What is a key position?
2. What is the definition of a high potential (HiPo)?
3. What is the organization's responsibility in identifying HiPos, and what should it be?
4. What is the definition of an exemplary performer?
5. What is the organization's responsibility in identifying and rewarding exemplary performers? What should it be?
6. How should the organization fill key positions?
7. What percentage of vacancies in key positions should be filled from within? from without? What percentage should be handled through other means?
8. What percentage of key positions should have at least one identifiable *backup* (successor)?
9. In what percentage of key positions should there be *holes*, i.e., no designated successors?
10. What is the maximum time that exemplary performers should remain in their positions?
11. What should be the maximum allowable percentage of avoidable turnover among high potentials? exemplary performers? What should be done to reduce it?
12. What should be the maximum allowable percentage of failures in key positions after individual advancement?
13. What percentage of key positions should be filled with employees from legally protected labor groups, such as women, minorities, and the disabled?

14. How desirable are international assignments for designated successors?
15. How should HiPos be prepared for advancement, and how should advancement be defined?
16. What should be the role and responsibility of each employee, manager, and the HR department in the process of developing HiPos?
17. How much should individual career goals be surfaced, considered, and tracked in succession planning?
18. How openly should the organization communicate about the status of individuals who are identified to be HiPos?

Of course, additional questions may also be posed to help clarify program purpose. Use the worksheet in Exhibit 4-3 to help clarify the mission of succession planning in an organization.

How Is a Mission Statement Prepared?

Prepare a mission statement by using any one of at least three possible approaches: "Ask, formulate, and establish," "recommend and listen," and "facilitate an interactive debate."

1. *The "ask, formulate, and establish" approach* is initiated when someone begins asking questions about succession planning in the organization. That launches a dialogue to establish program mission. Often that duty falls to human resources generalists, human resources development specialists, or management development specialists, although others—such as the CEO, a vice president of human resources or a specially appointed succession planning coordinator—could function as *change champions* to focus attention on the need for change. As a second step, change champions should compile the answers received from different decision makers. They should then formulate and circulate a proposal based on those answers. As a third and final step, decision makers hammer out their own responses, using the proposal as a starting point. In so doing, they establish a mission statement for a succession planning program.

A key advantage of this approach is that it requires little initial effort from busy top managers. Others undertake the groundbreaking work to collect information about succession planning, compile it, and base recommendations on it. (That is what officers in the armed services call "staff work.") On the other hand, a key disadvantage of this approach is that executives do not actively participate in the information-gathering process, so they will have no collective ownership in the results. A subsequent step is thus required to capture their support and thereby achieve consensus.

Exhibit 4-3. A worksheet to formulate a mission statement for succession planning.

Directions: Use this worksheet as an aid to formulate the mission of the succession planning program in your organization. Circulate the worksheet among decision makers. Ask them to respond individually. For each question posed, ask them to write an answer in the space below. Compile their responses and then feed them back as a catalyst for subsequent decision making about the mission statement of a succession planning program in the organization. Add paper or questions appropriate to your organization as necessary.

---

1. What is a key position?

2. What is the definition of a high-potential (HiPo)?

3. What is the organization's responsibility in identifying HiPos, and what should it be?

4. What is the definition of an exemplary performer?

5. What is the organization's responsibility in identifying and rewarding exemplary performers? What should it be?

6. How should the organization fill key positions?

7. What percentage of vacancies in key positions should be filled from within? from without? What percentage should be handled through other means?

(continues)

Exhibit 4-3 (*continued*).

---

8. What percentage of key positions should have at least one identifiable *backup* (successor)?

9. In what percentage of key positions should there be *holes* (that is, no designated successors)?

10. What is the maximum time that exemplary performers should remain in their positions?

11. What should be the maximum allowable percentage of avoidable turnover among Hi Pos? exemplary performers? What should be done to reduce it?

12. What should be the maximum allowable percentage *of failures* in key positions after individual advancement?

13. What percentage of key positions should be filled with employees from legally protected labor groups, such as women, minorities, and the disabled?

14. How desirable are international assignments for designated successors?

15. How should HiPos be prepared for advancement?

16. What should be the role and responsibility of each employee and the HR department in the process of developing HiPos?

17. How much should individual career goals be surfaced, considered, and tracked in succession planning?

18. How openly should the organization communicate with individuals who are identified to be HiPos about their status?

19. Draft a mission statement for the program. Ask:

   • How does it contribute to achieving the organization's mission and strategic plans?

   • What outcomes or results should be expected from it?

---

2. *The "recommend and listen" approach,* on the other hand, relies on considerable expertise by the HR generalists, HRD specialists, or MD specialists who use it. To use this approach they must start out with a thorough grasp of the organization's culture, top-management desires and values, and state-of-the-art succession planning practices. From that perspective, they *recommend* a starting point for the program, providing their own initial answers to the key questions abut program mission listed in Exhibit 4-3. They prepare and circulate their recommendations for a systematic succession planning program, usually in proposal form. They then *listen* to reactions from key decision makers, using the initial proposal as a catalyst to stimulate debate and discussion.

The advantage of this approach is that it usually has a shorter cycle time than "ask, formulate, and establish." It also relies more heavily on expert information about state-of-the-art succession planning practices outside the organization, thereby avoiding a tendency to reinvent the wheel. But these advantages exist only when those using the approach have a thorough grasp of the organization's current succession planning problems and practices, culture, decision-maker preferences, and state-of-the-art practices. Otherwise, it can provoke time-consuming conflicts among decision-makers that will only prolong efforts to achieve top-level consensus.

3. *The "facilitate an interactive debate" approach* is the most complex of the three methods of preparing a mission statement. HR generalists, HRD specialists, MD specialists, or others who use it function as group facilitators rather than as expert-consultants.

The first step is to prepare a forum for key decision makers to carry out an *interactive debate* about the succession planning program's mission. While the forum's content may be dictated by the CEO—or even by members of the board of directors—HR professionals set up the process for the debate. (*Content* refers to the issues on which the forum will focus; *process* refers to the means by which those issues will be examined.) That usually means that the CEO and the HR professional (or the CEO and an external facilitator) must work closely together to plot the best means by which to explore the most important succession planning issues facing the organization. Such a debate may take the form of an off-site retreat lasting several days or of numerous meetings spread across several months. During the debate, top-level decision makers work through small-group activities to clarify the mission, philosophy, and procedures governing the succession planning program.

The second step is to summarize results. Someone must prepare a written statement that contains key points of agreement after the retreat or after each meeting. That task usually falls to an HR professional or to an external facilitator, who prepares a presentation or handout. However, the CEO or other top-level decision maker feeds them back to the retreat participants.

The third and final step of this approach is to conduct follow-up activities to ensure agreement. Follow-up activities may be conducted in several ways. One way is to hold a follow-up meeting with the participants to surface any points of confusion or disagreement. That can be done in small groups (at the end of a retreat) or individually with participants (after the retreat). Another way is to establish a top-level committee to govern succession planning in the organization and/or at various levels or locations of the organization.

An interactive debate does focus initial attention on key issues that should be addressed to formulate a clear program mission statement. That is an advantage of the approach. But its chief disadvantage is that it requires much time and strong personal involvement from the CEO and others.

Writing Policy and Procedures

Why is the organization undertaking a succession planning program? What results are desired from it? How can consistent program operations be ensured? Decision makers may answer these questions by preparing written program policy and procedures.

What Is a Succession Planning Policy, And What Are Succession Planning Procedures?

Policy is a natural outgrowth of mission. Typically stated in writing, it places the organization on the record as supporting or opposing an approach to action. One research study revealed that approximately 36 percent of the responding sixty-four firms had developed a written succession planning policy.[3]

Procedures flow from policy and provide guidelines for applying it. Writing a policy on succession planning clarifies what the organization seeks to do; writing procedures clarifies how the policy will be applied. Typical components of a succession planning policy include a mission statement, philosophical statements, and procedures. A sample succession planning policy appears in Exhibit 4-4.

How Are Policies and Procedures Written?

Succession planning policy and procedures should usually be written only after decision makers agree on the program mission. Crises, problems, or issues of importance should provide clues about what to include in the policy and procedures. As decision makers prepare a mission statement, they will typically formulate what may rightfully be included in a written program policy and procedure.

In many cases the appropriate approach to use in writing policies and procedures stems from the approach used in preparing the mission statement. For instance, if an "ask and formulate" approach was used in formulating the mission statement, then prepare a draft succession planning policy and procedures to accompany the proposal submitted to executives. If a "recommend and listen" approach was chosen when preparing the mission statement, then draft a succession planning policy and procedures to accompany the mission statement in the initial proposal to management. If an "interactive debate" approach was chosen, then committees in the organization will usually be the means by which to draft policy and procedures, oversee refinements, and issue updates or modifications to policy and procedures.

Identifying Target Groups

Who should be the focus of the succession planning program? Should the program be geared to the top-level executive ranks only? Should it encompass other groups, levels, or parts of the organization? Answering these questions requires decision makers to identify target groups.

Most of what has been written about succession planning programs has directed attention to replacing top-level executive positions. Substantial research has been conducted on succession planning for the CEO.[4] Other writings have focused on the CEO's immediate reports. Relatively little has been written about succession planning for other groups, though many experts on the subject concede that the need has never been greater

Exhibit 4-4. A sample succession planning policy.

Mission Statement

The purpose of the succession planning program in [*company or organization name*] is to ensure a ready supply of internal talent for key positions at all times. This organization is fully committed to equal employment opportunity for all employees, regardless of race, creed, sex, religion, national origin, sexual orientation, or disability.

Policy and Philosophy

It is the policy of the [*company or organization name*] to help employees develop to the full extent of their potential and, to the extent possible for the organization, to help them achieve realistic career goals that satisfy both individual and organization requirements.

This organization is firmly committed to promotion from within for key positions, whenever qualified talent is available. This organization is also firmly committed to helping employees develop their potential so that they are prepared and qualified to assume positions in line with individual career goals and organization requirements.

Procedures

At least once each year, the organization will sponsor:
- *A replacement planning activity* that will assess how well the organization is positioned to meet replacement requirements by promotions or other personnel movements from within.
- *Individual performance appraisal* to assess how well individuals are meeting their current work requirements.
- *Individual potential assessment* to assess how well individuals are presently equipped for future advancement. Unlike a performance appraisal—which is typically focused on past or present performance—the focus of an individual potential assessment is on the future.
- *Individual development planning* to provide the means for action plans to help individuals narrow the developmental gap between what they already know or can do and what they must know or do to qualify for advancement.

The succession planning program will rely heavily on the processes listed above to identify individuals suitable for advancement. The program will work closely in tandem with an in-house career planning program, which is designed to help individuals identify their career goals and take proactive steps to achieve them.

---

for effective succession planning efforts at lower levels. Indeed, recent interest in multiskilling, team-based management, and cross-training stems from the recognition that more time, resources, and attention must be focused on systematically developing human capabilities at all levels and across all groups. The results of a 1990 study revealed that companies are already experiencing significant labor shortages. Indeed, 48 percent of the responding firms reported experiencing some or great difficulty in filling vacancies in supervisory or management positions, 61 percent reported experiencing difficulty in filling vacancies in professional positions, 64 percent in filling vacancies in technical positions, and 48 percent in filling vacancies in secretarial and clerical positions.[5]

The results of my recent survey on succession planning practices revealed that the respondents' organizations are not consistently identifying *and* developing successors across all job categories (see Exhibit 4-5).

Establishing Initial Targets

Where is the organization weakest in bench strength? The answer to that question should provide a clue about where to establish initial targets for the succession planning program. (See the activity in Exhibit 4-6.) If nec-

Exhibit 4-5. Targeted groups for succession planning.

Question: Succession planning may not be carried out with all groups in an organization. For each group listed below, indicate whether your organization makes a deliberate effort to identify and develop successors.

	Does your organization make a deliberate effort to identify successors?		*Does your organization make a deliberate effort to develop successors?*	
	Yes	*No*	*Yes*	*No*
Executives	27 (90%)	3 (10%)	22 (85%)	4 (15%)
Middle managers	28 (93%)	2 (7%)	21 (75%)	7 (25%)
Supervisors	13 (45%)	16 (55%)	17 (63%)	10 (37%)
Professionals	11 (38%)	17 (61%)	13 (48%)	14 (52%)
Technical workers	5 (17%)	24 (83%)	10 (38%)	16 (62%)
Sales workers	10 (37%)	17 (63%)	12 (50%)	12 (50%)
Clerical workers	2 (7%)	27 (93%)	5 (20%)	20 (80%)
Hourly production or service workers	2 (7%)	27 (93%)	6 (23%)	20 (77%)

SOURCE: William J. Rothwell, "Results of a 1993 Survey on Succession Planning Practices," unpublished, The Pennsylvania State University, 1994.

Exhibit 4-6. An activity for identifying initial targets for succession planning.

Directions: Use this activity to identify initial target groups for the succession planning program. For each job category listed in the left column below, indicate a priority (1 = highest priority) in the center column. Then, in the right column, briefly explain why the job category was assigned that priority. Circulate this activity to decision makers and ask them to complete it. Compile the results and feed them back to decision makers to emphasize what job categories were generally perceived to be the rightful targets for the succession planning program. Add paper as necessary. (If appropriate, modify the list of job categories so they coincide precisely with any special labels/titles associated with them in the organization.)

Job Category	Priority (1 = highest)	What is your reasoning?
1. Executives	_____	
2. Individuals preparing for executive positions	_____	
3. Middle managers	_____	
4. Individuals preparing for middle management	_____	
5. Supervisors	_____	
6. Individuals preparing for supervision	_____	
7. Professional workers	_____	
8. Individuals preparing to be professional workers	_____	
9. Technical workers	_____	
10. Individuals preparing to become technical workers	_____	
11. Sales workers	_____	
12. Individuals preparing to become sales workers	_____	
13. Clerical workers	_____	
14. Individuals preparing to become clerical workers	_____	

Job Category	Priority (1 = highest)	What is your reasoning?
15. Hourly production or service workers	_____	
16. Individuals preparing to become hourly production or service workers	_____	
17. Other job categories	_____	

essary, circulate the activity to top managers, or ask them to complete it in a meeting to formulate program parameters or in an initial program kickoff meeting.

You may wish to direct attention to three specific areas first, since they are common sources of problems: (1) successors for top management positions, (2) successors for first-line supervisory positions, and (3) successors for unique, tough-to-fill technical or professional positions.

Top management positions are fewest in absolute numbers, but they are often critically important for formulating and implementing organizational strategy. The top management ranks may grow weak in bench strength in organizations that experience significant employee reductions in the middle-management ranks as a result of layoffs, employee buyouts, or early retirement offers.

Supervisory positions are usually largest in absolute numbers, so continuing turnover and other personnel movements leave these ranks subject to greatest need for replacements. As a port of entry to management, supervision is also critically important because many middle managers and executives start out in supervision. Supervisors are often promoted from the hourly ranks and lack management experience, or else they are hired from outside the organization. Supervision is a trouble spot in organizations that do not have planned management development programs or that provide little or no incentive for movement into supervision—such as organizations in which unionized hourly workers earn substantially more than supervisors, who are ineligible for overtime pay but who must nevertheless work overtime.

Tough-to-fill technical or professional positions are often limited in number. Managers may toss and turn at night with worry about the mere thought of losing a member of this group, because recruiting or training a successor on short notice is difficult.

Choose one group, or all three, as initial targets for the succession planning program if the results of the Exhibit 4-6 activity demonstrate the need. Otherwise, use the results of the activity to identify the initial targets for the program. Verify the groups chosen with decision makers.

Expanding Succession Planning to Other Groups

Although the organization may have neither the time nor the resources to establish a systematic succession planning program that encompasses *all* people and positions, decision makers may agree that such a goal is eventually worth achieving. For that reason, periodically administer the Exhibit 4-6 activity to decision makers to assess in what order groups should be targeted for inclusion.

Of course, decision makers may wish to choose an alternative method than job category by which to prioritize groups. For instance, they may feel that bench strength is weakest in any of the following areas:

- Geographical locations
- Product or service lines
- Functions of organizational operation
- Experience with specific industry-related or product/service-related problems
- Experience with international markets

Ask decision makers where they perceive the organization to be weakest in bench strength. Then target the succession planning program initially to improve bench strength at that level. While continuing efforts at that level, gradually expand the effort to encompass other groups.

Setting Program Priorities

Much work needs to be done to establish a systematic succession planning program. But rarely, if ever, can it be accomplished all at once. Someone has to set both short- and long-term program priorities. That may be done by top-level decision makers, a full-time or part-time succession planning coordinator, or a committee representing different organizational groups or functions.

Initial priorities should be established to address the organization's most pressing problems, and to rectify the most serious weaknesses in bench strength. Subsequent priorities should be established to reflect a long-term plan for systematic succession planning in the organization.

In addition to the activities already described in this chapter—such as clarifying roles, formulating a mission statement, writing a program policy, clarifying program procedures, and identifying the program's targeted groups—others will have to be undertaken. Priorities should be established on what actions to take—and when—depending on the organization's needs. These activities include:

- Preparing an action plan to guide program start-up
- Communicating the action plan
- Training managers and employees for their roles in the systematic succession planning program
- Organizing kickoff meetings and periodic briefing meetings to discuss the program
- Counseling managers on handling unique succession planning problems, such as dealing with poor performers, managing high performers, grooming and coaching high potentials, addressing the special problems of plateaued workers, and managing workforce diversity
- Defining present and future work requirements, processes, activities, responsibilities, success factors, and competence
- Appraising individual performance
- Assessing individual potential
- Providing individuals with the means by which to carry out career planning within the organization
- Keeping records on performance and potential
- Preparing and following through on individual development plans (IDPs) to help close gaps between what people know or do and what they must know or do in the future to qualify for advancement and ensure leadership continuity
- Using and tracking innovative efforts to meet replacement needs
- Evaluating the benefits of systematic succession planning
- Designing and implementing development programs geared to meeting the needs of special groups (such as high potentials, plateaued workers, high performers, or low performers)
- Designing and implementing programs to meet special needs (such as reducing voluntary turnover among key employees after downsizing, handling workforce diversity, using succession planning in autonomous work teams, and integrating succession planning with such other organizational initiatives as total quality, reengineering, or customer service)

Depending on an organization's unique needs, however, some issues demand immediate attention—and action.

Take this opportunity to consider program priorities in your organization. Use the activity that appears in Exhibit 4-7 to establish initial program priorities. (If you are the coordinator of the succession planning program, you may choose to circulate the activity to key decision makers for their reactions, feed back the results to them, and use their reactions as a starting point for setting program priorities. Alternatively, share the activity with a standing committee on succession planning established in the organization, if one exists. Ask committee members to complete the activity and then use the results to set initial program priorities.) Revisit the priorities at least annually. Gear action plans to match the priorities.

Exhibit 4-7. An activity for identifying program priorities in succession planning.

Directions: Use this activity to help establish priorities for the succession planning program in an organization. For each activity listed in the left column below, set a priority by circling a number for it in the right column. Use the following scale:

1 = A top priority that should be acted on *now*
2 = A secondary priority that is important but that can wait a while for action
3 = A tertiary priority that should be acted on only after items prioritized as **1** or **2** have received attention

You may want to circulate this activity among decision makers as appropriate. If you do so, compile their responses and then feed them back as a catalyst for subsequent decision making. Add paper as necessary. (You may also wish to add other activities of interest.)

Activity		Priority	
1. Preparing an action plan to guide program startup	1	2	3
2. Communicating the action plan	1	2	3
3. Training managers and employees for their roles in the systematic succession planning program	1	2	3
4. Organizing kickoff meetings and periodic briefing meetings to discuss the program	1	2	3

Activity	Priority		
5. Counseling managers on handling unique succession planning problems	**1**	**2**	**3**
6. Defining present and future work requirements, processes, activities, responsibilities, success factors, and competencies	**1**	**2**	**3**
7. Appraising individual performance	**1**	**2**	**3**
8. Assessing individual potential	**1**	**2**	**3**
9. Providing individuals with the means by which to carry out career planning within the organization	**1**	**2**	**3**
10. Keeping records on performance and potential	**1**	**2**	**3**
11. Preparing, and following through on, IDPs	**1**	**2**	**3**
12. Using, and tracking, innovative efforts to meet replacement needs	**1**	**2**	**3**
13. Evaluating the benefits of systematic succession planning	**1**	**2**	**3**
14. Designing and implementing development programs geared to meeting the needs of special groups	**1**	**2**	**3**
15. Other			

Summary

Starting up a systematic succession planning program usually requires an organization's decision makers to:

- Clarify the desired program roles of management employees, facilitators, and participants.
- Prepare a program mission statement.
- Write a program policy and procedures.

- Identify groups targeted for program action, both initially and subsequently.
- Establish program priorities.

Subsequent steps in starting up the program are covered in the next chapter.

5

Refining the Program

Beyond start-up, additional steps need to be taken before an effective succession planning program can become operational. These steps include:

- Preparing a program action plan
- Communicating the action plan
- Conducting succession planning meetings
- Training on succession planning
- Counseling managers about succession planning problems in their areas

This chapter briefly reviews each topic listed above, providing tips for effectively refining a succession planning program during its early stages.

Preparing a Program Action Plan

Setting program priorities is only a beginning. Turning priorities into realities requires dedication, hard work, and effective strategy. Preparing a program action plan helps conceptualize the strategy for implementing effective succession planning.

The Value of an Action Plan

An action plan activates and energizes a succession planning program. It is a natural next step after setting program priorities because it indicates how they will be met.

Components of an Effective Action Plan

An action plan is akin to a project plan. It answers all the journalistic questions:

- *Who* should take actions?
- *What* action should they take?
- *When* should the action be taken?
- *Where* should the action be taken?
- *Why* should the action be taken?
- *How* should action be taken?

By so doing, an action plan provides a sound basis for program accountability.

How to Establish the Action Plan

Take these five steps when establishing an action plan:

1. List priorities.
2. Indicate what actions must be taken to achieve each priority.
3. Assign responsibility for each action.
4. Indicate where the actions must be performed.
5. Assign deadlines or time indicators to show when the actions should be completed, or when each stage of completion should be reached.

The result of these steps should be a concrete action plan to guide the succession planning program (use the worksheet appearing in Exhibit 5-1 to clarify the program action plan).

Communicating the Action Plan

Few results will be achieved if an action plan is established and then kept secret. Some effort must be made to communicate the action plan to those affected by it and to those expected to take responsibility for participating in its implementation.

Problems in Communicating

Communicating about a succession planning program presents unique problems that are rarely encountered in other areas of organization operations. The reason: Many top managers are hesitant to share information about their programs widely inside or outside their organizations.

They are reluctant to share information outside the organization for fear that succession plans will reveal too much about the organization's strategy. If a succession planning program is closely linked to, and sup-

Exhibit 5-1. A worksheet for preparing an action plan to establish the succession planning program.

Directions: Use this worksheet to help you formulate an action plan to guide the startup of a succession planning program in your organization. In column **1** below, list program priorities (*what* must be done first, second, third, and so on?) and provide a rationale (*why* are these priorities?). In column **2,** list the tasks that must be carried out to transform priorities into realities (*how* will priorities be achieved?). In column **3,** assign responsibility for each task. In column **4,** indicate (if applicable) special locations (*where* must the tasks be accomplished or the priorities achieved?). In column **5,** assign deadlines or time indicators.

Circulate this worksheet among decision makers—especialy top-level managers who are participating on a succession planning committee. Ask each decision maker to complete the worksheet individually. Then compile their responses, feed them back, and meet to achieve consensus on this detailed action plan. Add paper as necessary.

1	2	3	4	5
Program Priorities and Rationale	*Tasks*	*Responsibility*	*Locations*	*Deadlines/ Time Indicators*

portive of, strategic plans—as is desirable—then revealing information about it may tip off canny competitors to what the organization intends to do.

They are reluctant to share information inside the organization for fear that it will lead to negative consequences. High-performing or high-potential employees who are aware that they are designated successors for key positions may:

- Become complacent because they think advancement is guaranteed. That is called the *crown prince phenomenon*.
- Grow disenchanted if organizational conditions change and their status as successors is no longer assured.
- "Hold themselves for ransom" by threatening to leave unless they receive escalating raises or advancement opportunities.

Of course, the opposite can also happen: If high-potential employees are kept unaware of their status, they may seek advancement opportunities elsewhere. Equally as bad, good performers who are *not* presently identified as successors for key positions may grow disenchanted and demotivated, even though they may already be demonstrating their potential. A poorly handled communication strategy can lead to increases in avoidable turnover, thereby costing the organization precious talent and driving up training costs.

Choosing Effective Approaches

As part of the succession planning program, decision makers should review how the organization has historically communicated about succession issues, and consider how it should communicate about them. Establishing *consistent* communication strategy is vital.

Valuable clues about the organization's historical communication strategy may be found in how key job incumbents have been treated and how wage and salary matters are handled. If key job incumbents did not know that they were designated successors before they were eligible for advancement or if the organization's practice is not to publish salary schedules, then it is likely that a "closed" communication strategy is preferred. That means information is kept secret, and successors are kept in the dark about their status. On the other hand, if key job incumbents did know that they were designated successors before they were promoted or if salary schedules are published, then an "open" communication strategy is preferred. That means succession issues are treated with candor.

Choose an approach to communication based on the preferences of decision makers. If their preferences seem unclear, ask questions to discover what they are:

- How, if at all, should employees be informed about the succession planning program? (For instance, should the mission statement and/or policy and procedures on succession planning be circulated?)
- How should the organization characterize the use of employee performance appraisal, individual potential assessment, and individual development planning?
- How should decisions about individual selection, promotion, demotion, transfer, or development in place be explained to those who ask?
- What problems will result from informing individuals about their status in succession plans? From *not* informing them?
- What problems will result from informing employees about the succession planning program? From *not* informing them?

Ultimately, the organization should choose a communication policy that is consistent with the answers to those questions. Often the best approach is to communicate openly about the succession planning program in general, but to conceal the basis for individual personnel actions in line with good business practice and individual privacy laws. Individuals should be encouraged to develop themselves for the future but should understand, at the same time, that nothing is being "promised"; rather, qualifying is a first step but does not, in itself, guarantee advancement.

Conducting Succession Planning Meetings

It is a rare organization that does not need at least one meeting to lay the foundation for a systematic succession planning program. Often, four meetings are necessary during start-up: (1) a meeting of top decision makers to verify the need for the program, (2) a larger meeting to seek input from major stakeholders, (3) a smaller committee meeting of change champions to hammer out a proposal to guide program start-up, and (4) a meeting to introduce the program and reinforce its importance to those who will play critical roles in cultivating, nurturing, coaching, and preparing the leaders of the future at all levels. Later, periodic meetings are necessary to review program progress and ensure its continuous improvement.

Meeting 1: Verifying the Need

In the first meeting, a handpicked group—usually limited to the "top of the house"—assembles to verify that a genuine need drives the effort to make succession planning a more systematic process. In this meeting it is common to review current practices and problems that stem from an informal approach to succession planning. This meeting is usually prompted directly from a crisis or from the request of a change champion who wants to introduce a new way to carry out succession planning.

Meeting 2: Seeking Input

In the second meeting, a larger group of key decision makers is usually assembled to surface succession planning problems and to galvanize action. This meeting may take the form of an executive retreat. Executives should properly be involved in the program formulation process, since, regardless of the initial targeted group for the succession planning program and its initial priorities, such a program has important strategic implications for the organization. Despite recent moves to involve employees in organizational decision making, it has long been held that executives bear chief responsibility for organizational strategy formulation. That is borne out by research on executive roles.[1] It is also consistent with the commonsense view that someone must assume leadership at the outset of new initiatives.[2]

Planning an executive retreat of this kind should usually be a joint undertaking of the CEO and a designated coordinator for the succession planning program. (The coordinator may be the vice president of personnel or human resources, a high-level staff generalist from the HR function, the training director, an OD director, or a management development director.) A designated coordinator is needed because busy CEOs, while they should maintain active personal involvement in the succession planning program if it is to work, will seldom have the necessary time to oversee daily program operations. That responsibility should be assigned to someone so that it will not be lost in the shuffle of daily work responsibilities. Hence, naming a program coordinator is advisable. While a designated coordinator may be selected from a high level of the line (operating) management ranks—and that will be a necessity in small organizations not having an HR function—the individual chosen for this responsibility should have a strong commitment to succession planning, considerable knowledge about the organization's HR policies, procedures, and applicable HR laws, expertise in state-of-the-art management development and human resource development practices, in-depth knowledge about the organization's culture, and credibility with all levels of the organization's management. (It doesn't hurt, either, if the individual chosen for this role is a high potential in his or her own right.)

The CEO and succession planning coordinator should meet to hammer out an agenda to guide the executive retreat. Designed to collect input about the program, the retreat should be held soon after the CEO announces the need for a systematic succession planning program and names a program coordinator. Invitations should be extended to the CEO's immediate reports. The retreat should usually be held off-site, at a quiet and secluded location, to minimize interruptions. The retreat should focus on:

- Explaining the need for a more systematic approach to succession planning
- Formulating a (draft) program mission statement
- Identifying the target groups to be initially served by the program
- Setting initial program priorities

An executive retreat is worthwhile because it engages the attention, and involvement, of key players in the organization's strategic planning activities, thereby creating a natural bridge between succession planning and strategic planning. The retreat's agenda should reflect the desired outcomes. Presentations may be made by the CEO, the succession planning coordinator, and the vice president of HR. Third-party experts or consultants may be invited to share information about succession planning, including testimonials of succession programs in other organizations, war stories about the problems that can result when succession planning is ignored, and descriptions of state-of-the-art succession planning practices. An important component of any retreat should be small-group activities geared to surfacing problems and achieving consensus. (Many of the activities and worksheets provided in this book can be adapted for that purpose.) In many cases, a retreat will end when the CEO appoints a standing committee to work with the succession planning coordinator and to report back with a detailed program proposal at a later time.

In some organizations, the CEO or the succession planning coordinator may prefer that the retreat be facilitated by third-party consultants. That is desirable if the consultants can be located and if they possess considerable expertise in succession planning and in group facilitation. It is also desirable if the CEO feels that third-party consultants will increase the credibility of the program and emphasize its importance.

Meeting 3: Hammering Out a Proposal

A standing succession planning committee should be established to continue the program formulation process begun in the executive retreat. A committee format is really the best approach to (1) maintain high-level commitment and support, (2) conserve the time required to review the fruits of the committee's investigations, and (3) provide a means for senior-level involvement in succession planning.

The succession planning coordinator should be automatically named a committee member, though not necessarily committee chair. If the CEO can be personally involved, as is highly desirable, he or she should be the chair. Committee members should be chosen for their interest in succession planning, their track records of exemplary performance, their proven ability to develop people, and their keen insight into organization culture.

In most organizations, a committee of this kind should meet frequently and regularly during program start-up. Initial meetings should focus on investigating organizational succession planning needs, benchmarking practices in other organizations, and drafting a detailed proposal to guide the systematic succession planning program.

Meeting 4: The Kickoff Meeting

In the fourth meeting, the program is introduced to those previously involved in the second meeting and any others, as appropriate. This is typically called a kickoff meeting. In most cases, this meeting should focus on program details, and on the part that the meeting participants should play to ensure program success. In short, a kickoff meeting should seek answers to three questions: (1) What is the succession planning program in the organization? (2) what do the participants need to do to make the program successful? and (3) what results are sought from the program?

When organizing a kickoff meeting, pay attention to these six questions:

1. *Who* will be invited?
2. *What* exactly should participants know or be able to do upon leaving the meeting?
3. *When* should the kickoff meeting be held? For instance, would timing it so that it immediately follows a strategic planning retreat be desirable?
4. *Where* should the kickoff meeting be held? If maximum secrecy is desired, an off-site location should be chosen.
5. *Why* is the meeting being held? If the aim is to reinforce the importance of this new effort, then the CEO should usually be the keynote presenter.
6. *How* will the meeting be conducted?

Specific training can be offered later on establishing work requirements, appraising individual performance, assessing individual potential, clarifying individual career goals, establishing individual development plans (IDPs), and using succession needs to drive leadership training, education, and development activities.

Periodic Review Meetings

Conduct periodic review meetings after the succession planning has been established. These meetings should focus on such issues as these:

- The linkage between succession planning and organizational strategic plans (that may also be handled during strategic planning retreats)
- The progress made in the succession planning program
- Any need for revisions to any of the following: the program's mission statement, governing policy and procedures, target groups, priorities, action plans, communication strategies, and leadership training tied to the succession planning program
- The status of succession issues in each organizational component, including periodic meetings between the CEO and senior executives

The last of these should be familiar to executives in most major corporations. Once each quarter, senior executives from each part of the corporation should meet with the CEO and a top-level committee to review the status of succession planning in that part of the corporation. Common topics in such meetings include: (1) reviewing employee performance, (2) identifying and discussing high potentials, and (3) discussing progress made on individual development plans and critical strengths and weaknesses having to do with individual development. These meetings are crucially important to program success. They should serve to keep the succession planning program on target and to emphasize its importance to senior executives, who should be held accountable for "people development" as much as for market development or financial management.

Training on Succession Planning

Implementing a systematic approach to succession planning requires new knowledge and skills from those expected to cultivate the organization's internal talent. Some means must be found to train them so that they are the most efficient and effective in their new role.

Matching Training to Program Planning

Training to support succession planning should be designed to match program priorities. Indeed, to plan training on succession planning, examine program priorities first. Use program priorities as clues for designing initial training efforts.

In most cases, when organizations establish systematic succession planning, training should be undertaken to answer the following questions:

- What is the organization's succession planning program? What is its mission, policy, procedures, and activities?
- What are the desirable roles of management employees, succession planning facilitators, and individual employees in the succession planning program?
- What is the organization's preferred approach to clarifying present and future work requirements? How should it relate to succession planning as a source of information about activities, duties, responsibilities, competencies, and success factors in key positions?
- What is the organization's performance appraisal system, and how should it relate to succession as a source of information about individual job performance?
- What is the organization's individual career planning program (if one exists), and how does it relate to succession as a source of information about individual career goals and aspirations?
- What is the organization's high-potential assessment program (if one exists, as it should), and how does it relate to succession as a source of information about individual potential for future advancement?
- How do the organization's training, education, and development programs relate to preparing individuals for succession and advancement?
- What is an individual development plan? Why is planning for individual development important? How should programs for individual development be designed? implemented? tracked?
- How does the organization keep track of its human talent?
- How should the organization evaluate its succession planning program?
- How should the organization handle special issues in succession

planning, such as high performers, high potentials, and plateaued workers?

- How should the succession planning program be linked to the organization's strategy? to HR strategy? other plans (as appropriate)?

As a starting point for developing in-house training sessions on succession planning, refer to the draft training outlines appearing in Exhibit 5-2. Note that such training should be tailor-made to meet organizational needs.

As an alternative, decision makers may prefer to contract with qualified external consultants to design and deliver training on succession planning for the organization. Such consultants may be located through word-of-mouth referrals from practitioners in other organizations, those who have written extensively on succession planning, or such sources as *The ASTD's Buyer's Guide and Consultant Directory.* They are especially appropriate to use when in-house expertise is limited, external consultants will give the program credibility, the pressure is on to obtain quick results, or in-house staff members are unavailable. If decision makers decide to use external assistance, then the consultants should be invited in for a day or two to discuss what assistance they can provide. They should be asked for references from previous organizations with which they have worked. Before their arrival, they should also be given *detailed* background information about the organization and its existing succession planning practices and problems.

Many external consultants will begin by meeting individually with key decision makers and will then provide a brief group presentation about succession planning issues. Both can serve a valuable purpose. Individual meetings will emphasize the importance of the issue. Group meetings will help to informally educate participants about state-of-the-art practices outside the organization, which can create an impetus for change.

Ensuring Attendance at Training: A Key Issue

Perhaps the single most challenging aspect of offering training on succession planning is securing the critical mass necessary to ensure consistent approaches throughout the organization. It is particularly difficult to ensure that key managers will attend group training, and they are precisely the most important to reach because they exert the greatest influence on succession planning issues. But no matter what is done, some key managers will claim that they have too much work to do and cannot spare valuable time away from work to attend. Others will not attend and will offer

(text continues on page 133)

Exhibit 5-2. Sample outlines for in-house training on succession planning.

Purpose

To build skills in conducting employee performance appraisal, potential assessment, and individual development planning

Targeted Participants

Individuals, such as key position incumbents and immediate organization superiors of high potentials, who play important roles in implementing the action plan governing the succession planning program

Objectives

Upon completion of this training, participants should be able to:

1. Explain the organization's business reasons for establishing a succession planning program and the relationships between succession planning, strategic planning, and human resources planning.
2. Describe the mission, policy, procedures, and activities of the succession planning program.
3. Review the roles and responsibilities of managers in preparing employees to assume key positions in the organization.
4. Explain how the organization clarifies work requirements and identifies key positions.
5. Explain the role played by employee performance appraisal in succession planning and describe the organization's performance appraisal procedures.
6. Conduct effective employee performance appraisal interviews.
7. Explain the role played by employee potential assessment in succession planning and describe the organization's procedures for potential assessment.
8. Conduct effective employee potential assessments.
9. Explain the role played by individual development planning in succession planning and describe the organization's procedures for individual development planning.
10. Select and oversee appropriate internal development approaches.
11. Explain when promotion from within is—and is not—appropriate for filling key vacancies.
12. Review how the organization inventories human talent.

Session 1
Introducing Succession Planning

I. Introduction
    A. Purpose of the session
    B. Objectives of the session
    C. Organization (structure) of the session
II. Defining Succession Planning
    A. What is it?
    B. Why is it important generally?
III. Relating Succession Planning to the Organization
    A. What is the current status of the organization?
    B. What are the organization's strategic plans/goals?
    C. What are the organization's human resources plans and goals?
    D. What is the need for succession planning, given organizational strategy and human resources plans?
IV. The Purpose of the Succession Planning Program
    A. Mission
    B. Policy
    C. Procedures
    D. Activities
V. Roles in Succession Planning
    A. What should be the role of the immediate organizational superior?
    B. What should be the individual's role?
VI. Defining Work Requirements
    A. Job analysis
    B. Job descriptions and specifications
    C. Other approaches
VII. Identifying Key Positions
    A. How are they defined?
    B. Where are they located?
    C. How will key positions change in the future—and why?
VIII. Conclusion
    A. Summary
    B. Planning for on-the-job action
    C. Session evaluations

Session 2
Conducting Effective Employee
Performance Appraisals for Succession Planning

I. Introduction
    A. Purpose of the session

(continues)

Exhibit 5-2 *(continued).*

       B. Objectives of the session
       C. Organization (structure) of the session
  II. Defining Employee Performance Appraisal
       A. What is it?
       B. Why is it important?
  III. Relating Employee Performance Appraisal to Succession Planning
       A. Approaches
       B. Current method
       C. Relationship between appraisal and succession planning
  IV. Reviewing the Organization's Performance Appraisal Procedures
       A. Overview
       B. Step-by-step description of procedures
  V. Conducting Effective Performance Appraisal Interviews
       A. Overview
       B. Using the appraisal form to structure the interview
  VI. Role Plays (practice appraisal interviews)
  VII. Conclusion
       A. Summary
       B. Planning for on-the-job action
       C. Session evaluations

Session 3
Conducting Effective Employee
Potential Assessment for Succession Planning

  I. Introduction
       A. Purpose of the session
       B. Objectives of the session
       C. Organization (structure) of the session
  II. Defining Employee Potential Assessment
       A. What is it?
       B. Why is it important?
  III. Relating Employee Potential Assessment to Succession Planning
       A. Approaches
       B. Current method
       C. Relationship between potential assessment and succession planning
  IV. Reviewing the Organization's Potential Assessment Procedures
       A. Overview
       B. Step-by-step description of procedures

V. Conducting Effective Potential Assessment
   A. Overview
   B. Using potential assessment forms and procedures
   C. Gathering individual career planning information for use with potential assessment
VI. [*Optional*] Role Plays (practice assessment interviews)
VII. Conclusion
   A. Summary
   B. Planning for on-the-job action
   C. Session evaluations

Session 4
Conducting Effective Individual Development Planning

I. Introduction
   A. Purpose of the session
   B. Objectives of the session
   C. Organization (structure) of the session
II. Defining Individual Development Planning
   A. What is it?
   B. Why is it important?
III. Relating Individual Development Planning to Succession Planning
   A. Approaches
   B. Selecting appropraite approaches
   C. Relationship between individual development planning and succession planning
IV. Reviewing Approaches to Individual Development Planning
   A. Overview
   B. Step-by-step description of the approaches
V. Facilitating Effective Individual Development Planning
   A. Overview
   B. Approaches to individual development planning
   C. Relating individual career planning to individual development planning
VI. Conclusion
   A. Summary
   B. Planning for on-the-job action
   C. Session evaluations

no explanation. It may prove to be impossible to fit them into any group training schedule that is established.

No silver bullet exists to solve these problems. It amounts to a matter of commitment. If members of the board of directors and the CEO are genuinely committed to ensuring effective succession planning, then they will become personally involved to ensure the attendance of the targeted training participants. They will also attend themselves—and perhaps help deliver the training—and thereby demonstrate hands-on interest and support. Their participation and involvement will exert a powerful but subtle inducement for others to attend. But if they are unwilling to be involved, no amount of cajoling or threatening is an effective substitute. Moreover, *they* must set the example and follow the policies established for the organization.

Here are a few tips for securing attendance at group training on succession planning, assuming that adequate top-management commitment exists:

1. Draft a memo for the chairman or CEO to initial to go out with training invitations. Stress who will be in attendance, what issues will be discussed, and why the training is important.
2. Pick an opportune time. Check dates to make sure that those chosen for training do not conflict with other important dates.
3. If possible, tie the training on succession planning to other events—such as strategic planning retreats—in which the targeted participants are already scheduled to attend.
4. Field-test the training materials on a small, handpicked group of supportive managers. Be sure that the time is effectively used and that every training activity relates directly to succession planning practices in the organization.
5. If possible, videotape a well-rehearsed practice session and share it before the session with the chairman, CEO, or other key management personnel. Ask for their suggestions about how to improve it before the session.

Other Approaches to Training Management Employees To Enact Their Roles in Succession Planning

There will always be some management employees who are unable to attend group training on succession planning, even when vigorous steps have been taken to ensure attendance. That they had legitimate reasons for not attending will not alter the fact that they missed the training. They are the group most likely to operate in a way inconsistent with organizational policy because they missed the opportunity to learn about it firsthand.

Deal with this tough-to-reach audience through a form of guerilla warfare. Make sure that it is clear who they are. Then use any of the following tactics to train them:

- Meet with them individually, if their numbers are small enough to make that practical and if they are not so geographically dispersed that the expense of traveling to their locations is prohibitive. Deliver training personally.
- Videotape a practice session of the training and send it to those unable to attend. Then follow up with them later for their questions and reactions.
- Ask another manager who did attend—if possible, the CEO—to describe to them the key lessons of the training in his or her own words. (That should reinforce the importance of the message.)

Training Participants in Succession Planning

Training for participants in succession planning will be greatly affected by the organization's communication strategy. If decision makers do not wish to inform individuals of the organization's succession planning practices, then minimal training will typically be given; on the other hand, if the organization adopts a policy of openness, then training on succession planning may be offered.

There are three general ways by which to offer that training: (1) direct training, (2) training integrated with other issues, and (3) training tied to career planning.

1. *Direct training.* In direct training, employees are informed of the organization's succession planning policy and procedures. They are briefed on it in general terms, usually without specific descriptions of how the program is linked to existing organizational strategy. They learn how the succession planning program is linked to defining work requirements, appraising employee performance, assessing individual potential, and establishing individual development plans.

2. *Training integrated with other issues.* When training on succession planning is integrated with other issues, employees are told how their training, education, and development efforts factor into qualifying for advancement. No promises are made; rather, the value of planned learning activities is stressed as one means by which the individual can take proactive steps to qualify as a successor for key positions.

3. *Training tied to career planning.* Organizational succession planning and individual career planning represent mirror images of the same issue. Succession planning helps the organization meet its HR needs to ensure that it is equipped with the talent needed to survive and succeed. On the other hand, individual career planning helps the individual establish career goals and prepare for meeting those goals, either inside or outside the organization.

When training on succession planning is tied to training on career planning, individuals are furnished with information about work requirements at different levels and in different functions or locations. They also learn about performance requirements in different job categories and about future success factors. Armed with this information, they can establish their own career goals and take active steps to prepare themselves for advancement by seeking appropriate training, education, and development experiences.

Counseling Managers about Succession Planning Problems

Succession planning coordinators should make a point of meeting periodically and individually with executives to discuss succession planning issues in their work areas and to offer counseling about how to deal with those problems. If that counseling is requested, it indicates that executives have accepted succession planning, that they value advice about people management issues, and that they are making honest efforts to meet the succession planning needs of the organization.

The Need for Individual Counseling Sessions

Executives sometimes have need of third-party advice about people problems. In some cases they will be reluctant to share those problems with anyone, including the CEO, for fear that they will be perceived as unable to manage tough-to-handle management situations. Individual counseling with these executives by the succession planning coordinator can serve an invaluable purpose for improving succession planning practices. For this reason, the CEO and other decision makers in the organization should actively encourage such sessions.

Who Should Conduct the Sessions?

The succession planning coordinator should arrange to meet with senior executives on a regular basis. However, the coordinator must seize the initiative to arrange the meetings until he or she has gained sufficient credibility to be sought out.

The succession planning coordinator should call each senior executive and ask when they can meet. Although these individual meetings can be time-consuming, they are the best way to demonstrate commitment to the effort and get real payoffs from it. Individual meetings are usually best timed sometime *ahead* of periodic succession planning meetings, such as those held quarterly in many corporations. By meeting ahead of time, the succession planning coordinator and the executive in charge of that work area can discuss sensitive personnel issues which executives may be reluctant to bring up in group meetings, or share over the phone or by mail.

Essential Requirements for Effective Counseling Sessions

To conduct effective counseling sessions, succession planning coordinators should follow these general guidelines:

1. Send questions in advance, making the purpose of the session clear.
2. Tailor the questions to issues that will be treated in regularly scheduled group meetings with the CEO so that their relevance is immediately apparent.
3. Keep the meeting short and on target unless asked to offer advice on specific issues.
4. *Always assume that everything is said in strictest confidence.* (That point deserves strong emphasis.)
5. Be alert to casual remarks or questions that may seem to indicate problems, probing with additional questions to learn more as appropriate.

Common Succession Planning Problems—and Possible Solutions

Succession planning coordinators who meet to counsel managers on people problems unique to their areas should be prepared to deal with complex problems. Many events may derail the progress of otherwise high-potential employees, and a succession planning coordinator should be prepared to offer advice on what to do about those problems. Reclaiming high-potential employees on the verge of derailing their careers is an important role, and it is one that is often informally expected of the succession planning coordinator.

Over the years I have been asked to offer executives advice on how to counsel high potentials experiencing the following problems that were on the verge of derailing their futures:

- An executive engaged in a high-profile extramarital affair with a subordinate
- An executive accused of blatant sexual harassment (the accusation could not be substantiated)
- An executive, slated for the CEO spot, who was recognized as an alcoholic by everyone except himself
- A male executive who was grossly insubordinate to his female superior
- An executive renowned for her technical knowledge who was so abrasive that she was notorious for her inability to work harmoniously with her peers
- An executive who experienced a major personality conflict with his immediate superior

These are merely samples of the problems about which the succession planning coordinator may be asked to offer advice.

Although few succession planning coordinators are trained psychologists or psychiatrists, they should be able to apply the following steps, which I have found to be helpful when advising executives about people problems.

1. *Ask for information about the present situation.* What is happening now? Where is the executive obtaining information? When and how was this information revealed? Has the information been obtained firsthand, or is the executive relying on intermediaries, rumors, or speculation? What steps have been taken to separate fact from fancy?

2. *Ask for information about corrective actions already attempted.* What efforts, if any, have already been made to correct the problem? What were the results of those actions? What efforts have been made to alert the affected individual to the problem or to clarify desired behavior or performance?

3. *Determine the problem's cause, if possible, and assess whether it can be solved.* What does the executive believe is the cause of the problem? Does the person who is experiencing the problem know what to do? (If not, it may indicate a training need.) Is the person deliberately and maliciously engaging in undesirable behavior? (If so, it may indicate a disciplinary problem.)

Has anyone asked the person experiencing the problem to identify its cause(s) and possible solution(s)? Can the individual avoid derailing his or her career, or have matters already gone so far that others have lost all confidence in the possibility for improvement?

4. *Establish an action plan.* Emphasize to the executive receiving the

counseling the importance of properly managing the organization's human resources. Express strong confidence in the executive's ability to deal with the problem. Offer to help in any way possible. Suggest such steps as these: (1) Put the problem in writing and meet with the person having the problem so as to make it as clear as possible; (2) encourage the executive to clarify, in writing, what needs to be done, how it should be done, how much time for improvement will be permitted, and what will happen if it is not done.

5. *Follow up.* After meeting with the executive who has had a problem, the succession planning coordinator should make a point of following up later to see how the problem was resolved.

By following the five steps outlined above, succession planning coordinators should be able to identify and resolve people problems. That is a valuable service in its own right to an organization, and it can help get people who are in danger of derailing back on track.

Summary

This chapter focused on refining the succession planning program. It summarized what was needed to prepare a program action plan, communicate the action plan, conduct succession planning meetings, carry out training on succession planning, and counsel managers on succession planning problems—particularly those having to do with people problems—unique to their areas of responsibility.

To be successful, however, any succession planning program should be based on systematic analyses of present job requirements, future job requirements, present individual performance, and future individual potential. Conducting such analyses is not for the fainthearted, the ill prepared, or the uncommitted. These processes require hard work and diligence, as the next section of this book will show.

Part III

Assessing the Present And the Future

To be effective, succession planning should be based on reliable information about the organization's requirements and about individual performance and potential. To obtain that information, most organizations must establish the means by which to:

- Identify key positions.
- Assess work requirements in key positions.
- Appraise individual performance.
- Anticipate changes in work requirements.
- Assess individual potential.
- Use 360 degree feedback.

Only by approaching these activities systematically can the organization ensure planned succession. These issues are treated in Chapters 6 and 7, which compose Part III.

6

Assessing Present Work Requirements and Individual Job Performance

Leaders must know the present before they can plan the future.[1] They must be realistically aware of the organization's strengths and weaknesses before they can navigate around future external threats and seize the advantages presented by external opportunities. That can be a daunting task because leaders are biased observers: They are, after all, accountable in large measure for an organization's strengths and weaknesses. It is thus easy for them to overlook weaknesses, since the cause(s) may be rooted in their own past decisions; it is easy for them to overlook strengths, which they may take for granted. Managers, it has been shown, will persist in an ill-fated course of action because they fall prey to the *gambler's fallacy* that is based on the logic that "just a little more effort will lead to a big payoff."[2] But some efforts never pay off; rather, they merely lead to mounting losses. That is why organizations replace leaders after they experience repeated failures.

Many of the same basic principles apply to succession planning. Before leaders can effectively plan for succession they must be aware of the organization's work requirements and the strengths and weaknesses of its available leadership talent. Indeed, having the right person for the right job at the right time is a strategic issue of key importance that has long presented a major challenge to top managers. But to know who those people are and what they must do, the organization must first be able to furnish answers to such questions as these:

- What are the organization's key positions?
- What are the work requirements in key positions?
- How should individual performance be appraised?

- What methods should be used to keep track of the organization's
  work requirements and individual performance?

This chapter focuses on answering these questions. It thus emphasizes
examining *present conditions*. The next chapter focuses on anticipating *future conditions*. Taken together, they are a starting point for long-term and
systematic succession planning.

Identifying Key Positions

To achieve maximum benefits from a systematic succession planning program, begin by first identifying *key positions*. The reason: Key positions
underscore and dramatize important work processes that must be carried
out and important work results that must be continuously accomplished
by the organization. Key positions warrant attention because they represent strategically vital leverage points affecting organizational success.
When they are left vacant—or when the work is left undone for whatever
reason—the organization will not be able to meet or exceed customer expectations, confront competition successfully, or follow through on long-
term efforts of crucial significance.

How Can Key Positions Be Identified?

A *key position* is defined as one that exerts critical influence on organizational activities—operationally, strategically, or both. Key positions have
traditionally been viewed as those at the pinnacle of the organization's
chain of command. The most obvious reason is that important decision
making has been made at the top of most organizations and imposed
downward. But, as decision making has become more decentralized as a
result of increasing employee involvement and the application of principles linked to high-involvement work organizations, key positions have
become diffused throughout organizations. Hence, they may reside at
many points on the organization chart.

  Key positions are not identical across organizations. There are several
reasons why. One reason is that organizations do not allocate work exactly
the same. Position holders sharing job titles in different organizations do
not necessarily perform identical duties. A second reason is that top managers in different organizations do not share the same values. As a result,
they may vest job incumbents with more or with less responsibility, their
decision being influenced by their own perceptions (and values) about
what activities are most important. A third reason is that organizations do
not share identical strengths and weaknesses nor face identical environ-

mental threats and opportunities. Hence, a key position in one organization may not be a key position in another. Key positions are thus unique to a single organization.

Let's focus on six ways to identify key positions.

1. *By the consequences/uproar resulting from a pending or existing vacancy.* When the organization lacks a *key position incumbent*—defined as someone occupying a key position at any level, in any function, or at any location—it is apparent, because important decisions cannot be reached, orders cannot be shipped, production cannot proceed, customers' needs cannot be satisfied, or bills are left unpaid. In short, a vacancy in a key position creates an uproar because an important activity is placed on hold when the right talent is lacking to make an informed decision, complete a process, or achieve results. This delay can prove costly, placing an organization at risk to competitors who do not face such a handicap. Possible results include loss of customers, market share, and (in the worst cases) bankruptcy.

One way, then, to recognize a key position is by the consequences of—or uproar caused by—not filling a vacancy when it exists or is expected. I call this *the uproar method* of identifying key positions. Generally, the greater the uproar created by an existing or a pending vacancy, the greater the importance of that key position and the work process(es) over which it exerts influence.

2. *By organization charting.* Prepare a current organization chart. Show all functions. List the leader's name in each function, if the organization is sufficiently small to make that possible. Then list the number of people assigned to carry out the function. Pose these questions:

1. What does this function uniquely contribute to the organization's mission?
2. Could this function operate effectively if the leader were gone?

The answer to the first question provides valuable clues about organizational processes. It should be expressed in terms of the *inputs, transformational processes,* and *outputs* of that function relative to the organization's work. That tells why the function is important, and what it does to accomplish the results desired from it.

The answer to the second question yields clues about key positions.

If the answer to that question is no, then the next question to ask is, *Why is that leader so valuable?* What is it that makes him or her important—and potentially tough to replace? Does he or she possess specialized expertise or carry out specialized work duties? (If so, then it is a key position.) Do the staff members collectively assigned to that function lack the ability to achieve results in the absence of a leader? (If so, then a potential *replacement problem* has been identified that should be solved.)

If the answer is yes, then ask, *Why is the function able to operate without the leader?* Are others particularly key to its operation? If that is the case, then the leader does not occupy a key position, but one or more workers do.

If this activity is carried to its natural conclusion, key positions should be easily identified on the organization chart. Each key position is tied to a critically important organizational function/result/work process. A vacancy in any key position will represent a *hole*, a gap between an organizational requirement and the human talent needed to meet that requirement.

3. *By questioning.* Most senior executives have a keen grasp of their areas of responsibility. Ask them what they regard as key positions within their own areas. Do that by posing a question like this: What positions in your area of responsibility are so important that, if they suddenly became vacant, your part of the organization would face major problems in achieving results? Ask for the titles of the positions to be listed, not the names of job incumbents. Then ask, Why are these positions so important? Don't provide clues; rather, allow executives to furnish their own rationales. (That tactic is likely to lead to the best information.)

4. *By historical evidence.* Has the organization experienced crises or uproars in the past resulting from unexpected departures by key job incumbents? Use evidence of past uproars as indicators of where key positions are located. Scan personnel records to obtain the names and job titles of people who departed in the last few years. Then contact their former supervisors in the organization to find out *which* departures posed the greatest problems for the organization and *why* they posed problems. Were they in tough-to-fill positions? Did they possess unique, tough-to-replace knowledge and skills? What was it exactly that made these losses so important? How was the uproar handled? If a vacancy occurred in the same position again, would it still cause an uproar? Why? Compile the answers to these questions as evidence of key positions.

5. *By network charting.* Network charting is a technique of communication analysis that has recently been used in identifying employment discrimination.[3] But its applications are also potentially much more powerful in charting the decision-making process in organizations. The idea is a simple one. Trace the path of communication flows during one or more decisions to answer such questions as these: Who is included? Who is excluded? and Why are some individuals included or excluded?

A key assumption of network charting is that decision makers will seek information only from individuals who occupy important positions and/or who are viewed as credible, trustworthy, and knowledgeable about the issues on which decisions must be made. Significantly, it has also been shown that decision makers prefer to consult people like themselves—and exclude people unlike themselves—during decision-making processes. Hence, communication flows in the same way that succession decisions are made when left unchecked—that is, through *homosocial reproduction*,[4] the tendency of leaders to perpetuate themselves by sponsoring people who are in some way like themselves.

Network charting can be carried out by interviewing people or by retracing communication flows. But the best way, though time-consuming, is to shadow a key decision maker to determine firsthand *what positions* and *what individuals* are included, and why. In this application of network charting, the aim is not to uncover employment discrimination; rather, it is to determine which positions are considered key to decision making in each part of the organization. The results should yield valuable information about key positions in—and the route of work processes through—the organization.

6. *By combination.* A sixth and final approach is to combine two or more other approaches listed above. Academic researchers call this *triangulation*,[5] since it involves verifying information by double-checking it from multiple sources. Radar and sonar operators originated the approach, I believe, as a way to obtain a definite fix on an object. Practically speaking, however, many organizations have neither time nor resources to double-check key positions. Often, only one approach is used.

What Information Should the Organization Maintain About Key Positions?

Once key positions have been identified, additional questions will present themselves:

- Who occupies those key positions now? What are their qualifications? What background, education, experience, or other specialized credentials and attitudes did they bring to their positions?
- What are the work requirements in key positions? (See the next section.)
- When are those key positions likely to become vacant? Can some vacancies be predicted based on the announced retirement plans of key position incumbents?
- Where are key positions located in the organization? (Answer that question based on the organization's structure, job categories, and geographical locations.)
- How is performance appraised in the organization? How well do performance appraisal practices match up to information about work requirements by position?

- How well are the key position incumbents presently performing? Did their backgrounds, education, and experience properly equip them for the positions they now hold? If not, what are they lacking?
- How did key job incumbents secure their positions? Were they groomed to assume their positions, recruited from outside, transferred from within, or did they reach their positions through other means?

By answering these questions, the organization can begin to establish an *information system* to track key positions, key position incumbents, and individual performance.

Three Approaches to Determining Work Requirements in Key Positions

Once key positions have been identified, direct attention to determining the work requirements in those positions. After all, the only way that individuals can be prepared as replacements for key positions is to clarify first what the key position incumbents *do*. At least three ways may be used to do that. They are described below.

Conducting Job and Task Analysis

Job analysis summarizes or outlines activities, responsibilities, duties, or essential job functions. *Task analysis* goes a step beyond that to determine what must be done to carry out each activity or meet each responsibility, duty, or essential function. The result of a job analysis is called a *job description*; the result of a task analysis is called a *task inventory*.

Some authorities distinguish between the terms *job* and *position*:

> A *job* consists of a group of related activities and duties. Ideally, the duties of a job should consist of natural units of work that are similar and related. They should be clear and distinct from those of other jobs to minimize misunderstanding and conflict among employees and to enable employees to recognize what is expected of them. For some jobs, *several* employees may be required, each of whom will occupy a separate position. A *position* consists of different duties and responsibilities performed by only *one* employee.[6]

It is thus important to distinguish between a job description, which provides information about an entire job category (such as supervisors, managers, or executives), and a position description, which provides information unique to one employee. In most cases, the focus of determining work requirements for succession planning is on positions, since the aim is to identify work requirements unique to key positions.

▪ *What is a position description?* A position description summarizes the duties, activities, or responsibilities of a position. Hence, it literally describes a position in one organizational setting. It answers this question: *What are incumbents in the position expected to do in the organization?*

No universally accepted standards exist for either job descriptions or position descriptions.[7] In most organizations, however, position descriptions list at least the title, salary or wage level, location in the organization, and essential job functions. An *essential job function*, a legal term used in the Americans with Disabilities Act, is an activity that must be conducted by a position incumbent. More specifically, it is a *job activity*

> that's fundamental to successful performance of the job, as opposed to marginal job functions, which may be performed by particular incumbents at particular times, but are incidental to the main purpose of the job. If the performance of a job function is only a matter of convenience, and not necessary, it's a marginal function.[8]

Some organizations add other features to job descriptions, and the same features may be added to position descriptions as well. These additions may include, for instance, the approximate time devoted to each essential job function, the percentage of a position's total time devoted to each essential job function, the relative importance of each essential job function to successful performance, and a *job specification* listing the minimum qualifications required for selection.

▪ *How is position analysis conducted?* Position analysis is conducted in the same way as job and task analysis. As Kenneth E. Carlisle notes:

> The process of analyzing jobs and tasks involves at least three key steps. First, the job or task is broken down into its component parts. Second, the relationships between the parts are examined and compared with correct principles of performance. Third, the parts are restructured to form an improved job or task, and learning requirements are specified.[9]

Use the worksheet in Exhibit 6-1 as a guideline for preparing a current key position description. For ideas about what essential job functions to list, see *The Dictionary of Occupational Titles* (published by the U.S. Department of Labor), and works on the Americans with Disabilities Act and on management job descriptions.[10]

Exhibit 6-1. A worksheet for writing a key position description.

Directions: Give careful thought to the process of writing this position description, since it can be critically important in recruiting, selecting, orienting, training, appraising, and developing a job incumbent for a key position. The best approach is to ask the incumbent of the key position to write the description; then review it several levels up, down, and across the organization. [*In that way, it should be possible to obtain valuable information about the desired results necessary for this position at present—some of which even the current position incumbent may be unaware. For now, focus on what the position incumbent is* presently doing *and what others in the organization* want the key position incumbent to be doing in the future.]

Title [*Fill in the position title*]:

Salary level [*Note the present pay grade*]: _____
Organizational unit/department [*Note the present placement of the position in the organizational structure*]:

Immediate supervisor [*Note the title of the person to whom the position incumbent presently reports on the organization chart*]:

Position Summary [*In one or two sentences, summarize the purpose— or mission statement—for this position. Answer this question: why does it exist?*]:

Position Duties / Responsibilities / Activities / Key Results / Essential Functions [*Make a list in the left column below of the most important position duties, responsibilities, activities, key results, or essential functions. If necessary, use a separate sheet of paper to draft the list and then record the results of your deliberations in priority order. Be sure to list the most important duty, responsibility, activity, key result, or essential function first. Begin each statement with an action verb. Then, in the right column, indicate the approximate percentage of time devoted to that activity*]:

Position Duties/ Responsibilities/Activities/ Key Results/Essential Functions	Approximate Percentage of Time Devoted to Each
1.	
	_____%
2.	
	_____%
3.	
	_____%
4.	
	_____%
5.	
	_____%

• *Advantages and disadvantages of position descriptions.* Position descriptions are advantageous for identifying work requirements for three reasons. First, most organizations at least have job descriptions, which can be an important starting point on which to base more individualized position descriptions. Second, position descriptions can be the basis for making and justifying many personnel decisions—including selection, appraisal, and training—and not just decisions linked to succession planning. Third and finally, recent legislation—particularly the Americans with Disabilities Act—has made written expressions of work requirements important as legal evidence of what is necessary to perform the work.[11]

However, position descriptions are by no means foolproof. First, they tend to focus on activities, not so much on results. Second, they may leave out important personal characteristics of the job incumbent that are crucial to successful job performance. Third, they date quickly. Keeping them updated can be a time-consuming chore.

Assessing Competencies and Developing a Competency Model

Competency assessment is a possible step beyond job and task analysis as a means of clarifying key position requirements. In this context, *competency* refers to "an underlying characteristic of an employee (that is, motive, trait, skill, aspects of one's self-image, social role, or a body of knowledge) which results in effective and/or superior performance in a job"[12]; *compe-*

tency assessment identifies competencies; and a *competency model* "includes those competencies that are required for satisfactory or exemplary job performance within the context of a person's job roles, responsibilities and relationships in an organization and its internal and external environments." [13] In recent years much attention has been focused on competency assessment. One reason is that it is a means by which to push the assessment envelope beyond mere activities (what job incumbents *do*) and knowledge (what people must *know* to perform activities) to include underlying feelings and attitudes linked to successful performance.

Competency assessment has its roots in the work of David McClelland. [14] Its ability to push the assessment envelope beyond activities is becoming increasingly important as job performance becomes more complex—in both white-collar *and* blue-collar jobs—and more dependent on individual feelings and decision making than on cognitive or psychomotor skills. Competency assessment recognizes, as traditional job and task analysis typically do not, how much individuals *personalize* what they do. [15] Individuals in complex jobs adapt the work to fit their talents as much as the organization provides a framework to *socialize* them in cultural views about the "best" and "worst" ways to perform based on experience with "what works—and what doesn't." [16]

• *Defining "exemplary competence."* *Competent* is a word that is sometimes maligned, chiefly because it can be understood in more than one way. For instance, *The American Heritage Dictionary* defines the word as follows: "1. properly or well qualified; capable: *a competent worker.* 2. Adequate for the purpose; sufficient: *a competent performance.* 3. *Law.* Legally qualified or fit; admissible." On occasion, some managers understand the term to mean "just adequate to meet minimum job requirements," as in the second dictionary definition.

Even worse, the word's meaning can be vague. As Ron Zemke has noted:

> Competency, competencies, competency models, and competency-based training are Humpty Dumpty words meaning only what the definer wants them to mean. The problem comes not from malice, stupidity or marketing avarice, but instead from some basic procedural and philosophical differences among those racing to define and develop the concept and to set the model for the way the rest of us will use competencies in our day-to-day training efforts. [17]

Exemplary competence is perhaps best understood as an ideal, a description of what people must know, do, and feel to demonstrate better than merely adequate or sufficient competence. It is a desired future performance level, not just minimally adequate or the best performance presently possible. It thus signifies a goal or target that is achievable through an infinite number of possible behaviors or activities.

▪ *Summarizing approaches to competency assessment.* Different approaches to competency assessment have been devised. The most thoroughly researched treatment available of these approaches is found in David Dubois's *Competency-Based Performance Improvement: A Strategy for Organizational Change* (Amherst, Mass.: Human Resource Development Press, 1993).[18] While space is not available here to review each approach to competency assessment described at length by Dubois, those who are serious about succession planning will find the book to be a thoughtful treatment of the approaches currently available. Each may be applied to key positions and to high-potential individuals for purposes of succession planning. Summaries of these approaches appear in Exhibit 6-2.

While competency assessment is often conducted in a rigorous fashion, some who rely on competencies as an essential element in succession planning advocate a less rigorous—but faster and less expensive—approach to developing competency models.

The first step is to find a shopping list of management or leadership competencies from other sources (see the list appearing in Exhibit 6-3). The shopping list should be composed of "generic management/leadership competencies" to distinguish them from "organization-specific management/leadership competencies" that are tailored to an organization's unique culture and work demands and its success profile of the personal characteristics of high performers/high potentials. Of course, to be effective and useful, competencies such as those listed in Exhibit 6-3 must eventually have more detailed descriptions attached to them so that it is clear what underlying personal characteristics they do and do not include.

The second step is to call together a panel of up to fifteen suitable stakeholders to examine the competencies of a targeted job category. For instance, if the aim is to create an *executive success profile*—that is, a description of the desirable characteristics of an individual occupying a key position in the executive ranks—top managers are probably the most appropriate choices for the panel.

The third step is to present the panel members with the list of competencies and ask them to identify which ones should (and should not) be part of the executive success profile. That can be done in a meeting or in another way.

If it is done in a meeting, the group facilitator may ask the panel members to sort the competencies into those that are appropriate to the executive success profile, those that are neutral, and those that are not appropriate. This can be carried out in various ways, ranging from use

(text continues on page 158)

Exhibit 6-2. Approaches to competency assessment.

Approach	Brief Description	Steps in Applying the Approach
Job competence assessment method (JCAM)	"Relies on the use of a rigorous, empirical research procedure called job competence assessment, which helps determine what job competencies differentiate exemplary from average performance." (Dubois, 1993, p. 71)	1. Research the job components. 2. Research the attributes of the exemplary performers and construct the job competency model. 3. Validate the job competency model (Dubois, 1993, p. 73).
Modified job competence assessment method (MJCAM)	"Uses the JCAM research procedure, with the modification of having the exemplary and average performers write or otherwise record their critical behavior stories for use by the researcher." (Dubois, 1993, p. 71)	Replicate the steps for JCAM above.
Generic model overlay method (GMOM)	"Selects or obtains a prepared competency model and then overlays or superimposes it on a job within the organization." (Dubois, 1993, p. 71)	1. Complete the needs analysis, assessment, and planning step. 2. Research and develop a draft competency model.

3. Verify the draft competency model by having a group of exemplary job performers review the draft competency model.
4. Direct members of a focus group to review suggestions for modification to the model made by the exemplary performers (Dubois, 1993, p. 87).

| Customized generic model method (CGMM) | "Relies on the researcher's tentative identification of a universe of candidate generic competencies that fully characterize the attributes of the exemplary and average performers of a job in the organization." (Dubois, 1993, p. 71) | 1. Enlist initial client or client group support and develop a project plan.
2. Assemble and review all available information pertinent to the job. Prepare a job information paper or portfolio.
3. Research an initial set of job competencies.
4. Organize a focus group.
5. Convene the focus group and develop a draft "best-estimate" competency model.
6. Research the draft and develop the final competency model.
7. Brief the client or client group on project results (Dubois, 1993, p. 91). |

(continues)

Exhibit 6-2 *(continued).*

Approach	Brief Description	Steps in Applying the Approach
Flexible job competency model method (FJCMM)	"Relies on having a wide variety of comprehensive information sources for inclusion in the research base. A feature of this method is the identification and use of future assumptions about the organization and the job. . . . The use of this method results in the availability of job roles, job outputs, quality standards for the outputs, and behavioral indicators for each job competency." (Dubois, 1993, p. 72)	1. Assemble and review all available information that is pertinent to the job. Prepare a job information paper or portfolio. 2. Identify an expert panel consisting of senior organization leaders, managers, or exemplary subject-matter experts. 3. Develop present and future assumptions about the job in the context of the organization. 4. Develop a job-outputs menu, including (optional) quality criteria for each output.

5. Construct a job competencies menu and the behavioral indicators for each competency.
6. Determine a menu of job roles through a cluster analysis of the job outputs.
7. Construct one or more generic job competency models.
8. Brief the client or client group on the project results. Prepare the final project products (Dubois, 1993, p. 100).

ADAPTED, with the publisher's permission, from David Dubois, *Competency-Based Performance Improvement: A Strategy for Organizational Change* (Amherst, Mass.: Human Resource Development Press, © 1993). Reprinted by permission of HRD Press, Inc., 22 Amherst Rd., Amherst, MA 01002, 1-800-822-2801 (U.S. and Canada) or (413) 253-3488.

Exhibit 6-3. A shopping list of management and leadership competencies.

The individual is able to do the following:

- Act ethically.
- Apply an understanding of group dynamics.
- Budget.
- Build esprit de corps.
- Coordinate work activities.
- Cope with failure.
- Delegate.
- Demonstrate a service attitude with customers.
- Demonstrate humor.
- Demonstrate intellectual energy.
- Demonstrate knowledge of specialized subject matter.
- Develop others.
- Exercise creativity.
- Exercise tenacity.
- Exercise versatility.
- Find problems.
- Handle ambiguity.
- Handle interpersonal confrontations.
- Identify the source of conflicts.
- Inspire faith in others.
- Lead.
- Listen effectively.

- Maintain an effective balance between life at work and at home.
- Make decisions.
- Make effective recruitment and selection decisions.
- Manage conflict.
- Motivate others.
- Plan.
- Remain composed in stressful situations.
- Set priorities.
- Show appreciation for diversity.
- Show compassion.
- Show courage.
- Show a sense of urgency.
- Solve problems.
- Speak effectively.
- Take risks.
- Think strategically.
- Use computers.
- Work effectively with peers.
- Work effectively with subordinates.
- Work effectively with superiors.
- Write effectively.

of flipcharts to more innovative approaches involving playing cards or electronic presentation software.

If it is done outside a meeting, executives may be interviewed, surveyed, or otherwise contacted by the succession planning coordinator or other appropriate individual. More innovative approaches might involve electronic mail, audio teleconferencing, or video teleconferencing. An advantage of these innovative approaches is that they can permit international participation without necessitating expensive travel.

Of course, this less rigorous approach to competency assessment may be used with job categories other than executives. Because it is fast and inexpensive, it can be updated annually. However, the results are only as good as the process. That means that since the list of competencies are not unique to the organization, they may or may not reflect the "real" list in that corporate culture.

▪ *Advantages and disadvantages of competency assessment.* Competency assessment offers an alternative to traditional job analysis as a way of identifying characteristics linked to exemplary job performance. An advantage of competency assessment is its research-based rigor. Another is its ability to capture the (otherwise ineffable) characteristics of successful job performers and job performance. It can provide valuable information on key positions and high-potential employees on which to base succession planning practices.

Unfortunately, however, competency assessment does have disadvantages. One is that the term's meaning, as explained above, can be confusing. A second, and more serious, disadvantage is that rigorous approaches to competency assessment usually require considerable time, money, and expertise to carry out successfully. Rarely can they be done internally except by the largest organizations. The third, and final, disadvantage is that the results of competency assessment can date quickly. These can be genuine drawbacks when the pressure is on to take action and achieve results quickly.

Using "Rapid Results Assessment"

A new approach to competency assessment is needed to maximize the strengths and minimize the weaknesses of traditional approaches. Such a new approach may involve the marriage of a traditional approach to competency assessment, such as the Flexible Job Competency Model Method (see Exhibit 6-2), with the so-called DACUM method.

DACUM is an acronym formed from letters in the phrase *Developing A Curriculum*.[19] It has been widely used in job and task analysis for technical positions and in establishing occupational curricula at community colleges. Seldom, however, has it been described as a means by which to determine work requirements in management or professional positions because its traditional aim is to uncover job activities rather than duties or competencies.

To use DACUM in its traditional sense, select a facilitator trained in the approach. Convene a committee consisting of eight to twelve experts in the job. Then take the following steps:

1. Describe DACUM to the committee.
2. Review the job or occupation.
3. Identify the general areas of responsibility to be examined.
4. Ask committee members to identify the specific tasks performed in each area of responsibility.
5. Ask committee members to review and refine task and duty statements.
6. Ask committee members to sequence task and duty statements.
7. Ask committee members to identify entry-level tasks.[20]

The result of a typical DACUM committee or panel is a detailed matrix illustrating work activities arranged in order of difficulty, from the simplest to the most complex. In DACUM's traditional application, panel members approach descriptions of "personality characteristics" as an additional activity. For instance, at the conclusion of the DACUM session, panel members may be asked a question such as, What personal characteristics describe an effective job incumbent? That question may elicit such responses from panel members as "punctuality," "good attendance," or "ability to work harmoniously with coworkers." Rarely are such characteristics linked to specific, measurable behaviors—although the characteristics may be critical to successful job performance.

In practice, a DACUM panel usually meets in a quiet room for one or two days. The facilitator asks panelists to list work activities, in "round robin" fashion and in no particular order. Each activity is written with a felt-tipped pen on a sheet of paper and posted on a blank wall at the front of the room. Because panelists can list activities quickly, most DACUM facilitators need one or two confederates to assist them by writing the activities down on paper and posting the paper on the wall. Panelists who are unable to think of an activity are skipped. The process continues until all the panelists are unable to think of any more activities to list.

At that point, the facilitator calls a break. With the help of confederates—and perhaps one or more panelists or other job experts—the facilitator devises descriptive categories for the activities and then groups related activities into the categories. When finished, the facilitator reconvenes the panel. Panelists add, subtract, or modify categories and verify activities. Finally, they sequence categories and activities from most simple to most complex. These steps closely resemble classical brainstorming, which consists of two steps: *idea generation* and *idea evaluation*.[21]

To use DACUM as a tool for competency assessment, facilitators should take additional steps. Once a DACUM job matrix has been completed and verified, facilitators should adjourn the panel and plan to convene at another time. Once the panel is reconvened, facilitators should present panelists with the DACUM job matrix—either as an individualized handout or as a large wall chart. Facilitators should then progress around the room, focusing panelists' attention on each cell of the job matrix and asking panelists to (1) list underlying motives, traits, aspects of self-image, social roles, or the body of knowledge that effective job incumbents should exhibit to carry out that activity, and (2) work outputs or results stemming from each activity. The answers should be written inside each cell.

Once again, the panel should be adjourned briefly. As in the first panel meeting, facilitators should make an effort to eliminate duplication and economically list personal characteristics and work outputs for *each* activity. When facilitators are finished, they should again reconvene the panel and seek verification of the results and group consensus. If the meeting runs too long, facilitators may adjourn and follow up by written survey or electronic mail, thereby turning traditional brainstorming into a modified delphi process.[22]

The value of this approach should be apparent. First, *it is much faster than traditional competency assessment.* (That is a major advantage, and it is worth emphasizing.) Second, this approach—like traditional DACUM—has high face validity because it uses experienced job incumbents (or other knowledgeable people). It should gain ready acceptance in the organization. Third, it permits the personal involvement of key decision makers, thereby building the ownership that stems from participation. Fourth, and finally, it enjoys the advantage of being a competency-based approach in that the modified DACUM moves beyond the traditional focus on work activities or tasks to include descriptions of underlying characteristics and/ or outputs.

Of course, this new approach to competency assessment, which I have chosen to call *rapid results assessment,* does have its disadvantages. The results do not have the research rigor of other competency assessment approaches. Hence, rigor is sacrificed for speed. Second, the results of the approach will depend heavily on the credibility of the individual panelists. If inexperienced people or poor performers participate, the results will be greeted with suspicion.

Like traditional competency assessment, *rapid results assessment* can provide valuable information for succession planning. It can be kept updated because the process can be conducted annually. If the assessment process is focused on key positions—and if DACUM panels include immediate superiors, peers, incumbents, and even subordinates—it can yield useful information about role expectations for incumbents in these positions. It can also provide the basis, as DACUM does, to select, appraise, train, reward, and develop people who are being groomed for key positions.

Appraising Performance

For a succession planning program to be effective, it must be based on information about work requirements in key positions *and* about the performance of incumbents and prospective successors. Hence, employee performance appraisal should be an important source of information for succession planning. But what is performance appraisal, and how should it be linked to succession planning?

Defining Performance Appraisal

Performance appraisal is the process of determining how well individuals are meeting the work requirements of their jobs.[23] Just as most organizations prepare job descriptions to answer the question, *What do people do?*, most organizations also prepare performance appraisals to answer the question, *How well are people performing?* Performance appraisals are commonly used in making decisions about pay raises, promotions, and other personnel matters. They are also critically important for succession planning, since few organizations will advance individuals into key positions when they are not performing their present jobs adequately.

While a fixture of organizational life, employee performance appraisal has not been immune to criticism. Indeed, it is rare to find managers who will enthusiastically champion the performance appraisal practices of their organizations. In recent years, appraisals have been increasingly prone to litigation.[24] Moreover, appraisals were attacked by no less than the curmudgeonly guru of total quality management, W. Edwards Deming. Deming faulted employee performance appraisal for two primary reasons. First, he believed that performance appraisal led to management by fear. Second, appraisal "encourage[d] short-term performance at the expense of long-term planning."[25] It prompted people to look good in the short run, with potentially devastating long-term organizational effects.

The central point of Deming's argument is that people live up to the expectations that their superiors have for them. That is the Pygmalion effect, which takes its name from the ancient artist who fell in love with his own sculpted creation of the woman Galatea. The Pygmalion effect asserts that managers who believe that their employees are performing effectively will create a self-fulfilling prophecy. The underlying assumption, then, is that the world is influenced by viewers' beliefs about it.

When performance appraisal is conducted in a highly critical manner, it has the potential to demotivate and demoralize people. Indeed, research evidence indicates that performance appraisal interviews focusing on "what people are doing wrong" can actually lead to worse performance.

How Should Performance Appraisal Be Linked to Succession Planning?

Despite harsh attacks from critics, performance appraisal is likely to remain a fixture of organizational life. One reason is that, despite their flaws, written appraisals based on job-related performance criteria are superior in a legal defense to informal, highly subjective appraisals at a time when employees are increasingly prone to litigate. In the absence of written forms and formal procedures, managers do not cease appraising employees; rather, they simply do it in a less structured fashion. Worse yet, they may face no requirement to provide employees with feedback—with the result that they can never improve. Indeed, few can dispute that employees will not improve their performance—or develop in line with succession plans—if they have received no timely, concrete, and specific feedback on how they are doing or what they should do to improve. While annual performance appraisals are no substitute for daily feedback, they should be used together to help employees develop.[26] Otherwise, aside from the faulty memories and inarticulated impressions of supervisors and other employees, the organization will have no records of employee performance on which to base pay, promotion, transfer, or other decisions affecting workers' lives.

There are many approaches to performance appraisal. Much has been written on the subject.[27] (Different types of appraisals are summarized in Exhibit 6-4.) To be effective, however, performance appraisal should be based as closely as possible on the work that employees do. Used in conjunction with *individual potential assessments*, which compare individuals to future job assignment possibilities, they can be a powerful tool for employee improvement and development. For that reason, the best appraisal is one that examines employee performance point by point to present responsibilities.

One way to do that is to begin with a position description. Employees should then be appraised against each activity. In that way, the organiza-

(text continues on page 168)

Exhibit 6-4. Approaches to conducting employee performance appraisal.

Approach	Focus	Brief Description
Global rating	The individual's overall job performance.	The appraiser is asked to characterize an individual's overall job performance on a single scale or in a single essay response. *Chief advantage:* Appraisers can make responses quickly. *Chief disadvantage:* Performance is more complex than a single rating can indicate.
Trait rating	Traits related to the individual's performance. Examples of traits include "initiative" or "timeliness."	Appraisers are asked to characterize an individual's job performance over a specific time span using a series of traits. Often, trait ratings are scaled from "excellent" through "unacceptable." The appraiser is asked to check an appropriate point on the scale. However, traits can also be assessed by an essay response in which the appraiser is asked to write a narrative about the individual's performance relative to the trait.

(continues)

Chief advantage:
Appraisers can make responses quickly.

Chief disadvantage:
Traits can have different meanings, so consistency of rating and job relatedness of traits may be critical issues to deal with.

Dimensions/ activity rating	Each job activity, duty, responsibility, or essential function.

Think of a dimensional rating as a "job description that has been given scales to assess performance." Appraisers are asked to rate individual performance on *each* job activity, duty, responsibility, or essential job function. Responses may be provided by placing a mark on a scale or by writing an essay.

Chief advantage:
This approach to appraisal makes a deliberate effort to tie performance appraisal directly to job duties, thereby ensuring job relatedness.

Chief disadvantage:
To work effectively, both appraiser and performer must agree in advance on the duties. That means job descriptions must be updated regularly, which can be time-consuming.

Exhibit 6-4 *(continued)*.

Approach	Focus	Brief Description
Behaviorally anchored rating scales (BARS)	Job behaviors—observable activities—distinguishing exemplary from average performers.	A BARS performance appraisal typically consists of five to ten vertical scales that are developed through a critical incident process to distinguish effective from ineffective performance. Each scale represents actual performance. A BARS rating system is especially compatible with competency assessment. *Chief advantage:* Since each BARS is tied directly to job activities, this approach to performance appraisal enjoys high face validity. It can also lead to improved job performance by clarifying for performers exactly what behaviors are desirable and undesirable. *Chief disadvantage:* To work effectively, BARS requires considerable time and effort to devise. That can exceed the resources—or commitment—of many organizations.

Management by objectives (MBO)	Results of job performance rather than the processes used to achieve the results.	Before the appraisal period begins, the appraiser and performer jointly agree upon desired job results. At the end of the appraisal period, the results are compared with the objectives established at the beginning of the appraisal period.

Chief advantages:
The focus is on results rather than on methods of achieving them.
Both appraiser and performer are involved in establishing performance objectives.

Chief disadvantages:
Much time may be required for the appraiser and performer to reach agreement.
Writing performance objectives can turn the process into a paper mill.

tion can maintain precise and detailed records of employee performance in each facet of the individual's job and individuals will receive specific feedback about how well they are performing.

The problem is that such appraisals can be time-consuming to write and conduct. And, in the case of individuals who are performing poorly, their immediate organizational superiors must take the time to explain what needs to be improved and how it should be improved. To save time, some organizations attempt to develop simple, easy-to-fill-out appraisals to ease the paperwork burden on supervisors. Unfortunately, the easier an appraisal is to fill out, the less useful it is in providing feedback to employees.

To solve that problem, try developing free-form appraisals that use job descriptions (or competencies) themselves as the basis for appraisal (see Exhibit 6-5 for a worksheet to help prepare such an appraisal). Another approach is to develop appraisals so that they are geared only toward future improvement rather than past performance. In that way, they are focused less on what employees are doing wrong and more on what they can do right. If that approach is followed consistently, it can provide useful information to employees about what they should do to prepare themselves for the future and to qualify for succession.

Inventorying Talent

Organizations that have no means by which to keep records, and thus to preserve information, about present work requirements and individual job performance will have a difficult time locating qualified talent in the organization when vacancies occur in key positions. For that reason, every organization must establish some means to inventory present talent.

Succession planning inventories may take two forms: *manual* or *automated*.[28]

A *manual system* relies on paper files. It consists of individual personnel files or specialized records, assembled especially for succession planning, that take the form of a succession planning notebook or Rolodex file. These files contain information relevant to making succession decisions, such as:

- Descriptions of individual position duties or competencies (e.g., a current position description)
- Individual employee performance appraisals
- Statements of individual career goals or career plans
- Summaries of individual qualifications (for instance, educational and training records)

Exhibit 6-5. A worksheet for developing an employee performance appraisal linked to a position description.

Directions: Use this worksheet to develop a free-form employee performance appraisal *based specifically on the position description.* In the left column, indicate what the position description indicates are the duties, activities, responsibilities, key result areas, or essential job functions. Then, in the right column, indicate how performance in the position should be measured.

Position's Activities, Duties, Responsibilities	How Performance Should Be Measured for Each Activity, Duty, or Responsibility
1.	
2.	
3.	
4.	
5.	
6.	
7.	

- Summaries of individual skills (e.g., a personal skill inventory that details previous work experience and languages known)

Of course, other information may also be added. Examples may include individual potential assessment forms.

A manual inventory may suffice for a small organization having neither specialized expertise available to oversee succession planning activities nor resources available for automated systems. A chief advantage is that most of the information is filed in personnel files anyway, so no monumental effort is necessary to compile information on individual employees. However, a manual inventory can lead to difficulties in handling, storing, cross-referencing, and maintaining security over numerous (and sometimes lengthy) forms. Even in a small organization, these disadvantages can present formidable problems.

Automated inventories used in succession planning take any one of three typical forms: (1) simple word-processing files; (2) tailored succession planning software; or (3) succession planning software integrated with other personnel records.

Simple word-processing files are the next step beyond paper files. Special forms (templates) are created for succession planning using a popular word-processing program. Blank forms are placed on disk. Managers are asked to complete the forms on disk and return them, physically or electronically, to a central location. This approach reduces paper flow and makes handling, storing, and security easier to manage than is possible with paper records. Unfortunately, succession planning information that is inventoried in this manner will usually be troublesome to cross-reference.

Tailored succession planning software is becoming more common. Usually formatted for personal computers, this software ranges in price (at this writing) from a few hundred dollars to many thousands of dollars. The features run the gamut from simple to complex. Those who coordinate a succession planning program should review several such packages before purchasing one (see Exhibit 6-6 for a summary of software features and the addresses of many vendors).

The chief advantage of this software is that it is tailored specifically to succession planning. Indeed, it can give decision makers good ideas about desirable features to change, add, or subtract from the succession planning program. Handling, sorting, cross-referencing, and maintaining security over much information is greatly simplified. While software prices were relatively high even a few years ago, they are now affordable to most organizations employing fifty or more people.

The only major disadvantage of this software is that it can present

(text continues on page 177)

Exhibit 6-6. Software for succession planning.

Software System and Vendor's Name/Address	Key Features
Blueprint™ *Vendor:* Criterion, Inc. 9425 N. MacArthur Blvd. Irving, Tex. 75063 214-401-2100	This IBM-compatible software: • Is a true Windows software system. • Tracks employee and position information necessary to carry out succession planning. • Allows you to create detailed career development plans that track with your succesion plans. • Links career paths to candidate lists. • Allows preparation of replacement charts. • Is available in single-user and multiuser versions. • Provides for user customization of data, formulas, screens, reports, forms, graphics, and organization charts. • Client/server architecture.
Career Forecasting Reports **CARE-FOR**™ *Vendor:* Charles Russ Associates P.O. Box 6667 Shawnee Mission, Kans. 66206 913-338-1211	This IBM-compatible software: • Plans the movement of people up, down, in, and out of the organization. • Totally relates career development with succession planning. • Develops a five-year strategic plan for every person in the system with expected position openings. • Gives all minorities and protected classes access to upward mobility in compliance with the "glass ceiling" report. • Gives the most accurate picture of who is going where of any system, because it matches expected openings with real people to get the right person in the right job at the right time. • Generates three very user-friendly reports and hundreds of other reports using two simple but powerful report writers. • Is priced at $26,000 for a single user, which includes a complete turnkey installation, forty hours of consulting, and a free hotline.

(continues)

Exhibit 6-6 *(continued).*

Software System and Vendor's Name/Address	*Key Features*
Executive Resource System™ *Vendor:* Organization Metrics, Inc. 10 Winchester Rd. E. PO Box 550 Brooklin, Ont., Canada 905-655-8414	This IBM-compatible software: • Is a strategic human resources management tool. • Allows organizations to define and analyze required competencies at individual, group, and organization levels. • Allows preparation of development plans to address gaps between employee competencies and those required for the position; shows time and costs required. • Provides strategic planning view of the organizations' capabilities at any time in the future and allows comparison between strategic time frames. • Is custom coded for each organization. • Has intuitive, flexible Windows screens. • Is compatible with all LAN, WAN, and client/server platforms. • Is capable of interfacing with existing mainframe, mini-, or micro-based systems to eliminate duplicate data storage. • Has a flexible modular system design, allowing you to buy what you need, when you need it. • Is priced at $16,000 and above for a comprehensive system. • Site licenses are available.
Executive TRACK™ *Vendor:* HRSoft, Inc. 123 N. Main St. Fairfield, la. 52556 515-472-7720	This IBM-compatible software: • Serves more than 1,300 corporate customers in the United States and is thus the market leader for specialized, personal computer-based succession planning software. • Stores data on individuals and positions. • Permits on-line searches for candidates for key positions. • Can be used to prepare color-coded replacement charts and 'what if' scenarios.

Software System and Vendor's Name/Address	Key Features
	• Is capable of uploading and downloading from a mainframe HRIS. • Can be lined to other specialized software, available elsewhere, to track IDPs. • Has excellent security. • Allows screen, menu, and report customization by the end-user. • Is priced at $25,000 and above for a single user on a PC.
Genesys Human Resource Planning System® *Vendor:* Genesys Software Systems 5 Branch St. Methuen, Mass. 01844 508-685-5400	This IBM-compatible software: • Can be used on IBM PCs and some IBM mainframes. • Is part of a complete HRIS that integrates payroll, budgeting, and most HR applications—including succession planning, performance tracking, position data, and much more. • Lends itself to vendor customization.
Hay/McBer Xcel® *Vendor:* McBer and Company 116 Huntington Ave. Boston, Mass. 02116 617-437-7080	This IBM-compatible software: • Is a computer-assisted process that quickly and efficiently identifies the characteristics that predict success in a particular job. The McBer competency modeling method incorporates the use of a base of proven core competencies that determine superior performance. McBer consultants create a customized approach to modeling success according to the organization's unique culture. • Is installed in a customized way to meet the requirements of the client's Job Competency Assessment research projects and to facilitate the application of competency models in its organization. • Allows ratings of individuals that can be generated in a full 360-degree assessment process within the actual work setting, with superiors, peers, incumbents themselves, and employees completing the evaluation.

(continues)

Exhibit 6-6 *(continued).*

Software System and Vendor's Name/Address	Key Features
	• Permits data exchange with ASCII and SQL Servers. • Is designed to identify gaps between person and job (current, future), identify individuals whose current competencies closely match work requirements, identify careers in the organization that match individual competencies, and provide recommendations for individual development/training to help individuals qualify for advancement to new positions.
Occupational Skills Analysis System (OSAS)™ *Vendor:* Educational Data Systems 1 Parklane Blvd. Suite 701 W. Dearborn, Mich. 48126 313-271-2660	This IBM-compatible software: • Assists in the collection of job-related information at the task level. • Is useful in assessing individual performance, conducting occupational analysis, conducting job task analysis, developing OJT and apprenticeship requirements, developing training plans, and much more. • Is priced at approximately $2,995.
Panavue™ *Vendor:* Iris International, Inc. 2810 E. Oakland Park Blvd. Suite 304 Ft. Lauderdale, Fla. 33306 305-564-0408	This IBM-compatible software: • Can be used on IBM PCs. • Can interface with other systems through ASCII. • Permits data exchange with Lotus 1-2-3 and WordPerfect software. • Allows the user to summarize individual status, including position, salary grade, performance information, promotability, time in position and with the organization, classification, and some skills (e.g., foreign language fluency). • Allows the user to track compensation, experience and training, goal attainment, career development, and personal information.

Software System and Vendor's Name/Address	Key Features
	• Is priced between $15,000 and $25,000 for a single user.
RESTRAC PLAN™ (Formerly SuccessPlan) *Vendor:* RESTRAC (Formerly MicroTrac Systems) 1 Dedham Place Dedham, Mass. 02026 617-320-5600	This IBM-compatible software: • Is a Windows-based, true client-server application. • Tracks succession planning, career planning, training and development skills, and various position information. • Generates numerous status and planning reports, including successor reports, T&D reports, EEO reports, employee and position profiles, managers blocked, managers at risk, and high-potential reports. • Includes charting module for standard and custom organization charts. • Allows documents management for scanning, attaching, and searching internal resumés and performance appraisals. • Is priced at $30,000 and above.
SKILLS 2000™ *Vendor:* Educational Technologies 1007 Whitehead Rd. Ext. Trenton, N.J. 08638 609-882-2668	This IBM-compatible software: • Operates in a Windows environment and consists of four programs with a database of 1,734 skills statements. • Is used to survey skills of people, jobs, and training programs. • Includes a comparison program that enables users to select the best candidates for jobs/training. • Provides more than 50 reports, including resumés, job descriptions, critical skill profiles, basic skills profiles, and reading/math levels. • Is priced at $18,230.

(continues)

Exhibit 6-6 *(continued).*

Software System and Vendor's Name/Address	Key Features
Succession Plus™ *Vendor:* Nardoni Associates, Inc. 1465 Route 31 S. Annandale, N.J. 08801 800-338-9701	This IBM-compatible software: • Is geared primarily to senior management positions. • Allows for documentation of basic demographic data, resumé information, and development-related information as well as position data, position requirements, and listings of potential successors. • Produces numerous reports, including succession plans and summaries, individual resumés and development plans, position profiles, and succession/replacement charts. • Is priced at $21,000 and above.
Wingspread™ *Vendor:* Delphi Systems, Ltd. 6740 Pennsylvania Ave. Kansas City, Mo. 64113 816-333-6944	This IBM- and Macintosh-compatible software: • Is a human resources management tool based on a model of *leadership, management,* and *technical* skills derived from the research of R. Katz and J. Kotter. • Provides a factual underpinning for all standard and many innovative human resources functions. • Is built in the Omnis 7 4GL/GUI development and deployment environment; runs on IBM and Macintosh workstation or mainframe platforms; WAN and LAN distribution are standard. • Is of object-oriented design supporting powerful current and future artificial intelligence applications. • Is specifically tailored for each client installation; function modules grow from a robust core system as client needs mature. • Incorporates data from existing internal (i.e., HRMIS, financial, and other corporate MIS) and external (e.g., training

Software System and Vendor's Name/Address	Key Features
	and executive search) databases into its decision-making processes. • Operates from proprietary search, sort, composite, and virtual profile-generating algorithms that ensure accurate information.

SOURCE: Richard B. Frantzreb, ed., *The ASTD Training Support Software Directory* (Alexandria, Va.: The American Society for Training and Development, 1993), pp. H-7–H-45. Used by permission of the American Society for Training and Development. All rights reserved. Each vendor has also approved the description of its software and the use of its trademark for this book.

temptations to modify organization needs to satisfy software demands. In other words, software may not provide sufficient flexibility to tailor succession planning forms and procedures to meet the unique needs of one organization. That can be a major drawback. It is for this reason that succession planning software should be carefully reviewed, in cooperation with the vendor, prior to purchase. Of course, it may be possible for the vendor to modify the software to meet organizational needs at a modest cost.

Succession planning software may also be integrated with other personnel systems. In this case—and some large organizations attempt to keep all data in one place, usually in a mainframe system, in an effort to economize the problems inherent in multiple-source data entry and manipulation—succession planning information is included with payroll, training, and other records. Unfortunately, such software is usually limited in value for succession planning, at least at present. To be tailored to a large organization's uses, such software may have to undergo lengthy and large-scale programming projects. A typical—and major—problem with such mainframe HRIS programs is that they provide insufficient storage space for *detailed, individualized* record keeping tailored to unique succession planning needs. When that is the case, it may be easier to use a personal computer-based system, or else to mount a massive, expensive, and probably quickly dated programming effort to modify a mainframe program.

In many cases, those who oversee succession planning programs are well advised to develop their own assessment form to help them determine whether a software package will adequately meet the needs of their organization. (See Exhibit 6-7 as a starting point for developing such a software evaluation form.) Above all, resist "leaving these decisions to the technical professionals"; rather, take an active role in finding (or modifying) succession planning software to fit organizational uses. Don't be

(text continues on page 182)

Exhibit 6-7. An evaluation form for succession planning software.

Directions: Every organization will have its own requirements for software support for succession planning. Before selecting software, be clear about what those requirements are. Use this check sheet to help you identify them, and select software appropriate for the needs of your organization.

For each question posed in column **1**, circle **yes, no,** or **n/a** (for "not applicable") in column **2**. Only if you've circled **yes** in column **2** should you indicate the relative importance of that criterion in column **3**. Use the following scale:

1 = Not at all important
2 = Relatively unimportant
3 = Marginally important
4 = Somewhat important
5 = Very important

Jot notes to yourself about each question or issue in column **4**. When you complete this form, compare it to the responses of other decision makers in your organization.

1	2	3		4
	Applicability	Least	Importance Most	Notes
Question				
1. Do you wish to limit yourself to a PC-based system?	Yes No N/A	1 2 3 4 5		
2. Do you wish to have the capability to upload/download information from a mainframe Human Resource Information System (HRIS)?	Yes No N/A	1 2 3 4 5		

	Yes	No	N/A	1	2	3	4	5
3. Do you wish to have strong security on software designed to support succession planning?	Yes	No	N/A	1	2	3	4	5
4. Will this system be limited to only one user per site?	Yes	No	N/A	1	2	3	4	5
5. Do you wish to run this system on a local area network?	Yes	No	N/A	1	2	3	4	5
6. Will you use succession planning software for each of the following applications:								
a. Establishing work requirements/conducting job analysis?	Yes	No	N/A	1	2	3	4	5
b. Documenting results of job analysis?	Yes	No	N/A	1	2	3	4	5
c. Writing job or position descriptions?	Yes	No	N/A	1	2	3	4	5

(continues)

Exhibit 6-7 *(continued)*.

1	2			3					4
	Applicability			Importance					
Question	Yes	No	N/A	Least 1	2	3	4	Most 5	Notes
d. Identifying/ predicting future work requirements?	Yes	No	N/A	1	2	3	4	5	
e. Establishing performance requirements for jobs or positions?	Yes	No	N/A	1	2	3	4	5	
f. Recording skill or status information about individuals?	Yes	No	N/A	1	2	3	4	5	
g. Clarifying individual career goals?	Yes	No	N/A	1	2	3	4	5	
h. Plotting career paths?	Yes	No	N/A	1	2	3	4	5	
i. Recording performance information about individuals?	Yes	No	N/A	1	2	3	4	5	

j. Establishing replacement requirements for key positions?	Yes	No	N/A	1	2	3	4	5
k. Preparing replacement/ succession charts?	Yes	No	N/A	1	2	3	4	5
l. Conducting searches to replace key job incumbents?	Yes	No	N/A	1	2	3	4	5
m. Other essential applications?	Yes	No	N/A	1	2	3	4	5
7. Is price a major consideration for selection in your organization?	Yes	No	N/A	1	2	3	4	5
8. Other issues of special importance to your organization:							
a. _____	Yes	No	N/A	1	2	3	4	5
b. _____	Yes	No	N/A	1	2	3	4	5
c. _____	Yes	No	N/A	1	2	3	4	5

willing to sacrifice the needs of the succession planning program to expediency.

Summary

This chapter emphasized present conditions and addressed the following questions:

- What are the organization's key positions?
- What are the work requirements in key positions?
- How should individual performance be appraised?
- What methods should be used to keep track of the organization's work requirements and individual performance?

The next chapter focuses on anticipating *future* conditions as they are essential to succession planning. It thus discusses how to identify future work requirements in key positions, assess individual potential, and inventory high-potential talent.

7

Assessing Future Work Requirements and Individual Potential

Having information about present work requirements and individual job performance provides only a one-dimensional picture. To make the picture more complete—and thus provide the basis for effective succession planning—information is also needed about future work requirements and individual potential.[1] Hence, this chapter focuses on assessing future work requirements and individual potential. More specifically, this chapter addresses these questions:

- What key positions in the organization are likely to emerge in the future?
- What will be the work requirements in those positions?
- What is individual potential, and how should it be assessed?
- How can 360 degree feedback be used?

Identifying Key Positions for the Future

Neither key positions nor their work requirements will remain forever static. The reason, of course, is that organizations are constantly in flux in response to pressures exerted internally and externally. As a result, succession planning coordinators need to identify future key positions and determine future work requirements if they are to be successful in preparing individuals to assume key positions. They must, in a sense, cope with a *moving target effect* in which work requirements, key positions, and even high-potential employees are changing constantly.[2]

But how can they be certain what positions will be key to the organization in the future? Unfortunately, the unsettling fact is that there is no foolproof way to predict key positions with absolute certainty. About the best that can be done is to conduct careful reviews of changes in work and people and draw some conclusions about the likely consequences of change.

Applying Environmental Scanning

As a first step in predicting key positions in the future, begin by applying *environmental scanning*. It can be understood as a systematic process of examining external trends.[3] Focus attention on economic, governmental/legal, technological, social, geographical, and other issues affecting the organization's external environment. (Use the worksheet in Exhibit 7-1 for that purpose.) For best results, involve decision makers in this process, since key positions in the future should reflect the organization's strategic plans and changing work processes.

Applying Organizational Analysis

As a second step in predicting key positions in the future, turn next to *organizational analysis*. It is the systematic process of examining how an organization is positioning itself to address future challenges.[4] It can also be understood as any effort made to assess an organization's strengths and weaknesses. Consider these questions:

- How well positioned is the organization presently to respond to the effects of future trends?
- What action steps can the organization take to meet the threats and opportunities posed by future trends?
- How can the organization maximize its strengths and minimize its weaknesses as the future unfolds in the present?

As these questions are answered, pay particular attention to likely changes in:

- *Organizational structure*. What will be the reporting relationships? How will divisions, departments, work units, and jobs be designed?
- *Work processes*. How will work flow into each part of the organization? What will be done with it? Where will the work flow to?

Structure and processes are important issues because key positions are a function of decisions made about how to structure responsibility and organize the work process.[5] To direct attention to likely positions in the future, then, decision makers should examine how the organization will respond to external pressures by structuring responsibility and organizing work

(text continues on page 187)

Exhibit 7-1. A worksheet for environmental scanning.

Directions: What trends evident in the external environment will affect the organization in the future? Answering that question should prove valuable in strategic business planning, human resources planning, and succession planning. Environmental scanning attempts to identify those trends and, more importantly, to predict their effects.

   Use this simple worksheet to structure your thinking about trends that will affect your organization in the future and what their effects are likely to be. Answer each question; then compare your responses to what other decision makers in the organization have written.

---

1. What trends outside the organization are most likely to affect it in the next one to five years? Consider economic conditions, market conditions, financial conditions, regulatory/legal conditions, technological conditions, social conditions, and other trends that might uniquely affect the organization. List them below:

   a.

   b.

   c.

   d.

   e.

   f.

   g.

   h.

   i.

   j.

   k.

   l.

   m.

   n.

(continues)

Exhibit 7-1 (*continued*).

---

o.

p.

2. For each trend you listed in response to question 1, indicate how you think that trend *will affect the organization.* Describe the *trend's possible consequence(s), outcome(s), or result(s).* While you may not be able to do that with complete certainty, try to gaze into the crystal ball and predict what will happen as a result of a trend.

a.

b.

c.

d.

e.

f.

g.

h.

i.

j.

k.

l.

m.

n.

o.

p.

---

processes. Key positions will emerge and old ones will fade based on the way the organization chooses to respond to environmental demands. Use the activity appearing in Exhibit 7-2 to help decision makers address these issues.

Exhibit 7-2. An activity on organizational analysis.

Directions: How will your organization respond to the trends evident in the external environment that will likely affect it in the future? Use this worksheet to help you structure your thinking about how external environmental trends will affect work in the organization.

    This activity depends on your having completed the activity in Exhibit 7-1. Compare your responses to what other decision makers write. Use the responses to consider future work requirements in the organization.

---

1. For each consequence, outcome or result you listed in response to question 2 in Exhibit 7-1, indicate what functions/positions in the organization are most likely to be affected and how you think those functions/positions will—or should—be affected.

   • [*List affected functions/positions*]:

   • [*Describe how each consequence, outcome, or result will—or should— be affected*]:

2. How should the organization respond to future trends? Should workflow change? Should work methods change? Should the organization's structure change? Are any changes likely as a response to increasing external competitive pressure? How does the organization's strategic plan indicate that those challenges will be met? Will new key positions emerge as a result of changes in organizational strategy? Will old key positions fade in importance while new ones become more important?

   • [*Write narrative responses*]

Preparing Realistic Future Scenarios

As a third and final step in predicting key positions in the future, compare the results obtained from environmental scanning and organizational analysis. Draw an organization chart as decision makers believe it should appear in the future if the organization is to be successful. Write the expected future mission of each organizational function on the chart. (Do several versions of that chart at different time intervals—at, say, one year, three years, five years, and ten years into the future.) Then add the names of possible leaders and their successors.

This process is called *preparing realistic future scenarios*. It is based on the process of *scenario analysis*, which has been widely applied to futures research and strategic planning.[6] Use the activity appearing in Exhibit 7-3 to help decision makers structure their thinking in preparing realistic scenarios to identify future key positions. While not foolproof or fail-safe, this approach is one way to move beyond traditional thinking about succession planning to "lead" the target—what hunters do when they shoot ahead of a moving target.

Exhibit 7-3. An activity for preparing realistic scenarios to identify future key positions.

Directions: The future can be difficult to envision if predictions about it are vague. Use this activity to make predictions more tangible. Create a detailed description of the likely situation of your organization five years from now by answering the questions below on the basis of responses to Exhibits 7-1 and 7-2. Then compare what you and other key decision makers and strategists have written to develop an overall scenario that describes the "best-guess situation" of the way the future will appear for the organization.

---

1. How will the organization be functioning in one to five years, based on environmental scanning or organizational diagnosis? Describe the organization's situation, competition, profitability, and structure:

2. What positions do you believe will be critically important in one to five years? List the job titles below and explain why they will be key positions:

Three Approaches to Determining Future Work Requirements in Key Positions

Determining future work requirements means predicting possible or probable work activities, duties, and responsibilities in future key positions. Once likely future key positions have been identified, direct attention to predicting work requirements for those positions. More beyond present- or past-oriented descriptions to assess future work requirements in key positions. To that end, apply the three approaches described below.

Conducting Future-Oriented Job and Task Analysis

To conduct future-oriented job and task analysis for key positions,[7] focus attention on summarizing expected future activities, responsibilities, duties, or essential functions. Extend the analysis by examining future tasks linked to those activities, responsibilities, duties, or essential job functions. Write position descriptions as they should exist at a future time if the organization is to be successful in meeting the competitive challenges which it faces. In this way, the effects of organizational strategic plans on key positions can be mirrored, and thereby reinforced, in position descriptions and task inventories. By comparing present and future position descriptions, decision makers should be able to uncover important disparities, and accordingly, information about desirable developmental opportunities to groom individuals for advancement. Use the activity appearing in Exhibit 7-4 to prepare *future-oriented key position descriptions*.

However, future-oriented position descriptions are no panacea. They are prone to the same disadvantages as traditional (present-oriented) position descriptions: (1) a focus on activities, not results, (2) a lack of details about all elements essential to job success, including personal characteristics and attitudes, and (3) a requirement for continual, and time-consuming, revision because they date so rapidly. Additionally, they may be based on inaccurate (or simply wrongheaded) assumptions about the future. However, such disadvantages may be outweighed by their specificity and by helping individuals to envision the future into which they, and their organizations, are headed.

Assessing Future Competencies

Competency assessment uniquely lends itself to a future orientation.[8] To give a future orientation to competency assessment, simply direct attention to the future rather than to the present or past. Ask the organization's strategists to review each key position for underlying employee characteristics (including motives, traits, skills, aspects of self-image, social roles, or bodies of knowledge) that should, if assumptions about the future prove

Exhibit 7-4. An activity for preparing future-oriented key position descriptions.

Directions: An organization's strategic plans can seem vague to employees—and even to strategists—until they are made job-specific. Use this activity to help clarify how key positions should change to help the organization realize strategic goals and implement strategic business plans.

In the left column, list current job activities for a key position. Then, using the results of Exhibits 7-1, 7-2, and 7-3, list in the right column how those job activities should change between the present and one to five years in the future so as to enable the job incumbent to cope with expected environmental trends and organizational changes.

Ask each key job incumbent to complete this activity for his/her position. Then ask strategists to review the results of the activity for each key position in the organization. Use the results as a basis for succession planning.

Current Job Activities for Each Key Position	*How These Activities Should Be Carried Out in One to Five Years*

correct, simultaneously result in superior performance and actions consistent with organizational strategy. Apply each approach shown in Exhibit 6-2 with an emphasis on future, rather than past or present, competencies. Then use the resulting competency models as a guide to prepare individuals for advancement into key positions.

Alas, however, future competencies may not be identical to present or past competence. Indeed, they may even *conflict* with them. For instance, think about such examples as IBM after downsizing or AT&T after deregulation. In each case, what was required for future success was not what was historically required, or even desired, by the organization. That created a dilemma. Managers who succeeded under the old conditions were suddenly outmoded and were even unfit to counsel a new generation about what it would take for them to succeed. In these settings, managers had to identify, and cultivate, talent that was quite different from their own if their organizations were to survive. Exemplary future competence, then, represents a moving target, an ideal, a description of what people will probably have to know, do, or feel to perform successfully amid the uncertainties of the future.[9]

Future-oriented competency assessment, like future-oriented position descriptions, suffers from the same strengths and weaknesses as its traditional counterpart. While more rigorous than job analysis, competency assessment can be confusing to those who do not clearly understand what it is. The results of assessment can date quickly. In addition, future-oriented competency assessment usually requires considerable time and expertise to carry out successfully. That may require strategists to devote significant time and resources to it, which they may be reluctant to do.

Applying Future-Oriented "Rapid Results Assessment"

This approach to competency assessment has very real potential to help decision makers plan for future work requirements in key positions. Nor does it require substantial expertise, time, or resources to carry out. To use it, simply focus attention on *desirable future competencies.* Apply the steps depicted in Exhibit 7-5. Use those steps to assess competencies in each key position in the organization. Use the results as the basis to plan for individual development and organizational succession.

"Rapid results assessment" enjoys important advantages: It can be conducted quickly; it can be updated annually; it enjoys high face validity because it uses experienced job incumbents (or other knowledgeable people) on which to base position-specific information; it permits the personal involvement of key decision makers, thereby building their ownership in the results; and it can be used to move beyond a focus on mere work activities or tasks to include descriptions of underlying characteris-

(text continues on page 195)

Exhibit 7-5. Steps in conducting future-oriented "rapid results assessment."

| **Step 1** Orient the committee to the rapid results assessment procedure. |
- Assemble a group of five to thirteen knowledgeable individuals, including job incumbents and their immediate superiors.
- Brief group members on the need to predict changing work requirements.

| **Step 2** Review current information about the job/occupation/function. |
- Assemble information about one or more specific key jobs/positions in the organization.
- Focus attention on "what job incumbents do now."

| **Step 3** Review external environmental factors affecting the organization and likely ways the organization will respond to them. |
- Brief group members on trends in the external environment and the organization that may change—or require change—in job duties, activities, responsibilities, tasks, or essential job functions.

| **Step 4** Identify specific activities that are likely to be carried out in the key position in the future. |
- Ask group members to identify how they believe key positions will be affected by changing external environmental conditions.
- Go around the meeting room and ask each group member to list an activity that he or she envisions will be carried out in the future; continue this process until ideas are exhausted.

Step 5

Review and refine the future-oriented task and activity statements.

- Ask group members to review the activities they defined in the previous step, eliminating redundancy and identifying names for general categories.

Step 6

Sequence future-oriented task and activity statements.

- Ask group members to sequence the future-oriented task and activity statements they identified in the previous step so that they are arranged from easiest to most difficult to learn.

Step 7

Construct a "future-oriented task and activity" matrix.

- Develop a matrix on a sheet of paper that depicts a future-oriented tasks and activities matrix organized by category and arranged from easiest to most difficult to learn.

Step 8

Examine the appropriate "affective domain" issues for each future-oriented task and activity statement.

- Review *each* task/activity on the matrix and ask group members to identify appropriate feelings/value orientations that are properly associated with each task/activity. (Try to determine the competencies underlying each task activity on the matrix.)

(continues)

Exhibit 7-5 *(continued).*

Step 9

Examine appropriate performance standards for each future-oriented task and activity statement on the matrix.

- Review *each* task/activity on the matrix and ask group members to identify appropriate ways to measure/assess/appraise performance relative to the future-oriented task or activity.

Step 10

Establish procedures by which to use the matrix for selecting, appraising, and assessing potential and other important activities.

- Apply the results of the rapid results assessment to position succession planning on a future-oriented, rather than present- or past-oriented, footing.

tics or work outputs. However, it shares the disadvantages of its traditional counterpart: The results are not as rigorous nor as complete as other competency assessment methods will yield, and are heavily dependent on the credibility of the individual panelists. Additionally, as in other future-oriented approaches, it is only as good as the assumptions about the future on which it is based.

Assessing Individual Potential

The centerpiece of most succession planning programs is some means by which to assess individual potential. This effort seeks to determine how to make best use of the organization's existing human resource assets. However, assessing potential should not be confused with appraising performance: Performance appraisal is linked to present job performance; potential assessment is linked to future advancement possibilities. Potential assessment is a critically important activity if only because as many as one third of all leadership positions (it has been estimated) would not be filled by present incumbents if decision makers had it to do over again.[10]

What Is Individual Potential Assessment?

Individual potential assessment is a systematic process of examining individuals' possibilities for job change or movement. It is usually associated with determining whether individuals "have what it takes" to advance to positions of greater management responsibility or positions demanding greater technical expertise. It should be linked to, and serve as one basis for determining, employee training, education, and development activities, which (collectively) represent a vehicle to help individuals qualify for advancement.[11] It should also be linked to individual career planning activities, which have (unfortunately) been deemphasized in recent years due to widespread downsizing and economic restructuring.

What Is a High Potential?

The term *high potential* has more than one possible meaning. High potentials, who should be identified through the individual potential assessment process, represent the organization's inventory of future leaders. They are usually individuals who are capable of advancing two or more levels beyond their present placement, individuals who are slated for key positions, or those who have not reached a career plateau. (Other definitions are also possible.[12]) It is important to define the term in a way unique to each organization. In fact, each organization may have several definitions.

Distinguishing between Exemplary Performers and High Potentials

Individuals who are high potentials are almost always exemplary performers, who are identified through the performance appraisal process and who exceed minimum job expectations. Exceptional performance in the current job is usually a necessary prerequisite to advancement.[13] However, not all exemplary performers are high potentials because advancement potential is based on different criteria from present performance.

In any organization or organizational unit, individuals may be classified into four distinct groups based on their performance and their potential. To that end, think of a grid with two axes (see Exhibit 7–6).[14] One axis represents present performance and is divided between high and low performance; the second axis represents future potential and is divided between high and low potential. The result is a performance/potential grid that closely resembles the Boston Consulting Group's widely known portfolio analysis technique used in strategic planning.

1. As shown in Exhibit 7-6, *stars* (see the upper left cell of the performance/potential grid) are exemplary individual performers in their present positions. They are also perceived to have high potential for future advancement. A major corporate asset, they are properly regarded as *high potentials* and are a source of replacements for key positions. An effective HR strategy for stars involves a twofold effort to make the most of their current performance while systematically preparing them for advancement—and even accelerating their development, if possible. Above

Exhibit 7-6. How to classify individuals by performance and potential.

		High	**Low**
		Future Potential	
P R E S E N T	H I G H	*Stars* *HR Strategy* • Keep turnover low. • Take steps to accelerate their development.	*Workhorses* • Keep turnover low. • Keep them motivated and productive where they are.
P E R F O R M A N C E	L O W	*Question Marks* *HR Strategy* • Convert them to stars. • Counsel them so as to accelerate their development.	*Deadwood* • Convert them to workhorses. • Transfer or terminate them if they cannot be salvaged.

SOURCE: George S. Odiorne, *Strategic Management of Human Resources: A Portfolio Approach*, Figure 15, p. 305, adapted as shown. Copyright 1984 by Jossey-Bass Inc., Publishers. Code 8242.

all, the organization should make every effort to recruit and retain them, keeping their turnover minimal.

2. *Workhorses* (see the upper right cell of the performance/potential grid) are exemplary performers in their current jobs who are perceived to have poor future potential. Since they are highly productive where they are, they should remain there. An effective strategy for workhorses is to harness their skills while keeping them motivated and productive. Turnover in their ranks, as with stars, should be kept minimal.

3. *Question marks* (see the lower left cell of the performance/potential grid) are poor performers in their present positions who are perceived to have high future potential. The best HR strategy for dealing with them is to focus on improving their present performance, thereby turning them into stars. Their immediate supervisors should be trained to apply appropriate techniques—such as coaching, mentoring, and (when warranted) disciplinary steps—to make them more productive in their current positions. They cannot advance until their current performance improves.

4. Finally, *deadwood* (see the lower right cell of the performance/potential grid) consists of individuals who neither are good performers in their present jobs nor are perceived to have future advancement potential. Unfortunately, their ranks may have swelled over the years as a result of paternalistic management practices that emphasized camaraderie over productivity. More recently, however, deadwood has become an endangered species due to downsizing. A twofold HR strategy is most effective with deadwood. First, their immediate organizational superiors should make every effort to help them improve their present performance. If successful, that strategy will convert deadwood to workhorses. If unsuccessful, that strategy should be followed up by fair and evenhanded efforts to move them out of the job—or even out of the organization.

Approaches to Assessing Individual Potential

How can the organization assess potential? There are several ways to answer that question because approaches to assessing individual potential are as diverse as approaches to employee performance appraisal, which they may sometimes resemble.

1. *Global assessment.* One way to assess high potential is to ask senior executives to furnish the names of individuals in their areas of responsibility whom they feel have high potential according to the definition established in the organization. That is called *global assessment*. It is a simple approach (see Exhibit 7-7 for a worksheet to be used in making global assessments).

But it is not very effective for several reasons. First, few senior execu-

Exhibit 7-7. A worksheet for global assessments.

Directions: Use this worksheet to list individuals whom you consider to be high potentials in your area of responsibility. A high potential is a person who has the capacity to be promoted two or more levels. List the names below, provide their present titles, and the time they have spent in their present positions. Be prepared to discuss why you believe these individuals have the capacity to be promoted two or more levels. If possible, rank them by their potential—with 1 = highest potential. (Do *not* use current position as a basis for ranking; rather, use your judgment about individual ability.)

Names	*Titles*	*Time in Present Positions*

tives (except those in small organizations) will know everyone in their areas of responsibility. Second, unless the definition of *high potential* is made quite clear, senior executives are likely to respond to a request for names based on their perceptions. Those perceptions about individuals can be colored too much by recent events (*recency bias*), extremely bad incidents (*the horn effect*), or extremely good incidents (*the halo effect*). Indeed, perceptions can lead to personal favoritism, discrimination, or *pigeonholing* (in which individual potential is difficult to change once assessed).

2. *Success factors analysis*. A second approach to individual potential assessment is based on the process, known as *success factors analysis*, which involves discovering traits or other characteristics perceived to lead to organizational success or advancement. One research study, for instance, revealed that successful women share such characteristics as exemplary educational credentials, a track record of hard work and good performance, supportive mentoring relationships, effective interpersonal skills, and a willingness to take career and work risks.[15]

Success factors may be identified in various ways. One way is to ask executives what traits they think will lead to success in the organization. These traits may then be collected and listed in the way depicted in Exhibit 7-8. Executives can be asked to check off what they believe those traits are. Lists provided by numerous executives may be compiled and used as the basis for developing an *individual potential assessment form* like the one shown in Exhibit 7-9.

An alternative is to conduct *critical incident interviews* with organizational strategists. This approach is based on critical incident analysis, which has been used in training needs assessment. Critical incidents were first identified for pilots during World War II. They were asked what situations (*incidents*), if ignored, might lead to serious (*critical*) consequences.

If this approach is used, individual interviews should be conducted with strategists using a structured interview guide like the one shown in Exhibit 7-8. The results should then be analyzed and should become the basis for establishing success factors. These, in turn, can be used in assessing individual potential and, when appropriate, identifying developmental opportunities.

Philosophies of Individual Potential Assessment

There are three basic approaches to individual potential assessment. Each is based on a different philosophy. They are worth reviewing.

1. *Leader-driven individual potential assessment*. This approach, which might be called *leader-driven assessment*, is the traditional approach that was

(text continues on page 202)

Exhibit 7-8. A worksheet to identify success factors.

Directions: Use this worksheet to identify success factors. A "success factor" is a past experience or personal characteristic linked to, and correlated with, successful advancement in the organization. Identify success factors by asking individuals who have already achieved success—such as key position incumbents—about their most important developmental experiences and about what they did (or skills they demonstrated) in those experiences.

　　Pose the following questions to key position incumbents. Then compile and compare the results. Ask other key position incumbents in the organizations to review and validate or modify the results.

---

1. What is the single most difficiult experience you have encountered in your career? (Describe the situation below.)

2. What did you *do* in the experience you described in response to question 1? (Describe, as precisely as you can, what actions you took—and the results achieved.)

3. Reflect on your answer to question 2. What *personal characteristics* do you feel you exhibited or demonstrated in the action(s) you took? How do you feel they contributed to your present success?

Exhibit 7-9. An individual potential assessment form.

Directions: Ask management employees to rate subordinates—particularly those felt to be high potentials—against various success factors, skills, or abilities felt to be correlated with future success.

Ask key job incumbents to rate their subordinates on each of the following generic success factors. (It's best to use success factors specific to the unique organizational culture.) A separate form should be completed on each high potential. The completed forms may then be used as one source of information about individual strengths/weaknesses.

Ask the raters to circle the appropriate number below the scale and opposite each success factor listed in the left column and then ask raters to send their completed forms to the HR Department or to the organization's Succession Planning Coordinator. There are no "right" or "wrong" answers in any absolute sense. However, raters may vary in their potential assessments, depending on how they interpret the success factors and the rating scale.

Employee's name: _____ Job title: _____

Department: _____ Time in position: _____

Appraiser's name: _____ Job title: _____

Department: _____ Time in position: _____

Today's Date ___/___/9___ Plan Covering ___/___/9___ to ___/___/9___
mo./day/yr.　　　　　　mo./day/yr.　　　　　mo./day/yr.

Scale

Success Factors	Needs Improvement			Adequate			Exceeds Requirements		
Appraising	1	2	3	4	5	6	7	8	9
Budgeting	1	2	3	4	5	6	7	8	9
Communicating	1	2	3	4	5	6	7	8	9
Controlling	1	2	3	4	5	6	7	8	9
Dealing with change	1	2	3	4	5	6	7	8	9
Developing employees	1	2	3	4	5	6	7	8	9
Influencing others	1	2	3	4	5	6	7	8	9
Making changes	1	2	3	4	5	6	7	8	9
Making decisions	1	2	3	4	5	6	7	8	9
Managing projects effectively	1	2	3	4	5	6	7	8	9
Organizing	1	2	3	4	5	6	7	8	9
Planning	1	2	3	4	5	6	7	8	9
Representing the organization effectively	1	2	3	4	5	6	7	8	9
Staffing the unit	1	2	3	4	5	6	7	8	9

probably first used in business. Individual potential is assessed by the organization's strategists, and often solely by key position incumbents for
their own subordinates in their immediate areas of responsibility.

The process may be formal, in which the organization has established
forms for this purpose that are completed periodically on all employees
or on a select group of employees (such as those designated as high potentials). Alternatively, the process may be informal: Each function or organizational unit is asked to submit names of individuals who have
advancement potential.

This approach is characterized by secrecy. Employees have little or
no say in the process. Indeed, they are not always privy to knowledge
that it is being carried out. No effort is made to double-check individual
potential assessment results with individual career aspirations or plans to
ensure that an appropriate match exists.

An advantage of this approach is that it can be done quickly. Leaders
simply fill out forms and return them to the human resources department, the succession planning coordinator, or a designated executive. Employees do not challenge the results because they remain unaware of
them. The organization retains strong control over succession planning
and results.

A disadvantage of this approach, however, is that employees have no
stake in outcomes that they did not help to shape. If the results are ever
used in making succession decisions, employees may refuse promotions
or transfers that conflict with their career goals or that exceed their willingness to make personal sacrifices.

2. *Participative individual potential assessment.* In what might be called
the *participative assessment approach*, both individuals and their immediate
organizational superiors enact important roles in the assessment process.
Hence, it is participative.

Periodically, such as once a year, employees undergo an individual
potential assessment. It may be timed at the halfway point of the annual
performance appraisal cycle so that future-oriented potential assessment
is not confused with past- or present-oriented performance appraisal.

Although there are many ways to carry out the process, one approach
involves distributing individual assessment appraisal forms to employees
and their immediate organizational superiors. Employees and superiors
complete the forms, exchange them, and later meet to discuss the employees' advancement capabilities. As with performance appraisals, the forms
for individual potential assessment are usually prepared by and distributed from the human resources department, and the results are returned
to that department for filing in personnel records. (Alternatives to that
approach are possible. For instance, completed individual assessment appraisal forms may be retained by the leader of each organizational unit.)

An advantage of this approach is that it allows "reality testing." Individuals learn of possibilities for the future, which may interest them and motivate them; organizational representatives learn more about individual career goals and aspirations, thereby improving the quality of their succession plans. In this way, the assessment process provides an opportunity for mutual candor and for information sharing.

Key to this process is the individual potential assessment interview. It should be carried out in a quiet, supportive setting that is free of interruptions. The employee's immediate organizational superior should set the pace, discussing his or her perceptions about the individual's strengths and weaknesses for advancement, and the realistic possibilities for that advancement. An agenda can make an interview of this kind run smoothly.

Another advantage is that employees have a stake in the assessment process. If the organization should have need to make a succession decision, the likelihood is greater that employees will accept offers of promotions, transfers, or other assignments that match their career goals and organizational needs.

A disadvantage of this approach is that it can rarely be done quickly. Leaders and employees must devote time to it if it is to be worthwhile. Indeed, to gain the full benefits from it, leaders must be trained on effective interviewing skills.

Another disadvantage is that the value of participative assessment is a function of the interpersonal trust existing between leaders and their employees. However, trust is not always present. Nor is complete candor.

Several factors affect trust, among them: past dealings between the organization and individual, the perceived candor of the organization's representative, and the match between individual career goals and organizational opportunities.

To cite two examples: Suppose that an employee has personal aspirations that may eventually lead to her departure from the organization. She may be unwilling to share that information for fear of how it might affect her prospects for promotion. Likewise, leaders may be unable to share information about pending changes affecting the organization— such as a sale of a division or the dissolution of a product line—that may also impact career goals or succession plans.

3. *Empowered individual potential assessment.* Leaders provide guidance and direction for what might be called the *empowered assessment approach* but do not determine the outcomes or make final decisions affecting individual potential. Instead, they just share information and offer coaching suggestions. Individuals are expected to provide self-assessment and self-development.

Once a year employees are encouraged to complete individual potential assessment forms, share them with their immediate organizational superiors, and then schedule meetings to discuss them with their superiors. (Some may even decide to discuss their forms with their mentors or with others in a 360 degree relationship to them.) The form is usually created and supplied by the human resources department. However, it may or may not be called an *individual potential assessment form.* Alternative names might include *career planning assessment form, individual development planning form, leadership assessment form,* or even *management career planning form.*

In this approach, the initiative rests entirely with employees. They conduct their own individual assessments; they schedule assessment meetings with their immediate organizational superiors or with mentors in other parts of the organization; they are not required to participate in the assessment process, which remains voluntary. As with other approaches, however, it is usually kept separate from performance appraisals so as not to confuse present performance and future potential. Individual potential assessment becomes a tool to help individuals understand how to qualify for advancement within the framework of the organization's needs and their own career goals.

An advantage of this approach is that, like other empowerment efforts, it can be quite motivating to employees. Further, it discourages a philosophy of entitlement in which employees with a long service record feel that promotions are "owed" to them. Instead, the responsibility for advancement rests squarely on their shoulders, and they are expected to take an active role in setting their own career directions and finding the necessary resources to move in those directions.

Another advantage of this approach is that employees are not given the impression, which is possible with other approaches, that they are guaranteed advancement. Management should state the message, loud and clear, that "we can't guarantee promotions, but we can guarantee that those who have taken the steps to obtain the necessary qualifications for a higher-level position will be given due consideration."

However, the chief disadvantage of this approach is that the organization sacrifices control over employees. Indeed, it may not always be apparent whether replacements exist for each key position.

Empowered individual potential assessment is likely to grow in importance. One reason is that it matches current thinking about the need to decentralize decision making and give the control to those who deal with customers or consumers daily. A second reason is that this approach can unleash individual initiative rather than stifle it, thereby motivating people to *want* to qualify for advancement.

Using 360 Degree Feedback

Integrally related to individual potential assessment is *360 degree feedback,*[16] which takes its name from the 360 degrees that comprise a circle. The

Exhibit 7-10. Assessment methods to support 360 degree feedback.

Method	How is it used?	Advantages and Disadvantages
The interview Feedback about the individual is obtained by interviewing those surrounding him or her.	1. Target a group of individuals for 360 degree assessment. 2. Appoint someone to interview those surrounding the individuals, such as immediate superiors, peers, immediate reports, customers, suppliers, and other relevant groups. 3. Focus the questions on strengths, areas for improvement, and areas for development. 4. Feed the results of the interviews back to the individuals targeted for feedback. 5. Help the individuals establish their own developmental plans and activities to build on strengths, rectify areas for improvement, and develop themselves for the future.	*Advantages:* • Can be conducted quickly • Allows for probing *Disadvantages:* • Labor intensive • Expensive if travel is necessary
The survey Feedback is obtained by sending a written survey to those surrounding the individual.	Same steps in the method listed above, except that written questions should be prepared and tested before the survey is mailed.	*Advantages:* • Easy to prepare • Inexpensive to conduct *Disadvantages:* • Does not permit follow-up questions • Respondents may be loathe to write their true feelings if they are negative

(continues)

Exhibit 7-10 (continued).

| **The instrument**
A commercially available instrument is used to collect information about the individual who is to receive the feedback. | 1. Investigate commercially available instruments that may be purchased externally and applied to individuals employed by an organization.
2. Select an instrument and purchase sufficient quantities to use with the individuals targeted for participation.
3. Brief participants on what the instrument is, why it is being administered, how they should use the results, and how the organization will use the results.
4. Administer the instrument, collecting information from 360 degrees around the targeted participating individual.
5. Compile results.
6. Interpret results.
7. Meet with participants who were assessed to give them feedback and plan for the future. | *Advantages:*
• Easy to administer
• Easy to score and interpret if the instrument is accompanied by support material or vendor services
• The results are credible
• Instruments can help motivate people

Disadvantages:
• May be difficult to tailor to organization-specific needs and culture
• Can be unwieldy to use if more than a handful of people are to be subjected to 360 degree feedback |

fundamental idea of 360 degree feedback is to gather information about an individual from a circle of people most familiar with him or her. This circle may include organization superiors, peers, immediate organizational reports, and even customers, suppliers, or distributing retailers who come into contact with the individual. The individuals themselves may or may not participate in this activity, providing their own input through such alternative means as information about strengths and weaknesses on employee performance appraisals, career development activities, potential assessments, or individual development plans.

The 360 degree assessment is usually considered to be more powerful than assessment restricted to the perceptions of a high performer's or high potential's immediate superior. It can thus help to overcome biases that creep into assessments, whether those biases are intentional or not.

Several approaches may be used in 360 degree feedback (see Exhibit 7-10). But the most popular approach is to rely on commercially available instruments. Other approaches may be used so long as the aim is to collect information from different people and perspectives and the results are fed back to the targeted individual with the goal of identifying strengths and areas for improvement, assessing work performance, or clarifying development needs.

Conduct 360 degree feedback at least annually. Although the results may be used in appraising performance, they may also be appropriate for such future-oriented activities as assessing individual potential and planning for individual development. Be sure to feed back the results to the individual, but also exercise control over the results to ensure that appropriate privacy is maintained. Unless validated for selection purposes, instruments or other devices for 360 degree feedback should not be used as the *sole* determinants for reaching employment decisions.

Summary

This chapter showed that information about future work requirements and individual potential is essential to an effective succession planning program. When paired with information about present work requirements and individual job performance, it becomes the basis for preparing individual development plans to narrow the gaps between what individuals already know and do and what they must know and do to qualify for advancement.

Part IV

Closing The "Developmental Gap": Operating and Evaluating A Succession Planning Program

After analyzing work requirements, job performance and individual potential, the organization is ready to close individual development gaps. At this point, then, the organization is ready to operate a succession planning program. To that end, decision makers should begin by:

- Testing bench strength
- Formulating internal promotion policy
- Preparing individual development plans (IDPs)
- Developing successors internally
- Investigating, as appropriate, creative alternatives to simple replacement

This part treats each of these issues.

8

Developing Internal Successors

For a succession planning program to be effective, the organization must have some means by which to replace key job incumbents as vacancies occur in their positions. Promotion from within is a time-honored and crucially important, albeit traditional, way to do that.

But, to prepare individuals for promotion, the organization has an obligation to do more than merely identify present and future work requirements and performance. Some way must also be found to clarify, and systematically close, the developmental gap between what possible successors can already do and what they must do to qualify for advancement. *Individual development planning* is the process of clarifying that developmental gap; *internal development* uses planned training, education, development, and other means to close the gap and thereby meet succession needs.

This chapter focuses on determining the organization's collective succession needs, using promotion from within to meet those needs, clarifying individual developmental gaps, and closing those gaps systematically through planned training, education, and development. More specifically, then, this chapter addresses the following questions:

- What is bench strength, and how can the leaders of an organization test it?
- Why is internal promotion so important for succession, and when is it—and isn't it—appropriate for meeting succession planning needs?
- What is an individual development plan (IDP)? How should one be prepared, followed up, and evaluated?
- What are some important methods of internal development, and when should they be used?

Testing Bench Strength

Once key positions and work requirements have been identified, the organization should test bench strength. That is important because it provides information about the organization's collective succession needs. That information can, in turn, dramatize the importance of taking action to meet succession planning needs.

What Is Bench Strength?

Bench strength is the organization's ability to fill vacancies from within. *Testing bench strength* means determining how well the organization is able to fill vacancies in key positions from within.

Turnover saps bench strength. There are two kinds of turnover. *Unavoidable turnover* is outside the immediate control of the organization. It is the loss of personnel through death, disability, and retirement. It may also include turnover resulting from organizational action, such as layoff, early retirement, buyout, or other means. Although many line managers would like to include promotions and transfers from their areas in the definition of unavoidable turnover, most HR departments do not include internal movements in the definition.

On the other hand, *avoidable turnover* is initiated by employees. It is a loss resulting from resignation as individuals leave the organization, typically moving to positions in other organizations. Although turnover of any kind is costly because the organization must find and train replacements, avoidable turnover is worse than the unavoidable variety because it could be avoided if the organization could find some way to retain the employees.

Avoidable turnover from key positions is particularly distressing, because it creates unnecessary crises. (This is sometimes called *critical turnover.*[1]) One aim of any succession planning program should thus be to find ways to reduce avoidable turnover among key position incumbents—or at least find the means to keep it stable.

Approaches to Testing Bench Strength

To test an organization for bench strength, ask decision makers how they would replace key positions in their areas of responsibility, or ensure that work requirements will be met through other, more innovative, means. Use any of the means described below.

▪ *Replacement charting*. Prepare an organization chart to show the range of possible replacements for each key position in a work area (see the examples shown in Exhibits 8-1 and 8-2). Note how many *holes* can be identified. A *hole* is a position in which no internal replacement can be identified. The lower the percentage of holes relative to key positions, the greater is the organization's bench strength.

▪ *Questioning*. Ask senior executives to identify those who will replace key position incumbents in their areas in the event of a vacancy. Note how many "holes" by function can be identified. Track the "holes." The lower the percentage of "holes" to key positions, the greater is the organization's bench strength.

▪ *Evidence*. Using the results of an analysis of personnel records over the last few years, find out which departures created the worst problems for the organization. Note the number of such problems relative to total departures (turnover). The higher the percentage, the weaker the bench strength.

▪ *A combination of methods*. Use a combination of the methods identified above to assess bench strength. Note the percentage of holes. Feed that information back to decision makers to dramatize the value and importance of the succession planning program.

Formulating Internal Promotion Policy

The centerpiece of a systematic succession planning program is a written policy favoring internal promotion. Lacking such a policy, organizations may have difficulty keeping ambitious high potentials and exemplary performers who seek advancement. If they grow discouraged, they can contribute to a devastating increase in avoidable, and critical, turnover. It is thus essential for the organization to make all reasonable efforts to retain them. One way to do that is to place the organization "on the record" as favoring promotion from within. Not only does a promotion-from-within policy motivate employees by showing that their efforts can pay off through promotion, but promotion from within also saves the organization money in recruiting, selecting, and training a newcomer.[2] Respondents in one study some years ago revealed that they filled 85 percent of management openings and 58 percent of their white-collar openings by recruiting internally.[3]

Essential Components of an Internal Promotion Policy

To be effective, an internal promotion policy should

▪ Unequivocally state the organization's commitment to promoting employees from within whenever possible and whenever they are qualified to meet the work requirements of new positions.

(text continues on page 216)

Exhibit 8-1. A sample replacement chart format: typical succession planning inventory for the organization.

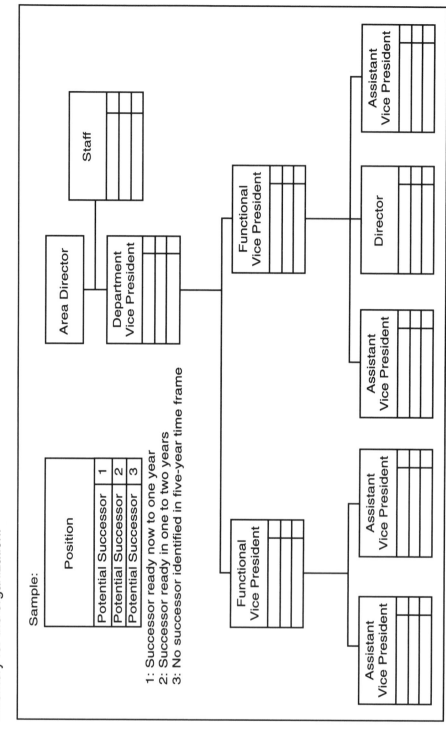

Sample:

Position	
Potential Successor	1
Potential Successor	2
Potential Successor	3

1: Successor ready now to one year
2: Successor ready in one to two years
3: No successor identified in five-year time frame

Source: Norman H. Carter, "Guaranteeing Management's Future Through Succession Planning," *Journal of Information Systems Management* (Summer 1986) p. 19. Used by permission of the *Journal of Information Systems Management* (New York: Auerbach Publications), © 1986 Warren Gorham Lamont.

Exhibit 8-2. Succession planning inventory by position.

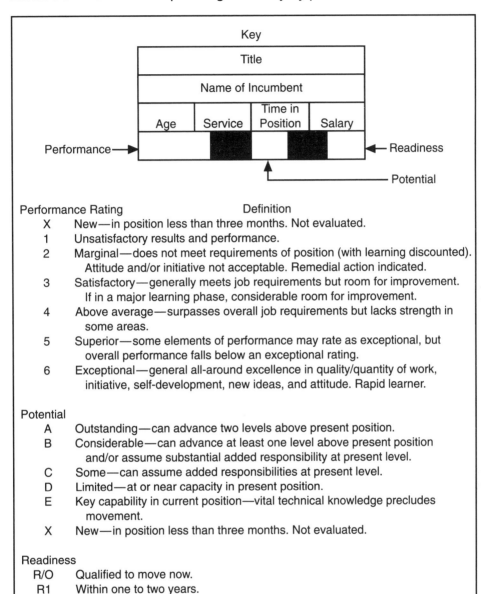

Performance Rating   Definition

X   New—in position less than three months. Not evaluated.

1   Unsatisfactory results and performance.

2   Marginal—does not meet requirements of position (with learning discounted). Attitude and/or initiative not acceptable. Remedial action indicated.

3   Satisfactory—generally meets job requirements but room for improvement. If in a major learning phase, considerable room for improvement.

4   Above average—surpasses overall job requirements but lacks strength in some areas.

5   Superior—some elements of performance may rate as exceptional, but overall performance falls below an exceptional rating.

6   Exceptional—general all-around excellence in quality/quantity of work, initiative, self-development, new ideas, and attitude. Rapid learner.

Potential

A   Outstanding—can advance two levels above present position.

B   Considerable—can advance at least one level above present position and/or assume substantial added responsibility at present level.

C   Some—can assume added responsibilities at present level.

D   Limited—at or near capacity in present position.

E   Key capability in current position—vital technical knowledge precludes movement.

X   New—in position less than three months. Not evaluated.

Readiness

R/O   Qualified to move now.

R1   Within one to two years.

R2   Within two to four years.

N/A   Current level appropriate.

SOURCE: Norman H. Carter, "Guaranteeing Management's Future Through Succession Planning," *Journal of Information Systems Management* (Summer 1986) p. 19. Used by permission of the *Journal of Information Systems Management* (New York: Auerbach Publications), © 1986 Warren Gorham Lamont.

- Define internal promotion.
- Explain the business reasons for that policy.
- Explain the legitimate conditions under which that policy can be waived and an external candidate can be selected.

Since an internal promotion policy will (naturally) build employee expectations that most promotions will be made from within, decision makers should anticipate challenges—legal and otherwise—to every promotion decision that is made. For that reason, the policy should be reviewed by HR professionals, operating managers, and legal professionals before it is implemented or widely communicated. In any case, reviewing the policy before adoption is more likely to build consistent understanding and ownership of it.

When Are Internal Promotions Appropriate—and Inappropriate—for Meeting Succession Planning Needs?

Internal promotion is appropriate to meet a vacancy in a key position when a qualified replacement from the organization is:

1. *Ready* to assume the duties of the key position by demonstrated mastery of at least 80 percent of the position requirements and progress toward meeting or exceeding the remaining 20 percent of the position requirements
2. *Willing* to accept the position, expressing a desire to do the work
3. *Able* to accept the position by having his or her own replacement prepared in a reasonably short time span and by being ready to assume the duties of a key position

But promotion from within is not appropriate for meeting succession planning needs when any of these conditions cannot be met. Alternatives to internal promotions are thus appropriate when a qualified internal candidate cannot be found after a reasonable search, when possible candidates refuse to accept a position, or when possible candidates cannot be freed up from their present duties in a reasonable time.

The Importance of Job Posting

Job posting is an internal method of notifying and recruiting employees for new positions in the organization. To begin such a program, the organization should establish a policy that position opening notices will be "posted" in prominent locations, such as next to building entrances and exits, near cafeteria entrances, on bulletin boards, or near restrooms. A typical job posting notice contains information about the position that is open, such as its title, pay grade, organizational location, and desirable starting date. Employees from all areas of the organization are encouraged to apply, and selection decisions are typically made on the basis of the applicant who brings the best qualifications to the job. In some organizations, however, seniority may be an overriding factor in making a selection decision. Also, posting may be restricted to include only some, but not all, job categories or functions in the organization.

In many cases, positions are posted internally while also advertised externally. In that way, both internal and external applicants are attracted. The organization can thus seek the most qualified applicant, whether or not that person is presently employed by the organization.

The major benefit of job posting is that it gives individuals a say in their career directions. Further, it permits the organization to consider applicants from outside the immediate work area, from which successors for key positions may frequently be selected.[4] It also reduces the chance of *employee hoarding* in which an employee's manager blocks promotions or transfers of high-potential or exemplary performers so they will remain forever trapped, though very productive, in the manager's work area.[5]

The major drawback to job posting has more to do with the management of such programs than with the posting concept itself. If employees are allowed to jump to new jobs merely to realize small wage increases, posting can be costly and demoralizing—especially to those responsible for training "mercenary job hoppers." Hence, to be used effectively as a tool in succession planning, all jobs should be posted; and all applicants should be subjected to a rigorous selection process to ensure that the most qualified applicant is picked. Careful restrictions should be placed on the process to ensure that employees remain in their positions for a period sufficient to recoup training costs.

Preparing Individual Development Plans

Testing bench strength should clarify the organization's collective succession planning needs. However, it does not indicate what individuals should do to qualify for advancement to key positions. That is the reason for preparing individual development plans (IDPs).

What Is an IDP?

An IDP results from a comparison of individual strengths and weaknesses on the current job and individual potential for advancement to possible key positions in the future. Preparing an IDP is a process of planning activities to narrow the gap between what individuals can already do and what they should do to meet the future work requirements in one or more key positions.

An IDP is a hybrid between a learning contract, a performance contract, and a career planning form. A *learning contract* is an agreement to learn. Contract learning has enjoyed a long and venerable history.[6] It is particularly well suited to participative, learning organizations that seek to balance individual career needs and interests with organizational strategy and work requirements. A *performance contract* is an agreement to achieve an identifiable, measurable level of performance.[7] Sometimes tied to performance appraisal, it is directed toward future performance improvement rather than past performance. Finally, a *career planning form* is a tool for helping individuals identify their career goals and establish effective strategies for realizing them in the future. A career planning form is typically linked to an organizational career planning program, which can reinforce and support succession planning.

An IDP goes a step beyond performance appraisal for the individual's present job and potential assessment of the individual's capability for advancement to key positions in the organization. It results in a detailed plan to furnish individuals with what they need to know or do to qualify for advancement into their next positions.

Developing an IDP usually requires a systematic comparison of the individual's present abilities (as indicated by job descriptions and performance appraisals) and future capabilities (as revealed through individual potential assessment). The IDP is designed to narrow the gap between them, providing a clear-cut plan by which to prepare the individual for advancement.

How Are IDPs Prepared?

Preparing an IDP shares strong similarities with preparing a learning contract. Take ten key steps in this process. (Exhibit 8-3 depicts these steps in a simple model).

1. *Select possible key positions for which to prepare the individual.* Begin by targeting a family of key positions in the organization for the individual. In most cases, that should be done only after a significant dialogue has taken place between the individual and an organizational representative. As Arthur Deegan notes:

> It is important that the individual understand the illustrative nature of the position you select as the targeted one and focus not on that specific job but on the family of jobs represented by it. Otherwise there

Exhibit 8-3. A simplified model of steps in preparing individual development plans.

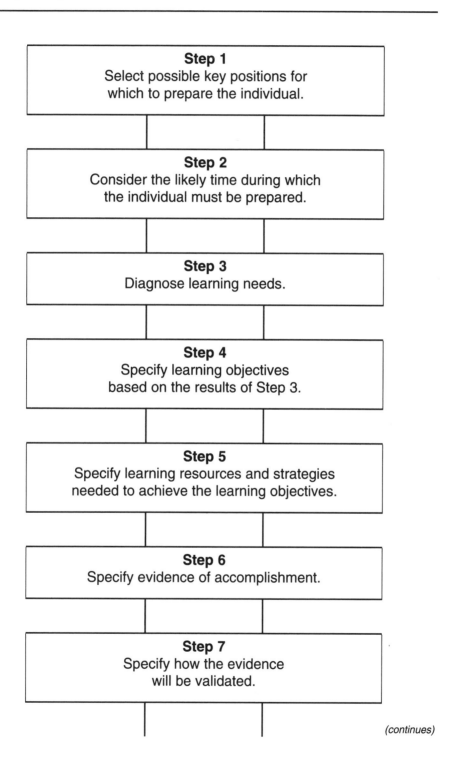

Step 1
Select possible key positions for
which to prepare the individual.

Step 2
Consider the likely time during which
the individual must be prepared.

Step 3
Diagnose learning needs.

Step 4
Specify learning objectives
based on the results of Step 3.

Step 5
Specify learning resources and strategies
needed to achieve the learning objectives.

Step 6
Specify evidence of accomplishment.

Step 7
Specify how the evidence
will be validated.

(continues)

Exhibit 8-3 (*continued*).

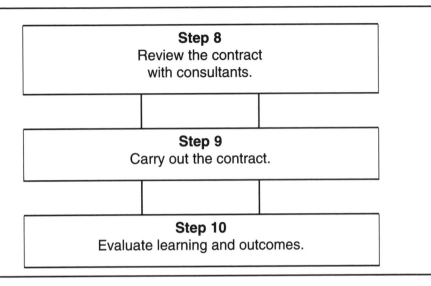

may be disappointment if that job is not offered even though a future offer might actually meet the person's needs better as well as those of the firm.[8]

Of course, if it is anticipated that the individual will be prepared for a specific key position that will soon become vacant, then planning should be focused on that position after discussion with the individual.

2. *Consider the likely time during which the individual must be prepared.* Time naturally affects what kind—and how many—developmental activities can be carried out. When individuals are slated for rapid advancement, there is little or no time for preparation. Hence, those developmental activities that are selected should be absolutely critical to effective job performance. There is thus a need to prioritize developmental activities. That should be done, of course, even when time is ample. The key issue in this step, then, amounts to determining how much time is available for development.

3. *Diagnose learning needs.* Exactly what is the difference between the individual's present knowledge and skills and the work requirements of key positions for which the individual is to be prepared? The answer to that question clarifies the developmental gap.

One way to determine this difference is to compare the individual's present work requirements and performance to those required in a targeted key position. As a simple example, that may mean comparing how well an employee could perform his or her immediate supervisor's job.

Another way to determine this difference is to ask the key position incumbent to compare what the individual is presently doing and how he or she is presently performing to what the key position incumbent does and how he or she must perform. Then ask the key position incumbent to recommend planned developmental activities to narrow the gap between what the employee already can do and what he or she must do to perform in the key position.

When diagnosing learning needs, be aware that the quality of the results depends on the quality of the diagnosis. While busy executives might prefer to short-circuit this process, that will usually prove to be counterproductive.

4. *Specify learning objectives based on the results of step 3.* Learning objectives are the outcomes or results that are sought from planned developmental activities. Needs represent deficiencies or problems to be solved; objectives, on the other hand, represent desired solutions. Each need should be linked to one or more learning objectives to ensure that each "problem" will be "solved."

Learning objectives should always be stated in measurable terms. As Robert F. Mager has noted, all learning objectives should have three components:

- *Performance.* What should the learner be able to do upon completion of training?
- *Criteria.* How will achievement of learning objectives be measured? What minimum performance standards must be achieved for the individual to demonstrate competence?
- *Conditions.* Under what conditions must the learner perform?[9]

Use the worksheet in Exhibit 8-4 to prepare learning objectives based on individual developmental requirements.

5. *Specify learning resources and strategies needed to achieve the learning objectives. Learning strategies* are the means by which learning objectives are to be achieved. There are many strategies by which to achieve learning objectives. Appropriate learning strategies depend on the learning objectives that are to be met. They answer this question: What planned learning activities will help narrow the gap between what individuals can already do and what they must do to meet key position requirements in the future?

Learning resources are what must be provided to achieve the learning objectives. Resources might include people, money, time, expertise, equipment, or information. People resources could include trainers, coaches, mentors, or sponsors. Money resources could include funding for participation in on-the-job or off-the-job developmental experiences. Time resources could include released time from work to participate in

Exhibit 8-4. A worksheet for preparing learning objectives based on individual development requirements.

Directions: Use this worksheet to help you prepare specific, measurable learning objectives to guide the process of meeting individual development needs.

In the left column, indicate activities, responsibilities, duties, tasks, or essential job functions to which the individual needs exposure in order to qualify for advancement. Then, in the right column, write specific and measurable learning objectives to describe what individuals should be able to know, do or feel upon completion of a planned development/learning experience tied to those activities, responsibilities, duties, tasks, or essential job functions. When you finish drafting the objectives, double check them to ensure that you have listed:

1. Desirable performance
2. Measurable criteria by which to assess how well the learning objective was achieved
3. The conditions in which the learning will be applied

Activities, Responsibilities, Duties, Tasks, or Essential Job Functions to which the Individual Needs Exposure in Order to Qualify for Advancement	*Specific and Measurable Learning Objectives*
1.	
2.	
3.	
4.	
5.	
6.	
7.	
8.	
9.	
10.	

planned training, education, or developmental activities. Expertise could include access to knowledgeable people or information sources. Equipment could include access, for developmental purposes, to specialized machines or tools. (Use the worksheet in Exhibit 8-5 to identify the resources necessary to develop individuals for key positions.)

6. *Specify evidence of accomplishment.* How can the organization track accomplishment of learning objectives? Answer that question by providing clear, measurable learning objectives and by providing regular feedback to the learner and those interested in the learner's development. If possible, use short, informal "project appraisals" or more formalized, written "developmental appraisals" to document individual progress, note accomplishments, and give the individual specific feedback that can lead to future performance improvement.

7. *Specify how the evidence will be validated.* Be clear about the means by which achievement of learning objectives will be validated. Will a knowledgeable expert, such as a key position incumbent, review the results? Will the learners be asked to complete oral interviews to demonstrate results? Will learners' performance on developmental projects be reviewed by those with whom they work? These questions must be answered separately for each learning objective and for each learning project or assignment on which the learners are to work in order to qualify for advancement.

8. *Review the contract with consultants.* Before the individual development plan is approved, it should be reviewed by knowledgeable experts. In this context, *experts* and *consultants* are meant to have broad meanings. For instance, experts and consultants might include any or all of the following:

- Members of succession planning committees
- Friends
- Spouses
- Immediate superiors or key position incumbents
- The learners' peers
- The learners' subordinates
- Academic experts
- Recognized authorities in other organizations

Depending on the organization, the individual, and the key position for which the individual is being prepared, other experts or consultants might prove useful. For instance, individuals may wish to identify their own mentors and ask for their advice while negotiating an IDP. In unionized settings, union representatives may also be included.

Ask the experts to provide information about issues on which they are qualified to comment. For instance, from their perspective does an IDP appear to have identified the right learning needs, established the

Exhibit 8-5. A worksheet for identifying the resources necessary to support developmental experiences.

Directions: Use this worksheet to help you identify the resources necessary to support planned learning/developmental experiences.

In the left column, indicate learning objectives and the planned learning/developmental experiences that will be used in helping an individual qualify for advancement. Then, in the right column, indicate the specific resources—such as information, money, trainers, equipment, and time—that will be needed to allow the individual to meet the learning objective and permit participation in the planned learning/developmental experience.

Learning Objectives and Planned Learning/Developmental Experiences Intended to Help an Individual Qualify for Advancement	*Specific Resources Needed to Achieve the Objective and Permit Participation in the Planned Learning/Development Experience*
1.	
2.	
3.	
4.	
5.	
6.	
7.	
8.	
9.	
10.	
11.	
12.	

right learning objectives, identified the most appropriate learning strategies and resources, and established the best means by which to evaluate results? Is the IDP practical and capable of being completed in the time allowed? What suggested changes, if any, do the "experts" recommend, and why?

9. *Carry out the contract.* I have found that the implementation of IDPs is the Achilles' heel of many otherwise well-conceived succession planning programs. While well conceived, many IDPs are not well executed. Hence, some means must be established to ensure accountability and monitor results during the time span encompassed by the IDP. That can be done by planning quarterly IDP review meetings with representatives from each major area of the organization so they can report on the progress made in their areas. Alternatively, a succession planning coordinator can pay visits to individual managers to review the progress made on IDPs in their areas of responsibility. The effect of these actions is to draw attention to the plans and to maintain an impetus for action.

10. *Evaluate learning and outcomes.* Be sure that results (learning outcomes) are measured against intentions (learning objectives and needs).

There are several ways to do that. One way is to establish periodic developmental assessments, much like project-oriented performance appraisals. If this approach is used, develop a simple feedback form to provide documentation of learners' progress on each developmental experience. They can then be reviewed upon completion of learning objectives or at agreed-upon intervals during the developmental experiences.

A second way is to provide a checklist on the IDP form to indicate whether learning objectives have been achieved. That is a simpler, albeit less ambitious and rigorous, approach than periodic developmental assessments. However, it is time-efficient and is thus more likely to be used by busy decision makers.

Use the sample IDP form shown in Exhibit 8-6 as a starting point for developing a form that is appropriate for your organization.

Developing Successors Internally

Internal development is a general term that refers to those developmental activities sponsored inside the organization that are intended to help an individual qualify for advancement by closing the gap between present work requirements/performance and future work requirements/potential. Indeed, it is the means by which individual potential is realized as the future unfolds in the present.

Exhibit 8-6. A sample individual development plan.

Directions: Use this individual development plan to help an individual qualify for advancement. This form should be completed by the individual's immediate superior, who should then discuss it with the individual. If the individual feels that modifications should be made, then the reasons for the changes should be discussed.

Employee's name: _____   Job title: _____

Department: _____   Time in position: _____

Appraiser's name: _____   Job title: _____

Department: _____   Time in position: _____

Today's date: ___ /___ /9___   Plan covering: _ /_ /9_ to _ /_ /9_

1. For what key position(s) should this individual be prepared? Over what time span?

2. What are the individual's career plans/objectives?

3. What learning objectives should guide the individual's development? [*Note to appraiser: Be sure to systematically compare the individual's current job description to a current job description for the targeted position[s] and list the identifiable gap below.*]

4. By what methods/strategies may the objectives be met? [*Provide a specific learning plan below, indicating learning objectives, strategies by which to achieve the objectives, deadlines for achieving each result, and a checklist showing whether the learning objective was achieved.*]
   a. *Objectives and strategy:*

      Deadlines/benchmark dates: _____ *Verified?*   **Yes No**

   b. *Objectives and strategy:*

      Deadlines/benchmark dates: _____ *Verified?*   **Yes No**

c. *Objectives and strategy:*

Deadlines/benchmark dates: _____ *Verified?* **Yes No**

d. *Objectives and strategy:*

Deadlines/benchmark dates: _____ *Verified?* **Yes No**

5. How can the relative success of each learning objective be measured?
   a. *Learning objective:*

   Evaluation approach:

   b. *Learning objective:*

   Evaluation approach:

   c. *Learning objective:*

   Evaluation approach:

   d. *Learning objective:*

   Evaluation approach:

Typical Methods of Internal Development

Many methods are used in internal development. As many as 88 ways have been devised to develop individuals in their present positions,[10] and as many as 300 ways have been devised to develop individuals.[11] My 1993 survey identified the following methods of internal development as most common:

1. Planned on-the-job training
2. Planned job rotation programs
3. Unplanned mentoring programs
4. Planned mentoring programs
5. Unplanned on-the-job training
6. Unplanned job rotation programs
7. In-house classroom courses purchased from outside sources and modified for in-house use
8. Off-the-job public seminars sponsored by vendors
9. Off-the-job public seminars sponsored by universities
10. Off-the-job degree programs sponsored by colleges and universities
11. In-house classroom courses tailor-made for employees
12. On-site degree programs sponsored by colleges/universities

The results of my 1993 survey are summarized in Exhibit 8-7. Each method is briefly summarized in Exhibit 8-8.

Another Way to View Methods of Internal Development

Other methods may also be used. They include:

1. *Who-based strategies.* These learning strategies focus on pairing up high potentials with individuals who have special talents, or management styles, worthy of emulation. Example: matching up a high potential with a participative manager, an authoritarian manager, or one who has demonstrated exceptional abilities in business start-ups, turnarounds, or shutdown efforts.

2. *What-based strategies.* These learning strategies focus on exposing high potentials to specific developmental experiences, such as projects, task forces, committees, jobs, or assignments that require the individual to master or demonstrate analytical skills, leadership skills, or skills in starting up an operation, shutting down an operation, converting a manual to an automated process, or another project of a specific kind. Additionally, service on interteam, interdepartmental or interdivisional committees can give the individual visibility and exposure to new people and new functions.

3. *When-based strategies.* These learning strategies expose high potentials to time pressure. Examples: meeting a nearly impossible deadline or beating a wily competitor to market.

4. *Where-based strategies.* These learning strategies expose high potentials to special locations or cultures. Examples: sending high potentials on

(text continues on page 238)

Exhibit 8-7. Methods of grooming individuals for advancement.

Directions: There are many ways to implement succession plans, since individuals may be "groomed" in different ways. Review the list of possible methods by which to groom individuals in column **1**. Then, in column **2**, check (√) **Yes** or **No** to indicate whether your organization is using it, and, in column **3**, circle the number indicating how effective you feel that method is in developing people to assume future job responsibilities. In column 3, use the following scale:

1 = Not at all important
2 = Not very important
3 = Somewhat important
4 = Important
5 = Very important

1	2		3						
	Is your organization using this method to develop people?		How effective do you feel the method is for developing people to assume future job responsibilities?						Import-ance Ranked by Mean
			Not Important				Very Important		
Possible methods by which to groom individuals	Yes (√)	No (√)	1	2	3	4	5	Mean	
1. Planned on-the-job-training	28 (97%)	1 (3%) N = 29	2 (7%)	0	0	7 (24%) N = 29	20 (69%)	4.48	1
2. Planned job rotation programs	21 (72%)	8 (28%) N = 29	1 (4%)	2 (7%)	2 (7%)	7 (26%) N = 27	15 (56%)	4.22	2

(continues)

Exhibit 8-7 (continued).

	1	2		3							
		Is your organization using this method to develop people?		How effective do you feel the method is for developing people to assume future job responsibilities?							
				Not Important				Very Important			Importance Ranked by Mean
Possible methods by which to groom individuals		Yes (√)	No (√)	1	2	3	4	5	Mean	
3. Unplanned mentoring programs		23 (77%)	7 (23%) N = 30	0	0	6 (23%)	10 (38%) N = 26	10 (38%)	4.15	3 ⎤ Tie
4. Planned mentoring programs		15 (50%)	15 (50%) N = 30	1 (4%)	1 (4%)	4 (15%)	8 (30%) N = 27	13 (48%)	4.15	3 ⎦
5. Unplanned on-the-job training		25 (86%)	4 (14%) N = 30	0	3 (12%)	4 (15%)	9 (35%) N = 26	10 (38%)	4.00	4
6. Unplanned job rotation programs		20 (69%)	9 (31%) N = 29	1 (4%)	3 (12%)	5 (20%)	5 (20%) N = 25	11 (44%)	3.88	5
7. In-house classroom courses purchased from outside sources and modified for in-house use		26 (87%)	4 (13%) N = 30	1 (3%)	2 (7%)	5 (17%)	14 (48%) N = 29	7 (24%)	3.83	6

Item								Mean	Rank
8. Off-the-job public seminars sponsored by vendors	29 (97%)	1 (3%) N = 30	0	2 (7%)	7 (26%)	13 (48%)	5 (19%)	3.78	7
9. Off-the-job public seminars sponsored by universities	29 (97%)	1 (3%) N = 30	0	1 (4%)	10 (37%)	10 (37%) N = 27	6 (22%)	3.78	7
10. Off-the-job degree programs sponsored by colleges/universities	25 (83%)	5 (17%) N = 30	0	4 (15%)	8 (30%)	10 (37%) N = 27	5 (19%)	3.59	8
11. In-house classroom courses tailor-made for management level employees	28 (93%)	2 (7%) N = 30	0	2 (7%)	5 (17%)	15 (50%) N = 30	8 (27%)	3.59	8

Tie (items 8 and 9, rank 7)

Tie (items 10 and 11, rank 8)

(continues)

Exhibit 8-7 *(continued).*

	1		2		3						
	Possible methods by which to groom individuals	Is your organization using this method to develop people?		How effective do you feel the method is for developing people to assume future job responsibilities?							Import-ance Ranked by Mean
		Yes (√)	No (√)	Not Important				Very Important	Mean		
				1	2	3	4	5		
12.	On-site degree programs sponsored by colleges/universities	3 (10%)	26 (90%) N = 29	6 (24%)	7 (28%)	6 (24%)	4 (16%) N = 25	2 (8%)	2.56	9

13. Other (*please describe briefly*):
- Task forces and cross-functional teams while remaining in the same job
- Cross-functional teams assigned
- Management reading programs
- Visits/discussions with other organizations
- Task-force leader/participant, key projects, job enrichment
- Planned and unplanned managerial coaching
- On-the-job coaching and being a good model or example for other leaders

SOURCE: William J. Rothwell, "Results of a 1993 Survey on Succession Planning Practices," unpublished, The Pennsylvania State University, 1994.

Exhibit 8-8. Key strategies for internal development.

Strategy	How to Use It	Appropriate and Inappropriate Uses
1. Off-the-job degree programs sponsored by colleges/ universities	• Clarify job-related courses tied to the work requirements of key positions. • Compare individual skills to work requirements. • Identify courses related to individual needs. • Tie work requirements to degree/course requirements, if possible.	*Appropriate:* For meeting specialized individual needs that are not shared widely enough to warrant on-site training *Inappropriate:* For meeting highly specialized needs unique to one employer
2. On-site degree programs sponsored by colleges/ universities	• Same basic procedure as listed in Strategy 1.	*Appropriate:* • When funding and time are available • When several people share similar needs • When in-house expertise is not available *Inappropriate:* • When conditions listed above cannot be met • For meeting highly specialized needs
3. Off-the-job public seminars sponsored by vendors	• Compare work requirements to the instructional objectives indicated by information about the off-the-job seminar.	*Appropriate:* • When needs are limited to a few people • When in-house expertise does not match the vendor's

(continues)

Exhibit 8-8 (*continued*).

Strategy	How to Use It	Appropriate and Inappropriate Uses
		Inappropriate: • For meeting needs unique to one employer
4. Off-the-job public seminars sponsored by universities	• Same as Strategy 3.	*Appropriate:* • Same as number 3 above *Inappropriate:* • Same as number 3 above
5. In-house classroom courses tailor-made for employees	• Define specific instructional objectives that are directly related to work requirements in key positions. • Use the courses to achieve instructional objectives for many individuals.	*Appropriate:* • When adequate resources exist • When in-house expertise is available • When needs can be met in a reasonable time *Inappropriate:* • For meeting requirements unique to one organization • For meeting objectives requiring lengthy and experiential learning

6. In-house classroom courses purchased from outside sources and modified for in-house use	• Identify a learning need shared by more than one person. • Find published training materials from commercial publishers and modify them for in-house use. • Deliver to groups.	*Appropriate:* • When several people share a common learning need • When expertise exists to modify training materials developed outside the organization • When appropriate training materials can be located
7. Unplanned on-the-job training	• Match up a high-potential employee with an exemplary performer in a key position. • Permit long-term observation of the exemplar by the high potential.	*Appropriate:* • When time, money, and staffing are not of primary importance *Inappropriate:* • For quickly preparing high potentials to be successors for key job incumbents
8. Planned on-the-job training	• Develop a detailed training plan based on a "tell, show, do, follow-up approach" to instruction.	*Appropriate:* • When a key job incumbent is an exemplar • When time and safety considerations will permit one-on-one instruction *Inappropriate:* • When the conditions listed above cannot be met

(continues)

Exhibit 8-8 (continued).

Strategy	How to Use It	Appropriate and Inappropriate Uses
9. Unplanned mentoring programs	• Make people aware of what mentoring is. • Help individuals understand how they can establish mentoring relationships and realize the chief benefits from them. • Encourage key job incumbents and exemplars to serve as mentors.	*Appropriate:* • For establishing the basis for mentoring without obligating the organization to oversee it • For encouraging individual autonomy *Inappropriate:* • For encouraging diversity and building relationships across unlike individuals • For transferring specific skills in a planned, orchestrated way
10. Planned mentoring programs	• Match up individuals who may establish useful mentor-protégé relationships. • Provide training to mentors on effective mentoring skills and to protégés on the best ways to take advantage of mentoring relationships.	*Appropriate:* • For building top-level ownership and familiarity with high potentials • For pairing up unlike individuals on occasion *Inappropriate:* • For building specific skills quickly

11. Unplanned job rotation programs	• Arrange to move individuals into positions that will give them knowledge, skills, or abilities they will need in the future, preferably (but not necessarily) geared to advancement. • Track individual progress.	*Appropriate:* • When sufficient staffing exists • When individual movement will not create a significant loss of productivity for the organization *Inappropriate:* • When the conditions listed above cannot be met
12. Planned job rotation programs	• Develop a specific learning contract (or IDP) that clarifies the learning objectives to be achieved by the rotation. • Ensure that the work activities by which the individual gains experience are directly related to future work requirements in key positions. • Monitor work progress through periodic feedback to the individual and through performance appraisal geared to the rotation and related to future advancement.	*Appropriate:* • When there is sufficient time and staffing to permit the rotation to be effective *Inappropriate:* • When timing and staffing will not permit planned learning

international job rotations or assignments to give them experience with doing business in another culture or sending them to another domestic site for a special project. However, international assignments can be tricky: an estimated 20 percent to 50 percent of those sent on such assignments return early, and the cost of each "failure" can exceed $200,000.[12] Like any job rotation or temporary assignment, international assignments should be preceded by a well-prepared plan that clarifies what the individual is to learn, and why it is worth learning.

5. *Why-based strategies.* These learning strategies focus on giving high potentials exposure to mission-driven change efforts that are, in turn, learning experiences. Examples: asking high potentials to pioneer start-up efforts or to visit competitors or "best-in-class" organizations to find out why they do what they do.

6. *How-based strategies.* These learning strategies focus on furnishing high potentials with in-depth, "how-to" knowledge of different aspects of the business in which they are otherwise weak. Examples might include lengthy job assignments, task force assignments, or job rotations that expose high potentials to other areas of the business with which they are unfamiliar.

Using Action Learning in Succession Planning

Action learning, although it has been around for years, has recently commanded increasing interest.[13] Indeed, it has become one of the hottest topics in management and leadership development circles. It may offer an alternative to the more rigorous, albeit sometimes more expensive-to-design, planned learning experiences based on the instructional systems design model (see a comparison of the two models in Exhibit 8-9). It is also compatible with coaching and on-the-job training, which are popular methods for preparing managers and grooming leaders.

One reason I believe that action learning has become so popular lately is that it offers learners the opportunity to meet their own learning objectives and developmental needs in real time and in the real world rather than in downtime and in artificially constructed settings (a particularly important advantage in downsized organizations). Another reason is that it permits executives and managers, whose planned learning experiences have historically been highly individualized, to work together in teams so that they can learn from each other as well as from the action learning assignment.

A typical action learning set begins with a problem, goal, objective, or issue. (The term *set* is used instead of *planned learning experience* because

Exhibit 8-9. A comparison of instructional systems design and action learning: contrasting models for use in developing leadership talent.

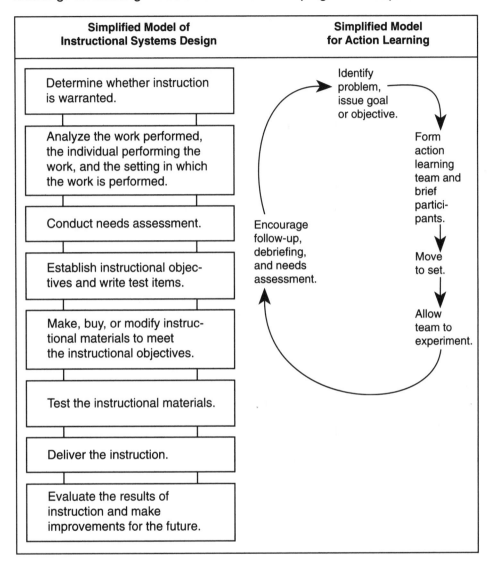

the learning occurs in a work setting.) Learners are brought together, sometimes from remote locations, to form a team, and are chosen for team membership based on their expertise. They are then briefed on the problem, goal, objective, or issue to be investigated and are told at least (1) what results are desired upon completion of the assignment, (2) when the assignment is to be completed, (3) what resources (people, time, money) they may draw upon in the course of their assignment, (4) where they may obtain additional information, and (5) why the assignment is important.

Team members are then left to their own devices to research, experiment, and test out solutions. The time they are given may be limited (a few hours or days) or extended (for an international assignment, a year or more). The facilitator intervenes only when requested, helping team members work together more effectively and offering advice about where to get more information. The facilitator's role is thus one of process consultant, resource, and enabling agent rather than trainer.

Team members may go through repeated trials to find a solution to the problem, appropriate actions for handling the issue, or an appropriate strategy for meeting a goal or objective. When they reach a point where it appears that repeated efforts will not be beneficial, the team is disbanded. Before the team is disbanded, however, the facilitator helps members (1) reflect on what they learned through their experience, (2) reflect on the results achieved, and (3) assess their own individualized (and perhaps even team-based) training, education, and development needs for the future. Reflection on the learning experience is usually considered a key to success.

Experiences of this kind can, of course, be designed in such a way as to give prospective successors the opportunity to investigate a problem or issue that is directly related to their future advancement opportunities. It also offers the organization a chance to see them in action and to identify developmental needs.

Action learning is also appropriate for building cross-functional knowledge, skills, and competencies. A prospective CEO, for instance, may be teamed up with functional experts from many areas to work in a set. That allows team members to share what they know and to acquire knowledge about other functional areas.

Summary

Promotion from within is an important way to implement succession plans. To that end, the organization should test bench strength, establish an unequivocal internal promotion policy to ensure internal promotion when appropriate, prepare individual development plans (IDPs) to close the gap between what individuals presently do and what they must do to qualify for advancement, and use internal development when appropriate to realize the learning objectives established on IDPs.

But internal promotion and internal development are not the only means by which succession planning needs can be met. Alternative means, which usually fall outside the realm of succession planning, are treated in the next chapter. In these days of business process reengineering, those involved in succession planning should have some awareness of approaches to meeting work requirements other than traditional succession methods that rely on job movements.

9

Assessing Alternatives
To Internal Development

The traditional approach is to prepare successors for key positions internally. Most descriptions of succession planning treat it as nothing more than a form of replacement planning. In this process, several key assumptions are usually made: (1) Key positions will be replaced whenever a vacancy occurs, (2) employees already working in the organization, and often within the function, will be the prime source of replacements, and (3) a key measure of effectiveness is the percentage of key positions that can be filled from within, with minimal delay and uproar, whenever a vacancy occurs. Some organizations add a fourth: The relative racial and sexual diversity of replacements should be enhanced so that protected labor groups are well represented among the qualified internal successors for key positions.

A traditional approach to succession planning has major advantages, of course. First, it makes succession predictable. Each time a vacancy in the key position occurs, people know precisely what to do: Find a replacement. Second, since a high percentage of successors are assumed to be employed by the organization already, investments in leadership development can be justified to minimize losses in productivity and turnover.

However, when succession planning is treated in this way it can occasionally become a mindless exercise in filling in the blank name on the organization chart. Concern about that should be sufficient to lead strategists to explore innovative alternatives to the traditional replacement-from-within mentality. This chapter focuses on some alternatives and on when they should be used instead of the traditional approach to succession planning.

Assessing Alternatives

The natural response to a problem [writes James L. Adams in *Conceptual Blockbusting*] seems to be to try to get rid of it by finding an answer—often taking the first answer that occurs and pursuing it because of one's reluctance to spend the time and mental effort needed to conjure up a richer storehouse of alternatives from which to choose. This hit-and-run approach to problem-solving begets all sorts of oddities.[1]

Succession planning can fall victim to the same natural response to which Adams refers: Whenever a vacancy occurs, the organization is confronted with a problem. The "natural response" is to find an immediate replacement. There may also be a tendency to "clone the incumbent," that is, find someone who resembles the present position incumbent in order to minimize the need to make adjustments to a new person.

But replacement is not always appropriate. Consider a replacement unnecessary when any one of the seven questions listed below can be answered yes. (Review the flowchart in Exhibit 9-1 as a simplified aid in helping with this decision process.)

1. *Is the key position no longer necessary?* A replacement is not necessary when a key position is no longer worth doing. In that situation, a position is no longer "key." Decision makers can simply choose not to fill the key position when a vacancy occurs. Of course, if this question is answered no, then a replacement may still have to be found.

2. *Can a key position be rendered unnecessary by finding new ways to achieve comparable results?* A replacement may not be necessary if the work outcomes of the key position can be achieved through new ways. In this sense, then, succession planning can be affected by *business process reengineering,* defined by best-selling authors Michael Hammer and James Champy as "the fundamental rethinking and radical redesign of business processes to achieve dramatic improvements in critical, contemporary measures of performance, such as cost, quality, service, and speed."[2] If the organization can reengineer work processes and thereby eliminate positions that were once "key" to an "old" process, then replacing a key job incumbent will be unnecessary. In short, key positions may be reengineered out of existence.

To that end, try applying the model suggested by Rummler and Brache to process improvement:

- Identify a critical issue or process that is to be reengineered.
- Select a leader and members for a process improvement team.
- Train team members on process improvement methods.
- Develop flowcharts to show where and how work flows into a system, how it is transformed through work methods, and where it goes when the products or services are provided to the "customers."

(text continues on page 250)

Exhibit 9-1. Deciding when replacing a key job incumbent is unnecessary: a flowchart.

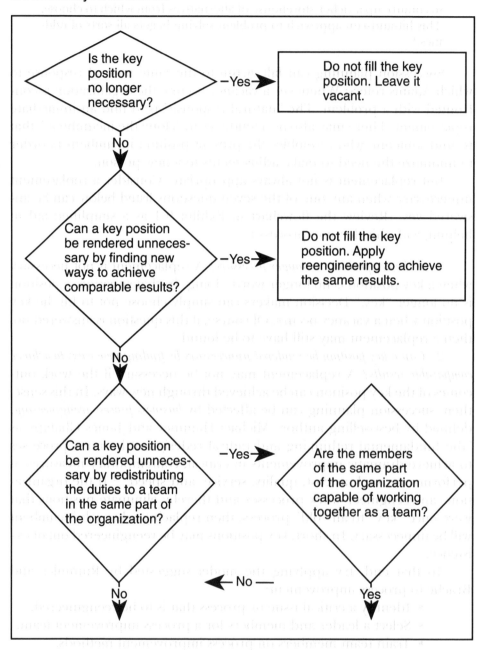

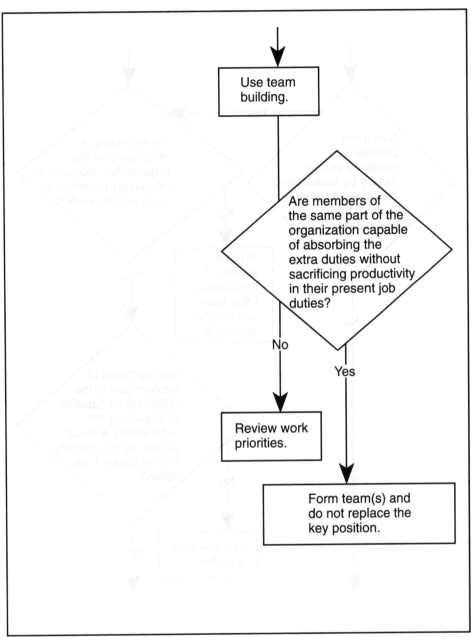

(continues)

Exhibit 9-1 (*continued*).

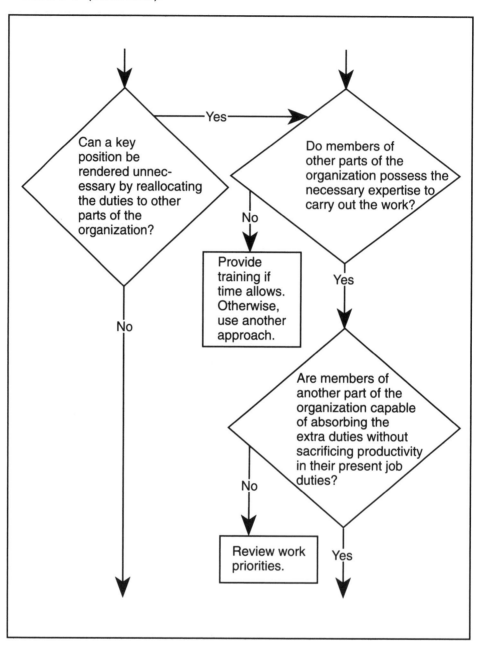

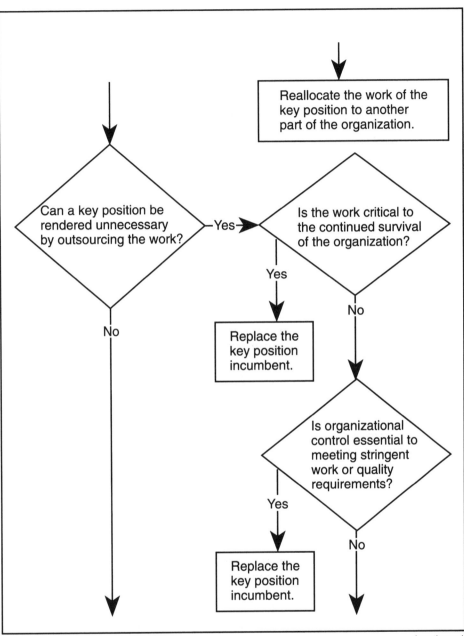

(continues)

Exhibit 9-1 (*continued*).

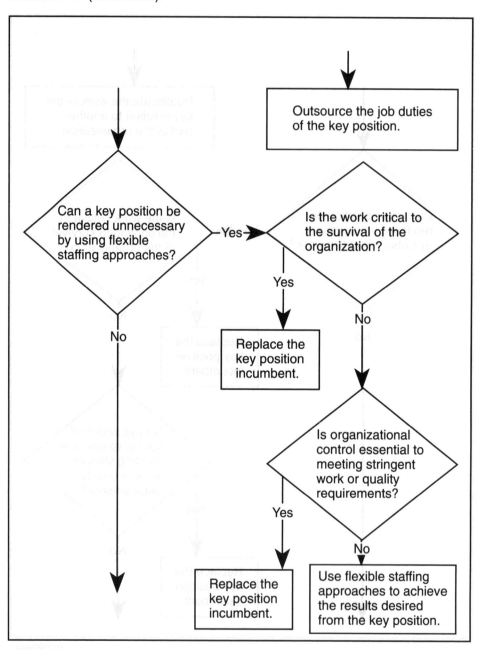

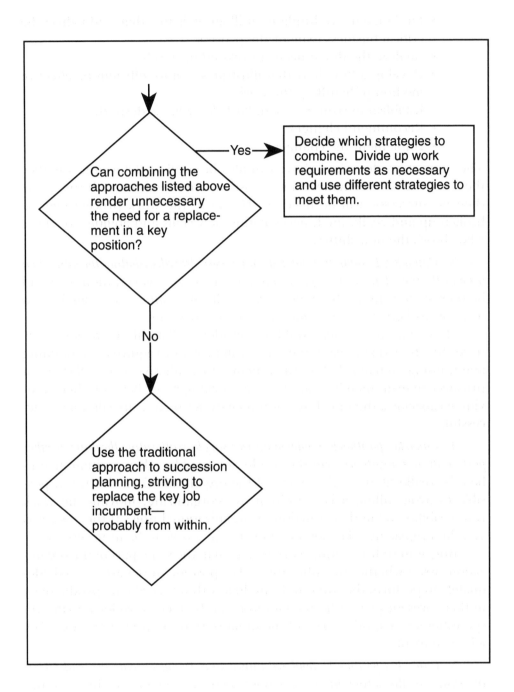

- Find missing, redundant, or illogical factors that could affect the critical business issue or the process.
- Analyze the disconnects uncovered in step 5.
- Develop a flowchart that illustrates a more efficient or effective method of handling the work.
- Establish measures or standards for what is desired.
- Recommend changes.
- Implement the changes.[3]

The same steps described above can also be used to determine whether there are ways to reengineer a key position out of existence. If there are, then no successor will be needed. (However, the work process may be broken up and reallocated, necessitating new skills and abilities for those who absorb the new duties.)

3. *Can a key position be rendered unnecessary by redistributing the duties to a team in the same part of the organization?* If the answer is yes, then it should be possible to achieve the same work results by vesting responsibility in a team of workers from the same function or work unit.

However, two caveats should be considered. First, if the workers have never functioned as a team, then they will probably require team building and training on team skills to turn them into a cohesive group. Second, if prospective team members are already working at, or beyond, their individual capacities, then loading additional duties on a team will not be successful.

4. *Can a key position be rendered unnecessary by reallocating the duties to other parts of the organization?* Can the results achieved by a key position incumbent be reallocated to other parts of the organization? In short, is it possible to avoid filling a key position by reorganizing, moving the work responsibility to another function or organizational unit? If the answer is yes, then replacing a key job incumbent may prove to be unnecessary.

But, as in redistributing work to a team in the same part of the organization, assess whether the inheritors of key position duties are trained adequately to perform the work and can do it without sacrificing productivity in their present jobs. If both conditions can be met, consider moving responsibilities to another part of the organization to avoid replacing a key job incumbent.

5. *Can a key position be rendered unnecessary by outsourcing the work?* Can the same results achieved by a key position be moved outside the organization and conducted by a contractor? If the answer is yes, then replacing a key job incumbent may be unnecessary. The same results may be achieved more cost-effectively than by replacing a key job incumbent.

Pay particular attention to two key issues when answering the question: *criticality* and *control*. If the work is critical to the continued survival of the organization, then outsourcing it may be unwise because that may vest too much influence in an individual or group having little or no stake in the organization's continued survival. If the work must adhere to stringent and specialized requirements that few external sources are qualified to meet, then outsourcing may also prove to be unwise because controlling the activities of an external contractor may become more time-consuming than performing the work in-house.

6. *Can a key position be rendered unnecessary by using flexible staffing approaches?* Can the same results achieved by a key position be met through flexible staffing approaches other than outsourcing, such as the use of permanent part-time or temporary part-time staff, rotating employees, or internships? If the answer is yes, then replacing a key job incumbent may be unnecessary.

However, as in outsourcing, pay attention to *criticality* and *control*. If the work is critical to the continued survival of the organization, then using innovative staffing approaches may prove to be unwise because it will place too much influence over the organization's survival in the hands of an individual or group having little or no stake in the organization's continued existence. If the work must meet stringent, specialized requirements which require an extended time span for mastery, then innovative staffing may prove to be impractical because part-time talent may not be able to achieve or maintain mastery.

7. *Can combining the approaches listed above render unnecessary the need for a replacement in a key position?* Finally, can the need to replace a key job incumbent be avoided by relying on a combination of the approaches listed above? In other words, is it possible to split apart the key results or outcomes desired from the key position and handle them separately, through reengineering, team-based management, organizational redesign, or other means? If that question can be answered yes, then it should be possible to ensure that the organization achieves the same results as those provided by the key job incumbent—but without the need for a replacement.

Use the worksheet in Exhibit 9-2 to decide when it is possible to answer yes to any one, or all, of the questions listed above.

Deciding What to Do

There is no foolproof way to use alternatives to replacement from within. The important point is to make sure that alternatives to simple replacement are always considered. Often, that responsibility will rest with HR generalists, HRD specialists, SP coordinators, and even CEOs or others

Exhibit 9-2. A worksheet for identifying alternatives to the traditional approach to succession planning.

Directions: Use this worksheet to help you identify alternative approaches to succession planning—that is, describe ideas to avoid simple replacement from within the organization and within the function.

Identify by title the key position you are examining. Then answer the questions about it appearing in the left column. Write your responses in the right column, making notes about ways by which you can use alternatives to the traditional approach to succession planning. When you finish, share your responses with others in the organization. Ask for their thoughts, and, if possible, compare their comments to yours. Add paper as necessary.

There are no right or wrong answers to this activity; rather, the aim is to provide you with an aid to creative ways by which to meet succession planning needs.

Title of key position:

Questions about Key Position:	*Ideas for Avoiding Simple Replacement from Within*
Is the key position no longer necessary?	
Can a key position be rendered unnecessary by finding new ways to achieve comparable results?	
Can a key position be rendered unnecessary by redistributing the duties to a team in the same part of the organization?	
Can a key position be rendered unnecessary by reallocating the duties to other parts of the organization?	
Can a key position be rendered unnecessary by outsourcing the work?	
Can a key position be rendered unnnecessary by using flexible staffing approaches?	
Can combining the approaches listed above render unnecessary the need for a replacement in a key position?	

who bear major responsibility for succession planning. A good strategy is to raise the issue at two different—and opportune—times: (1) during review meetings to identify successors and (2) on the occasions when a vacancy occurs in a key position and permission is sought to fill it.

During the review process, ask operating managers how they plan to meet replacement needs. At that time, raise the alternatives, and ask them to consider other possibilities as well, such as hiring someone from outside the organization. Be sure that only key positions are being considered in succession planning efforts in order to focus attention on areas of critical need.

When a vacancy occurs, or is about to occur, in a key position, raise the issue again. Ask operating managers what alternatives to simple replacement they have considered. Briefly review some of them to ensure that succession is driven by work requirements and not by custom, resistance to change, or other issues that may prove to be needlessly costly or inefficient.

Summary

This chapter reviewed alternatives to traditional replacement from within. Alternatives may be used when any one or all the following seven questions may be answered yes:

1. Is the key position no longer necessary?
2. Can a key position be rendered unnecessary by finding new ways to achieve comparable results?
3. Can a key position be rendered unnecessary by redistributing the duties to a team in the same part of the organization?
4. Can a key position be rendered unnecessary by reallocating the duties to other parts of the organization?
5. Can a key position be rendered unnecessary by outsourcing the work?
6. Can a key position be rendered unnecessary by using flexible staffing approaches?
7. Can combining the approaches listed above render unnecessary the need for a replacement in a key position?

Pose these questions during periodic succession planning review meetings and on the occasions when a vacancy occurs in a key position. Be sure that key positions are filled only when absolutely necessary to achieve essential work requirements.

10
Evaluating Succession Planning

After a succession planning program has been implemented, top managers will eventually ask, Is this effort worth what it costs? How well is it working? Is it meeting the organization's needs?

Simple answers to these questions will prove to be elusive because a succession planning program will affect many people—and will usually have to satisfy conflicting goals, interests, and priorities. But the questions do underscore the need to establish some way to evaluate the program. This chapter, then, will explore three simple questions: (1) What is evaluation? (2) What should be evaluated in succession planning? (3) How should a succession planning program be evaluated?

What Is Evaluation?

Evaluation means *placing value or determining worth.*[1] It is a process of determining how much value is being added by an activity or program. It is through evaluation that the need for program improvements are identified and are eventually made. Evaluation is typically carried out by an evaluator or team of evaluators against a backdrop of client expectations about the program and the need for information on which to make sound decisions.

Interest in Evaluation

How human resources programs are evaluated has been a popular topic of numerous books, articles, and professional presentations.[2] Treatments of it have tended to focus on such bottom-line issues as cost-benefit analysis and return on investment,[3] which should not be surprising in view of the perception of HR practitioners that these issues are of chief interest to top managers. Training has figured most prominently in this literature, probably because it has the dubious reputation of being the first HR program to be slashed when an organization falls on hard times.[4]

On the other hand, writers on evaluation have tended to pay far less attention to succession planning than to training. One reason could be that systematic succession planning is less common in organizations than training is. A second reason could be that evaluations of succession planning are informally made on a case-by-case basis whenever a vacancy occurs in a key position: If a successor is ready, willing, and able when needed, the succession planning program is given the credit; otherwise, it is blamed. While the value of succession planning should, of course, be judged on more than that basis alone, that is probably too often how a succession planning program is viewed—on a case-by-case basis by its chief stakeholders.

Key Questions Governing Evaluation

To be performed effectively, evaluation for succession planning should focus on four key questions:

1. Who will use the results?
2. How will the results be used?
3. What do the program's clients expect from it?
4. Who is carrying out the evaluation?

The first question seeks to identify the audience; the second question seeks to clarify what decisions will be made based on evaluation results; the third grounds evaluation in client expectations and program objectives; and the fourth provides clues about appropriate evaluation techniques based on the expertise of the chosen evaluator(s).

What Should Be Evaluated?

Some years ago Donald Kirkpatrick developed a four-level hierarchy of training evaluation[5] that may be usefully modified to help conceptualize what should be evaluated in succession planning.

Kirkpatrick's Hierarchy of Training Evaluation

The four levels of Kirkpatrick's training evaluation hierarchy consist of *reaction, learning, behavior,* and *organizational outcomes,* or *results.* Reaction forms the base of the hierarchy and is easiest to measure. It examines customer satisfaction—that is, how much did participants like what they learned? Learning, the second level on the hierarchy, has to do with immediate change. In other words, how well did participants master the information or skills they were supposed to learn in training? The third level of the hierarchy, behavior, has to do with on-the-job application. How much change occurred on the job as a result of learner participation in training? The highest level of Kirkpatrick's hierarchy, the fourth and final one, is organizational outcomes, or results. It is also the most difficult to measure. How much influence did the results or effects of training have on the organization?

Modifying Kirkpatrick's Hierarchy of Training Evaluation for Succession Planning

Use Kirkpatrick's hierarchy of training evaluation to provide a conceptual basis for evaluating a succession planning program. (Examine the hierarchy of succession planning evaluation depicted in Exhibit 10-1).

Make the first level *customer satifaction,* which corresponds to Kirkpatrick's *reaction* level. Pose the following questions:

- How satisfied with the succession planning program are its chief customers?
- How satisfied are its customers with each program component—such as job descriptions, competency models, performance appraisal processes, individual potential assessment processes, individual development forms, and individual development activities?
- How well does succession planning match up to individual career plans? How do employees perceive succession planning?

Make the second level *program progress,* which is meant to correspond to Kirkpatrick's *learning* level. Pose the following questions:

- How well is each part of the succession planning program working compared to stated program objectives?
- How well are individuals progressing through their developmental experiences in preparation for future advancement into key positions?

Make the third level *effective placements,* which is meant to correspond to Kirkpatrick's *behavior* level. Pose these questions:

- What percentage of vacancies in key positions is the organization able to fill internally?

Exhibit 10-1. The hierarchy of succession planning evaluation.

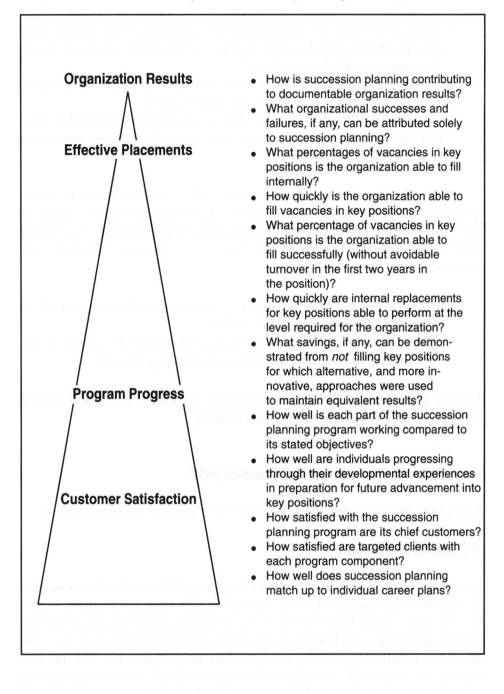

Organization Results

- How is succession planning contributing to documentable organization results?
- What organizational successes and failures, if any, can be attributed solely to succession planning?

Effective Placements

- What percentages of vacancies in key positions is the organization able to fill internally?
- How quickly is the organization able to fill vacancies in key positions?
- What percentage of vacancies in key positions is the organization able to fill successfully (without avoidable turnover in the first two years in the position)?
- How quickly are internal replacements for key positions able to perform at the level required for the organization?
- What savings, if any, can be demonstrated from *not* filling key positions for which alternative, and more innovative, approaches were used to maintain equivalent results?

Program Progress

- How well is each part of the succession planning program working compared to its stated objectives?
- How well are individuals progressing through their developmental experiences in preparation for future advancement into key positions?

Customer Satisfaction

- How satisfied with the succession planning program are its chief customers?
- How satisfied are targeted clients with each program component?
- How well does succession planning match up to individual career plans?

- How quickly is the organization able to fill vacancies in key positions?
- What percentage of vacancies in key positions is the organization able to fill successfully (that is, without avoidable turnover in the first two years in the position)?
- How quickly are internal replacements for key positions able to perform at the level required for the organization?
- What savings, if any, can be demonstrated from *not* filling key positions for which alternative, and more innovative, approaches were used to achieve results?

Make the fourth level *organizational results,* which is meant to correspond to Kirkpatrick's *outcomes,* or *results.* Direct attention to the impact of the succession planning program on the organization's ability to compete effectively, which is (admittedly) difficult to do. Consider the following questions:

- How is the succession planning program contributing, if at all, to documentable organizational results?
- What successes or failures in organizational strategic plans, if any, can be attributed to the succession planning program?

Use the guidelines in Exhibit 10-2 and the worksheet in Exhibit 10-3 to consider ways to evaluate succession planning.

How Should Evaluation Be Conducted?

Evaluation may be conducted *anecdotally, periodically,* or *programmatically.*

Anecdotal Evaluation

Anecdotal evaluation is akin to using testimonials in evaluating training.[6] It examines the operation of the succession planning program on a case-by-case basis. As vacancies occur in key positions, someone, often the succession planning coordinator, documents in *incident reports* how they are filled (see Exhibit 10-4 for an example of an incident report). The incident reports are eventually brought to the organizaiton's succession planning commmittee for review and discussion. They provide a solid foundation for troubleshooting problems in succession planning that the organization

(text continues on page 263)

Exhibit 10-2. Guidelines for evaluating the succession planning program.

Type/Level	Purpose	Strengths	Weaknesses
Customer satisfaction	To measure client feelings about the program and its results	• Easy to measure. • Provides immediate feedback on program activities and components.	• Subjective. • Provides no objective measurement of program results.
Program progress	To measure results of each component of the succession planning program	• Provides objective data on the effectiveness of the succession planning program.	• Requires skill in program evaluation. • Provides no measurement of skills of benefit to the organization.
Effective placements	To measure the results of the succession decisions made	• Provides objective data on impact to the job situation.	• Requires first-rate employee performance appraisal system.
Organizational results	To measure impact of the succession planning program on the organization	• Provides objective data for cost-benefit analysis and organizational support.	• Requires high level of evaluation design skills; requires collection of data over a period of time. • Requires knowledge of the organization's strategy and goals.

(continues)

Exhibit 10-2 *(continued).*

Type/Level	Examples	Guidelines for Development
Customer satisfaction	• "Happiness reports" • Informal interviews with "clients" at all levels • Group discussion in succession planning meetings	• Design a survey form that can be easily tabulated. • Ask questions to provide information about what you need to know: attitudes about each component of the succession planning program. • Allow for anonymity and allow the respondents the opportunity to provide additional comments.
Program progress	• Examine individual movements through the organization.	• Design an instrument that will provide quantitative data. • Include "pre" and "post" level of skill/knowledge in design. • Tie evaluation items directly to program objectives.
Effective placements	• Performance checklists • Performance appraisals • Critical incident analysis • Self-appraisal	• Base measurement instrument on systematic analysis of key positions. • Consider the use of a variety of persons to conduct the evaluation.
Organizational results	• Organizational analysis • Speed of replacement • Cost of replacements • Cost of nonreplacements • Turnover	• Involve all necessary levels of organization. • Gain commitment to allow access to organization indices and records. • Use organization business plans and mission statements to compare organizational needs and program results.

Exhibit 10-3. A worksheet for identifying appropriate ways to evaluate succession planning in an organization.

Directions: Use this worksheet to help you identify appropriate ways to evaluate the succession planning program in your organization.

In column **1,** indicate the various stakeholder groups (such as top managers, key position incumbents, line managers, and the succession planning coordinator) who will be primarily interested in evaluation results on succession planning in your organization. In column **2,** indicate what levels of evaluation—customer satisfaction, program progress, effective placements and organizational results—will probably be of prime interest to each stakeholder group. Then, in column **3,** indicate how evaluation of succession planning should be carried out in your organization.

1	2	3
Stakeholder Groups for Evaluation	Levels of Evaluation that Will Probably Be of Prime Interest to Each Group	How Evaluation of the Succession Planning Program Should Be Carried Out in Your Organization
1.		
2.		
3.		
4.		
5.		
6.		
7.		
8.		
9.		
10.		
11.		
12.		

Exhibit 10-4. A sample "incident report" for succession planning.

Directions: The purpose of this incident report is to track successor/ replacement experiences in your organization.

Answer the questions appearing in the spaces below. Be as truthful as possible; the collective results of many incident reports will be used to identify program initiatives for the succession planning program.

Fill out this report for each position filled from within. [*This report should be completed in addition to any personnel requisitions/justification forms that you must complete.*] Submit the completed form to [*name*] at [*organization address*] within three weeks after filling the vacancy.

Name of departing employee: _____ Job title: _____
Department: _____ Time in position: _____
Reason for leaving (if known): _____
Name of replacing employee: _____ Job title: _____
Department: _____ Work unit/team: _____
Time in position: _____ Today's date: ___ /___ /9___

1. Describe how this position is being filled (internally/externally).

2. Was there an identifiable "successor" who had been prepared to assume this position previously? If so, briefly explain how the individual was being prepared; if not, briefly explain reasons for not preparing a successor.

3. Who was selected for the position, and why was he/she selected?

4. If an individual other than an identifiable successor was chosen for the position, explain why.

_____ **Approval** _____

Management Employee: _____ Title: _____
                                    [*Signature*]

Address: _____

Phone: _____

is confronting. They can then be used as a basis for planning how to avoid similar problems in the future.

Anecdotal evaluation dramatizes especially good and bad practices. It draws attention to them and provides an impetus for change. That is a chief advantage of this approach.

On the other hand, a chief disadvantage is that anecdotal evaluation suffers from a lack of research rigor. It is not necessarily representative of typical succession planning practices in the organization. (Indeed, it focuses on special cases, horror stories, and war stories.) It may thus draw attention to unique, even minor, problems with succession planning in the organization.

Periodic Evaluation

Periodic evaluation examines components of the succession planning program at different times, focusing attention on program operations at present or in the recent past. Rather than evaluate critical incidents (as anecdotal evaluation does) or all program components (as programmatic evaluation does), periodic evaluation examines isolated program components. For instance, the succession planning coordinator may direct attention to:

- The program mission statement
- Program objectives, policy, and philosophy
- Methods of determining work requirements for key positions
- Employee performance appraisal
- Employee potential assessment
- Individual development planning
- Individual development activities

Periodic evaluation may be conducted during regular succession planning meetings and/or in succession planning committee meetings. Alternatively, the organization's decision makers may wish to establish a task force or a subcommittee of the succession planning committee, or even involve a committee of the board of directors in this evaluation process.

A chief advantage of periodic evaluation is that it provides occasional, formal monitoring of the succession planning program. That process can build involvement, and thus ownership, of key stakeholders while simultaneously surfacing important problems in program operation.

A chief disadvantage of periodic evaluation is that it makes the improvement of succession planning an incremental rather than a continuous effort. Problems may be left to fester for too long before they are investigated.

Programmatic Evaluation

Programmatic evaluation examines the succession planning program comprehensively against its stated mission, objectives, and activities. It is an in-depth program review and resembles the human resources audit that may be conducted of all HR activities.[7]

Programmatic evaluation is usually carried out by a formally appointed committee. The succession planning coordinator is usually a member. Representatives of key line management areas, and the CEO or members of the corporate board of directors, may also be members.

Examine the steps in Exhibit 10-5 and the checksheet in Exhibit 10-6 as starting points for conducting a program evaluation of succession planning. (Compare your responses to the questions in Exhibit 10-6 to the survey responses appearing in Exhibit 2-1 to assess how well your organization's succession planning program matches programs in other organizations.)

Summary

This chapter addressed three simple questions: (1) What is evaluation? (2) what should be evaluated in succession planning? and (3) how should a succession planning program be evaluated?

Evaluation was defined as the process of placing value or determining worth. It is through evaluation that the need for improvements is identified and these improvements are eventually made to the succession planning program. Evaluation should focus on several key questions:

- Who will use the results?
- How will the results be used?
- What do the program's clients expect from it?
- Who is carrying out the evaluation?

Focus the evaluation of succession planning on four levels, comparable to those devised by Donald Kirkpatrick to describe training evaluation. Those four levels are: *customer satisfaction, program progress, effective placements,* and *organizational results.*

Conduct evaluation *anecdotally, periodically,* or *programmatically.* Anec-

(text continues on page 273)

Exhibit 10-5. Steps for completing a program evaluation of a succession planning program.

Step 1 Assemble a committee to conduct the program evaluation	1. Assemble a group of five to eight people who have their own roles to play in the succession planning program. (Ideally the group should consist of the CEO, succession planning coordinator, vice president of human resources, and two or more key operating managers.)
Step 2 Brief committee members on the need to evaluate the succession planning program and the steps to be followed in the evaluation effort.	1. Call a meeting, providing an agenda and briefing materials to committee members beforehand. 2. Explain the value of evaluating the succession planning program. 3. Provide benchmarking information from other companies, if available. 4. Provide information from incident reports and other indicators of the program's progress. 5. Agree on evaluation objectives, approaches, and steps.

Step 3
 	
Conduct background research on the relative effectiveness of the succession planning program.
	1. Conduct research by:
	  • Collecting information on the program's operations and results.
	  • Collecting information from other organizations to use in benchmarking.

(continues)

Exhibit 10-5 *(continued).*

Step 4 Analyze results, make recommenations for program improvements, and document evaluation results.	1. Analyze results. 2. Prepare recommendations for program improvements. 3. Write report and prepare oral presentation.
Step 5 Communicate results.	1. Circulate written report. 2. Present oral report/briefing to those responsible for the succession planning program.
Step 6 Identify specific actions for program improvement.	1. Work with those who bear responsibility for succession planning, such as key operating managers, to establish program improvement objectives.
Step 7 Take continuing action for program improvement.	1. Take continuing action for improvement through training, briefings, and other means.

Exhibit 10-6. A checksheet for conducting a program evaluation for the succession planning program.

Directions: Use this check sheet as a starting point for deciding what to evaluate in your organization's succession planning program. Ask members of a program evaluation committee to complete the following check sheet. Have them compare notes and then use the results to establish priorities for evaluating the components of the organization's succession planning program. Add, delete, or modify characteristics in the left column as appropriate.

For the succession planning program, has your organization:	Does your organization's succession planning program have this characteristic?		How important do you believe this characteristic to be for an effective succession planning program?				
			Not Important				Very Important
1. Tied the succession planning program to organizational strategic plans?	Yes	No	1	2	3	4	5
2. Tied the succession planning program to individual career plans?	Yes	No	1	2	3	4	5
3. Tied the succession planning program to training programs?	Yes	No	1	2	3	4	5

(continues)

Exhibit 10-6 *(continued).*

For the succession planning program, has your organization:	*Does your organization's succession planning program have this characteristic?*		*How important do you believe this characteristic to be for an effective succession planning program?*				
			Not Important				*Very Important*
4. Prepared a written program purpose statement?	Yes	No	1	2	3	4	5
5. Prepared written program goals to indicate what results the succession planning program should achieve?	Yes	No	1	2	3	4	5
6. Established *measurable* objectives for program operation (such as number of positions filled per year)?	Yes	No	1	2	3	4	5
7. Identified which groups are to be served by the program, in priority order?	Yes	No	1	2	3	4	5

	Yes	No	1	2	3	4	5
8. Established a written policy statement to guide the program?	Yes	No	1	2	3	4	5
9. Articulated a written philosophy about the program?	Yes	No	1	2	3	4	5
10. Established a program action plan?	Yes	No	1	2	3	4	5
11. Established a schedule of program events based on the action plan?	Yes	No	1	2	3	4	5
12. Fixed responsibility for organizational oversight of the program?	Yes	No	1	2	3	4	5
13. Fixed responsibility of each participant in the program?	Yes	No	1	2	3	4	5
14. Established incentives/rewards for identified successors in the succession planning program?	Yes	No	1	2	3	4	5

(continues)

Exhibit 10-6 *(continued).*

For the succession planning program, has your organization:	*Does your organization's succession planning program have this characteristic?*		*How important do you believe this characteristic to be for an effective succession planning program?*				
			Not Important				*Very Important*
15. Established incentives/rewards for managers who have identified successors?	Yes	No	1	2	3	4	5
16. Developed a means to budget for a succession planning program?	Yes	No	1	2	3	4	5
17. Devised a means to keep records for individuals who are designated as successors?	Yes	No	1	2	3	4	5
18. Created workshops to train management employees about the succession planning program?	Yes	No	1	2	3	4	5

	Yes	No				
19. Created workshops to train individuals about career planning?	Yes	No	1	2	3	4	5
20. Established a means to clarify *present position responsibilities?*	Yes	No	1	2	3	4	5
21. Established a means to clarify *future position responsibilities?*	Yes	No	1	2	3	4	5
22. Established a means to appraise individual performance?	Yes	No	1	2	3	4	5
23. Established a means to compare individual skills to the requirements of a future position?	Yes	No	1	2	3	4	5
24. Established a way to review organizational talent at least annually?	Yes	No	1	2	3	4	5
25. Established a way to forecast future talent needs?	Yes	No	1	2	3	4	5

(continues)

Exhibit 10-6 *(continued).*

For the succession planning program, has your organization:	Does your organization's succession planning program have this characteristic?		How important do you believe this characteristic to be for an effective succession planning program?				
			Not Important				Very Important
	Yes	No	1	2	3	4	5
26. Established a way to plan for meeting succession planning needs through IDPs?	Yes	No	1	2	3	4	5
27. Established a means to track development activities to prepare successors for eventual advancement?	Yes	No	1	2	3	4	5
28. Established a means to evaluate the results of the succession planning program?	Yes	No	1	2	3	4	5

dotal evaluation is akin to using testimonials in evaluating training. Periodic evaluation examines isolated components of the succession planning program at different times, focusing attention on program operations at the present or in the recent past. Programmatic evaluation examines the succession planning program comprehensively against its stated mission, objectives, and activities.

Epilogue

Special Issues In Succession Planning

No organization is immune to changing external environmental conditions. However, *what* external conditions affect an organization will vary—depending on such variables as the organization's industry, size, and relative prominence. Moreover, *how* those conditions affect an organization will depend on the ways that its leaders choose to address them. These principles hold as true for succession planning programs as for strategic planning.

In this Epilogue, I will focus on the following important issues affecting succession planning that stem, in whole or part, from changing external environmental conditions:

- Accelerating the development of high potentials through HiPo programs
- Avoiding critical turnover after downsizing
- Building diversity and multiculturalism into succession planning
- Adapting succession planning to team environments

I will conclude the chapter with three predictions about the future of succession planning.

Accelerating the Development of High Potentials Through HiPo Programs

High potentials (HiPos) represent powerful assets for any organization. They are usually a driving force behind creative adaptation to the external environment and a source of future leaders. In some organizations, strategists are not content with merely defining what a HiPo is and placing stars on individual foreheads; rather, strategists actively support special programs to accelerate HiPo development.[1] The aim is thus to cultivate HiPos so they realize their potential faster than they otherwise would. That is viewed as desirable both for individuals and the organization.

What Is a High-Potential Program?

A *high-potential program* is a planned effort to systematically accelerate the preparation of individuals who are perceived to have the potential for advancement. A high-potential program demands considerable commitment from the organization and the individual. It typically involves full-time or significant part-time duties that are intended to prepare individuals for future advancement.

What Else Are They Called?

High-potential programs are rarely called by that name. There are two reasons.

First, if individuals are called HiPos, they might develop a crown prince or princess syndrome in which they picture themselves as destined for future advancement no matter how they perform. Most organizations would prefer to avoid the perception that some employees have advancement guaranteed no matter what they do.

Second, individuals not called HiPos might feel demotivated and demoralized. (They might include exemplary performers who are not perceived to be capable of advancing for whatever reason.) They would challenge how others were chosen for the high-potential ranks, and would be particularly likely to do so if the high-potential ranks are easily distinguishable from other employees *and* if protected labor groups are underrepresented among the HiPos.

More commonly, HiPo programs operate under such names as management trainee program, supervisory development program, management development program, executive rotation program, or multinational executive program. HiPo programs are carefully planned to prepare individuals for advancement to higher levels of responsibility or for exercising and increasing technical expertise. They last for a significant time, and may use any or all developmental techniques such as off-the-job degree programs sponsored by colleges/universities, on-site degree programs sponsored by colleges/universities, off-the-job public seminars sponsored by vendors, off-the-job public seminars sponsored by universities, in-house courses prepared inside the organization or purchased from outside sources, unplanned on-the-job training, planned on-the-job training, unplanned mentoring programs, planned mentoring programs, unplanned job rotation programs, planned job rotation programs, or other approaches.

Who Participates?

HiPo programs may be prepared for any location, level, or job category. While they are probably most common at the mangement entry level, HiPo programs may also be developed for such other job categories as professional or technical employees. At higher levels—middle managers and above—job rotations, including multinational assignments, are among the single most common ways to develop HiPos.[2]

CASE STUDY: A HIGH-POTENTIAL PROGRAM

In the minds of most training professionals on-the-job training (OJT) evokes an image of a training method appropriate for hourly workers only. But OJT can have much broader applications than that.[3] It may also be used with supervisors, managers, technical employees, professionals, and even executives. However, the term *coaching* is (admittedly) used more often to describe OJT with the latter employee groups.

In the early 1990s, the Superco Insurance Company—the name is fictitious but the company is real and well-known—faced a crisis. As a result of a generous early retirement offer and several waves of downsizing, top executives perceived that the company had grown "weak in bench strength" at all management levels. They resolved to take strong, immediate corrective action. But, at first, they were unsure what to do.

One company executive decided that the creation of a supervisory trainee program might be the appropriate solution to the problem. She was aware that numerous companies had previously experienced great success with such programs.[4] Accordingly, she discussed the idea with top managers, conducted research to identify the exact parameters of the "talent shortage" potentially facing the company, and (working on a committee with others) prepared a detailed proposal to establish and implement a supervisory trainee program.

The basic idea was a simple one that was based on an investigation of critical incidents in the lives of the company's successful supervisors, managers, and executives.[5]

Forecasting Supervisory Needs

The first step was to clarify existing needs, particularly at the critically important supervisory level which served as a feeder for middle and top management ranks. Company decision makers decided to conduct an annual survey of line (operating) managers about their anticipated needs for supervisory talent in their respective areas. (In this company, supervisors are frontline management employees who oversee and guide hourly workers on a daily basis.) Based on anticipated supervisory needs, the company would recruit potential entry-level talent from inside and outside the organization. It was decided that, as part of the goals of the supervisory trainee program, the company would seek a widely diverse and multicultural group of recruits to reflect (among other distinctions) different ages, sexes, races, and ethnic heritages. The selection process would be rigorous and uncompromising.

Components of the Supervisory Trainee Program

The "chosen few" hired into the supervisory trainee program—it was anticipated that there would be only a dozen positions for the program each year—would participate in a combination of classroom training, OJT, job rotation, and short work assignments. Each recruit would spend at least fourteen months in the supervisory trainee program with no possibility of promotion out of the program during that time. (This policy prevented managers from skimming the best recruits from the program early, thereby short-circuiting their exposure to different parts of the company and leaving behind only those trainees with less perceived potential.)

The First Six Weeks

All trainees would receive a first-day orientation, conducted by the human resources department, which would introduce them to their benefits and company work rules. About a month after the date they were hired, trainees would receive an in-depth classroom orientation to the organization, its strategic plan, its products, and its customers.

Following orientation but during their first six weeks of employment, they were expected to participate in a "tour" in which they conducted informational interviews with 80 to 100 of the company's 300 exempt employees. While on a tour, supervisory trainees would meet individually with company management representatives to ask questions about their divisions, departments, and work units. (All tours began with a one-on-one discussion with the company's chairman, and that meeting gave trainees the proper impression that they were very important people in the organization.) At the end of the tour, trainees were expected to have completed the preparation of a "tour guide" that described the names, organization charts, work processes, key forms, and other information about each area they had visited. That tour guide became their source of information about who does what in the company and how they do it. (Copies of earlier guides, pre-prared by their predecessors, were available to serve as models.)

The First Year

Although trainees would remain on the payroll of the human resources department until they were finished with their program, they would ro-tate through at least three major operating divisions after their tour. During a four-month rotation, trainees would be guided by a learning contract that described the responsibilities during the rotation, the ex-pected outcomes, and time frames for completion of assignments. At the end of each rotation, trainees would receive a formal training prog-ress report to describe their performance and enumerate future train-ing needs. While on rotation, trainees would report on a daily basis directly to a line (operating) manager.

The company's executives believed that all trainees should per-form useful work, and not just participate in training. This view was in keeping with the company's philosophy that the supervisory trainee program represented a form of boot camp in which trainees would be put through the paces and challenged at every turn so as to build the right work ethic early in their development.

Each trainee was destined to receive different kinds of rotations to build the competencies essential to success in the organization. An *analytical rotation* was designed to give trainees responsibility for meeting the requirements of a troubleshooting assignment, tapping the expertise of experienced workers in the process. A *customer service rotation* was designed to expose trainees directly to the company's customers (insurance policyholders and sales representa-tives). A *presupervisory rotation* was designed to give trainees expo-sure to the actual work duties of a supervisor by making them an understudy or assistant to a top-performing supervisor. Most trainees, it was decided, would begin with an analytical rotation because that helped to acquaint them with the organization. All trainees would eventually participate in a presupervisory rotation, which was deemed the most important, because they were destined to enter a supervisory position upon program completion.

While on rotation, trainees received planned OJT and individual-ized coaching from company supervisors, managers, and executives.[6] Often they were paired with experienced hourly employees or assigned to an experienced, exemplary supervisor. They were expected to perform while learning but also to learn while performing. (However, because they were given coaching or classroom training about what to do before they needed to do it, many managers liked to joke that trainees did not face a sink-or-swim experience because the company had "thrown them a life preserver.") Their learning contract provided written documentation of the training they were to receive and the results they were expected to achieve. In other respects, their rotations were based on "best practices" in company management rotation programs.[7]

One afternoon each week they attended classroom training. The topics varied. Typically, they would hear about a topical issue from someone within the company, an industry representative, a customer, or a vendor. On occasion, they would participate in hands-on exercises in which they were asked to work through critical incidents about supervision that had actually occurred in the organization and were gathered from experienced workers or from their own successful predecessors.

After completing the structured training program, each trainee would become eligible for promotion to supervision. Company managers were not required to select them. Trainees thus competed for promotions with promising hourly employees and experienced supervisors from the industry recruited from outside. Trainees were thus under some pressure to prove themselves throughout the supervisory training program. They understood at the time they were hired that they could be terminated for poor performance during training. (However, company policy required *progressive discipline* to be applied even with trainees in order to ensure that they were given ample opportunities to improve prior to termination.)

Program Results

After three years the supervisory trainee program was hailed as a resounding success by the company's supervisors, managers, and executives. Turnover in the program remained extraordinarily low, and morale among trainees remained exceptionally high. As a final tribute to the program's success, some managers started discussing the possibility of requiring all future supervisors—even those promoted from within or hired from outside with experience—to come from the program. There were even discussions about establishing similar but parallel programs for other job categories, including technical workers, salespersons, and hourly employees.

Reviewing the Case: Guidelines for Establishing And Operating Successful HiPo Programs

What conclusions can be drawn from this case study? Here are a few guidelines for establishing and operating successful HiPo programs:

1. Ensure personal involvement and support of senior managers and those with significant experience.
2. Gear the program to meet perceived organizational succession planning needs.
3. Focus the program on practical work results so that people learn while doing and do while learning.
4. Allow cross-fertilization of talent in the organization.
5. Combine learning techniques. Do not rely on the isolated use of job rotation, classroom training, or other techniques.

Note that a HiPo program can become an important source of future talent for the organization, and can do so in a way that is neither prohibitively expensive nor unproductive.

Use the worksheet in Exhibit E-1 to structure decision making about planning and installing a HiPo program in an organization.

Avoiding Critical Turnover after Downsizing

Economic restructuring and downsizing have profoundly changed the face of workplaces in the United States in recent years. Although some organizations are learning that downsizing must be planned and managed[8]—and that is the good news—"the bad news is that serious, unintended consequences still result from poorly planned and hastily implemented downsizings. Cutbacks in some companies are still managed in ways that attenuate the human costs imposed on those losing their jobs."[9] Although most writing on the subject has focused on those who lost their jobs due to downsizing, less attention has been devoted to the survivors.[10]

Why Downsizing Can Create Problems

However, there is good reason to pay attention to survivors of downsizing because how they react can affect the organization's future profitability, and even its future existence. When a downsizing occurs, work must be reallocated. Someone must begin performing tasks which others once performed. Often that process is not well planned.[11]

Exhibit E-1. A worksheet for planning and installing a HiPo program.

Directions: Use this worksheet to plan and install a HiPo program in your organization.

   Answer each question; then circulate your responses to other managers in the organization for their review and comments. Ask the organization's succession planning coordinator or HR director to compile the results and schedule a meeting to review how to establish and operate a HiPo program.

---

1. How do you define a high-potential employee at the entry level in your organization?

2. Into what job categories is your organization most interested in recruiting HiPos?

3. For what characteristics or competencies should you look to identify a HiPo?

4. Into what job categories should you recruit HiPos?

5. How should you recruit HiPos?

6. How should a rigorous but nondiscriminatory selection process work for HiPos?

(continues)

Exhibit E-1 *(continued).*

---

7. How should HiPos be oriented to your organization?

8. How should HiPos be trained for their first jobs?

9. How should HiPos be developed for advancement?

10. How should HiPos be mentored?

11. How should HiPos be rewarded?

12. How should HiPos be appraised?

13. How should career development activities be carried out for HiPos?

One result is that work is unevenly distributed, with exemplary performers and high potentials given more than their fair share because the organization's leaders are confident that they can handle the additional workload. It does not take long for this differential workload to become apparent: Exemplary performers and high potentials are often the first to notice that they are doing more but are receiving the same rewards as those doing much less. (That was always true, but the difference will tend to be in starker contrast after a downsizing.)

At that point, they may accept the increased workload quietly. Alternatively, they may choose to:

1. Ask their immediate organizational superiors to increase their rewards to match their contributions.
2. Deliberately reduce their efforts to match what other workers, who are not exemplary or high-potential, are doing.
3. Seek a move to another job in the organization where the match between reward and contribution is more equitable.
4. Seek employment outside the organization in an effort to achieve a better match between rewards and contributions.
5. Take all of actions 1 through 4.

If they choose action 4, then critical turnover increases as high potentials gradually find employment in other organizations.

Avoiding the Loss of Exemplary Performers and High Potentials

If leaders are not responsive to the issues described in the previous section, they may stand by and watch with horror as their exemplary workers and high potentials slowly leave the organization. There is already much anecdotal evidence to suggest that is happening—or has happened—in many organizations already.

What can be done to avoid this hemorrhage of key talent from the organization? Here are a few suggestions:

1. Pay attention to planning for workload redistribution before and during the downsizing. Involve workers in this process.

2. Establish, or review and improve, an exit interview program at the time a downsizing is announced. Track the exemplary workers and HiPos who leave. Be sure to find out why they are leaving and what can be done to prevent others from doing so. Feed this information back to decision makers and/or to members of a succession planning committee.

3. Use attitude surveys selectively to take the pulse of the organization and its workers. Act preemptively to address complaints of workers who are feeling the pressure of increased work due to downsizing.[12]

4. Review wage and salary policy immediately, if possible. Take steps to allow reviews when warranted due to work redistribution. (Explore a

pay-for-knowledge program if the organization is genuinely committed to encouraging internal development consistent with systematic succession planning).[13]

If these steps do not hold avoidable turnover down, then make turnover of key talent an agenda item for discussion at future meetings of the organization's succession planning committee. Be sure, too, to alert the CEO and/or board of directors to the problem and involve them in brainstorming ways to solve it.

Building Diversity and Multiculturalism Into Succession Planning

Diversity and multiculturalism are different, albeit related, topics. At present they rank among the hottest topics in management circles. Interest in diversity and multiculturalism has been gaining momentum since the publication of an electrifying report entitled *Workforce 2000* that described the changing workforce in the United States.[14]

What Are Diversity and Multiculturalism?

Diversity means *differences. Managing diversity,* then, means *managing differences.* As workplaces in the United States become more heterogeneous, it becomes increasingly important for organizational members to appreciate, and even celebrate, differences and *not* equate differences with inferiority. Indeed, diversity can lead to increased organizational competitiveness because different perspectives can lead to increased creativity.[15]

Multiculturalism refers to the *ability to work with many cultures.* As the global village shrinks under the influence of media and fast-paced information systems, organizational members find that they must increasingly interact with people from more than one national culture. Understanding of, and appreciation for, different cultures is thus increasingly important in business.

Diversity and *multiculturalism* can be overlapping terms. Both refer to differences. Workplaces in the United States can be characterized by diversity (with people of different races and sexes and from different ethnic backgrounds working together) *and* can also be multicultural (with people of different cultures working together). In most cases, however, managers probably think of "managing diversity" as an exercise in overseeing the work of *people* unlike themselves, while they think of "managing multiculturally" as an exercise in overseeing the work in *places* unlike their own.

Why Is There Interest in Diversity and Multiculturalism?

Among key predictions made by *Workforce 2000* about the changing workplace and workforce in the United States:

- The average age of an American worker will increase from 36 in 1985 to 39 in the year 2000.
- An estimated 25 million new workers will enter the workforce in the United States between 1985 and 2000. Only 15 percent of net new workers will be native white men, 42 percent will be white women, 13 percent will be native nonwhite women, 13 percent will be immigrant men, 9 percent will be immigrant women, and 7 percent will be native nonwhite men.
- Most new jobs in the United States economy (about 90 percent) will be in the service sector; only 8 percent will be in manufacturing.
- By the year 2000, only 27 percent of new jobs will fall into low-skill categories. In comparison, about 40 percent of jobs fall into low-skill categories now.[16]

As a result of these predicted trends, employers are expected to face stiff competition for dwindling numbers of young employees, who make up traditional entry-level talent in most organizations. That may make it more difficult to attract and retain them.

In addition, the groups that are expected to grow in the workforce are those that have been traditionally underutilized: women and immigrants. Since the workforce of tomorrow—and that is also, to some extent, the workforce of today—is changing to include more women, minorities, and immigrants, organization leaders are facing a growing need to show sensitivity to many different perspectives and viewpoints. In recent years, many efforts have been made to build appreciation for diversity and multiculturalism in the workplace.[17]

Succession Planning, Diversity, and Multiculturalism

Organization leaders have the obligation to encourage social justice and responsibility. To that end, they should establish some means by which to increase the awareness of, and sensitivity to, diversity. Moreover, they should equip their future leaders with the ability to compete multiculturally.

- *Diversity and succession planning.* There are at least three ways that diversity and succession planning programs can be integrated.

One way is to take pains to identify high-potential workers from protected labor groups, such as women, minorities, and the disabled. The organization should then ensure that they are given opportunities to participate in high-potential programs. In that way, the organization takes positive steps to accelerate their individual development while giving away nothing except a chance to succeed faster than would otherwise be the case.

A second way is to identify a *talent pool* of high-potential individuals from protected labor groups. Their development can then become a topic of special interest, with the view in mind of helping them qualify for advancement faster than might otherwise be the case. They can also be furnished with mentors or even sponsors from parts of the organization outside their own, in order to provide them with individual coaching and counseling about how best to succeed.

Third and finally, the organization can choose to link any internal diversity program with the succession planning program. In that way, a special quesiton will be focused on in succession planning: How can we increase the diversity and multicultural composition of our workforce at all levels, including successors for key positions? That question can be explored periodically in succession planning meetings and in meetings about diversity.

▪ *Multiculturalism and succession planning.* Perhaps the best way to give future organization leaders the skills they need to help their organizations compete multiculturally is to include at least one international assignment while they are being prepared for the future. Many large organizations do that already.[18]

A particularly good approach is thus to build an international assignment (job rotation) into the individual development plans of high potentials whenever possible. However, the track record with overseas assignments is not a good one. Many companies report failures with them, and they can (if handled improperly) lead to a hemorrhage of high potentials. Here are some tips for making international assignments successful:

1. Involve the family.
2. Provide training on the language and culture of the new country before the assignment begins.
3. Clarify why the assignment is important to the individual.
4. Ensure that lines of communication are kept open between the organization's headquarters and the site where the high-potential is headed.

Be sure to establish an "exit interview" program for all American expatriates who return—or who leave the organization's employ while overseas. It is very important to find out why they leave and to take positive steps to keep that from happening repeatedly.

Adapting Succession Planning to Team Environments

The Total Quality Movement has led to increasing interest in teams as a means by which to increase employee involvement in decision making. The implications of teams for succession planning are significant because teams build cross-functional expertise among employees. Indeed, self-directed teams even increase management expertise by (potentially) giving nonmanagement employees experience in managerial work.

What Is a Team?

A team is a cohesive group of employees who work closely together in pursuit of a common goal. However, teams may be understood in different ways, as described below. A team installation effort is akin to pushing into real-time *quality circles,* which consist of coworker cohorts who meet off the job to focus creative attention on improving the ways they do the work. In teams, workers apply creativity and innovation *while they work.*

Transitioning from Functional to Team Organizations

When a functional (traditional) organization moves to a team environment, it usually progresses through four distinct phases: (1) functional work groups, (2) nominal teams, (3) family teams, and (4) self-directed, or autonomous, teams. These four phases also represent different stages on a continuum from a traditional (function, or nonteam) structure to an autonomous team structure.

1. *Functional work groups* are traditional work groups. Supervisors are responsible for each group. Decision making is from top down; communication flows from top down. Each employee is viewed as an individual contributor. Performance is evaluated individually, and rewards are allocated accordingly.

2. *Nominal teams* exist in name only. Supervisors are given new titles—*team leaders, team facilitators,* or *job coaches*—but their behavior remains unchanged from functional work groups. Decision making continues to flow from top down, as does communication. Employees and their immediate organizational superiors are told to funciton as team members, but they are not sure what that means or what they are expected to do. Typically, team training has not been conducted, though it should begin before or during this step. Without additional effort, such as training, cross-training, incentives, and structural changes to reflect a team environment, nominal teams will not make the transition to the next step.

Either they will revert to functional work groups or the organization will commit appropriate resources to team training and team building, which leads to family teams.

3. *Family teams* are cohesive work groups whose members have received training on teams. They represent a transitional stage between functional (traditional) and self-directed (autonomous) work teams. Members of family teams are committed to the team. They understand the difference between working as a solitary contributor and working as a team member. The organization has shored up the team environment by introducing changes to job descriptions, creating incentives for team contributions, increasing cross-training, and making structural changes to reflect teams. Supervisors have become true team leaders and have thus become more facilitative and less directive; decision making and communication flow about equally from top down and from bottom up.

4. *Self-directed, or autonomous, teams* are highly cohesive work groups operating without a resident superior. Team members have been cross-trained on work duties and have also been trained on team-based management and team skills. At this point, the team members split up and assume the duties that their supervisor once handled, such as taking attendance, passing out pay stubs, walking around to monitor operations, conducting selection interviews, conducting disciplinary interviews, and appraising employee performance. To perform these duties successfully, and to avoid any miscues that might also place the organization in legal jeopardy, team members will usually require leadership training. Decision making and communication flow from bottom up; employees are empowered to make decisions and are involved in solving problems affecting them.

In addition to the four work groups just mentioned, there are *ad hoc,* or *temporary, teams,* which are formed when a unique problem demands special expertise. Many organizations have met with success by pooling employees from different work groups for extended time spans to solve a problem requiring cross-functional or cross-departmental knowledge. When used effectively, this approach becomes a setting for action learning.

Teams and Succession Planning

On first appearance it might seem that teams, particularly self-directed teams, would decrease the need for systematic succession planning. After all, teams can function as *talent pools* in which many individuals have been cross-trained on different jobs. (Indeed, increasing individual capability is a major advantage of teams.) Moreover, as team members in self-directed teams absorb supervisory duties, thereby eliminating supervisory positions, the absolute numbers of key positions are reduced as supervisory and management duties are reallocated across team members.

Often the introduction of teams can lead to a decrease in the need for simple replacement planning in the supervisory ranks. However, it actually results in an increase in the need to conduct supervisory training, since many workers enter the potential talent pool for advancement to middle management. That can make eventual advancement to middle management more difficult, and more daunting, for individuals. Further, the leadership knowledge, skills, and attitudes required of middle managers—and executives—should change dramatically in a team environment. Instead of directing supervisors, middle managers and executives must master the new skills of inspiring, leading by example, questioning, and coaching.

Planning Succession in Teams

Use the worksheet in Exhibit E-2 to structure your thinking about planning for succession in a team environment.

Three Predictions about the Future of Succession Planning

Allow me to conclude this book with three predictions about the future of succession planning. In my opinion, that future is not difficult to foretell, assuming that current trends unfold as expected.

I. *Succession planning will become the focus of greater attention.* As a result of widespread downsizing and other economic restructuring efforts during the 1990s, strategists will discover that their organizations are weak in bench strength. Middle management, the traditional training ground for top management, has been cut back dramatically; supervision, the traditional training ground for middle management, has been reduced as a result of employee involvement programs, Total Quality Management efforts, and team installations. Where will the future leaders of organizations come from? The answer to that question is not at all apparent unless organizations take the step of installing effective succession planning.

II. *Succession planning software will become more sophisticated, easier to use, and less costly.* Even small organizations will find that the price is right and that the technology is growing more user friendly. That will prompt greater interest in, and sophistication about, succession planning as users acquire that software and learn about the issues underlying it.

III. *Succession planning will move beyond single organizations and will increasingly include innovative alternatives.* Succession planning will move

Exhibit E-2. A worksheet for planning succession in a team environment.

Directions: Use this worksheet to consider how to conduct succession planning in a team environment.

   In the left column, list *all* work activities performed by team members (think of it as a "team job description," if you wish). In the right column, list the names of all team members (adding paper as necessary). Then, place an **X** below the name of each individual opposite the team activities on which he or she has been trained or has demonstrated acceptable performance. Use the worksheet to identify gaps in the team in which one or more people need to be cross-trained to serve as possible successors or backups to carry out the activity. (If you wish, carry out a similar activity on a different worksheet to indicate individual potential.)

Work Activities Performed by Team Members	*Names of Individual Team Members*
1.	
2.	
3.	
4.	
5.	

beyond the fill-in-the-box approach to replacement. Decision makers will be increasingly willing to seek innovative approaches to meet succession needs. Among other approaches, succession planning coordinators will thus be increasingly likely to:

- Use executive recruiters.
- Use national resumé databases to uncover specialized talent.
- Increase the use of college internship programs and special summer employment programs to try out possible high potentials before extending offers for longer-term emplyment.
- Use contractual assistance, looking upon the contractors as possible high potentials.
- Share information about employee expertise with other organizations to identify the most qualified candidates for advancement to a dwindling number of key positions.

Summary

The shape of the succession planning program is affected by changing external environmental conditions and by the ways that the organization chooses to react to them. In this Epilogue, I focused on how to accelerate the development of high potentials through special HiPo programs, avoid the loss of high potentials due to downsizing, build appreciation for diversity and multiculturalism into succession planning, and adapt succession planning to team environments. I concluded the chapter with three predictions about the future of succession planning.

Notes

Preface

1. Warren Bennis and Burt Nanus, *Leaders: The Strategies for Taking Charge* (New York: Harper & Row, 1985), p. 2.
2. "Turnover at the Top," *Business Week*, December 19, 1983, p. 104.
3. Lynda C. McDermott, *Caught in the Middle: How to Survive and Thrive in Today's Management Squeeze* (Englewood Cliffs, N.J.: Prentice-Hall, 1992).
4. As quoted in Michael J. Kami, *Trigger Points: How to Make Decisions Three Times Faster, Innovate Smarter, and Beat Your Competition by Ten Percent (It Ain't Easy)* (New York: McGraw-Hill, 1988), p. 134.
5. Arthur Deegan, *Succession Planning: Key to Corporate Excellence* (New York: Wiley-Interscience, 1986), p. 5.
6. As quoted in Harper W. Moulton and Arthur A. Fickel, *Executive Development: Preparing for the 21st Century* (New York: Oxford University Press, 1993), p. 29.
7. E. Zajac, "CEO Selection, Succession, Compensation and Firm Performance: A Theoretical Integration and Empirical Analysis," *Strategic Management Journal* 11:3 (1990), p. 228.
8. R. Sahl, "Succession Planning Drives Plant Turnaround," *Personnel Journal* 71:9 (1992), pp. 67–70.
9. "Long-Term Business Success Can Hinge on Succession Planning," *Training Directors' Forum Newsletter* 5:4 (1989), p. 1.
10. See the description of these results reported in James F. Bolt, *Executive Development: A Strategy for Corporate Competitiveness* (New York: Harper & Row 1989), p. 18. The survey was conducted by A. Elliott Carlisle and Kent Carter, and the results were published in the March-April 1988 issue of *Business Horizons*.
11. Oliver Esman, "Succession Planning in Small and Medium-Sized Companies," *HR Horizons, 103* (1991), pp. 15–19; Barton C. Francis, "Family Business Succession Planning," *Journal of Accountancy* 176:2 (1993), pp. 49–51; T. Roger Peay and W. Gibb Dyer, Jr., "Power Orientations of Entrepreneurs and Succession Planning," *Journal of Small*

Business Management 27:1 (1989), pp. 47–52; and Michael J. Sales, "Succession Planning in the Family Business," *Small Business Reports* 15:2 (1990), pp. 31–40.

12. William J. Rothwell and H. C. Kazanas, *The Complete AMA Guide to Management Development: Training, Education, Development* (New York: AMACOM, 1993).

Chapter 1

1. Henri Fayol, *Administration Industrielle et Generale* (Paris: Societe de l'Industrie Minerale, 1916).

2. Norman H. Carter, "Guaranteeing Management's Future Through Succession Planning," *Journal of Information Systems Management* 3:3 (1986), pp. 13–14. Reprinted with permission from Journal of Information Systems Management (New York: Auerbach Publications), © 1986 Warren Gorham Lamont.

3. Richard Hansen and Richard H. Wexler, "Effective Succession Planning," *Employment Relations Today* 15:1 (1989), p. 19.

4. See Chris Argyris and Donald Schon, *Organizational Learning: A Theory of Action Perspective* (Reading, Mass.: Addison-Wesley, 1978); Peter Senge, *The Fifth Discipline: The Art and Practice of the Learning Organization* (New York: Doubleday/Currency, 1990).

5. Walter R. Mahler and Stephen J. Drotter, *The Succession Planning Handbook for the Chief Executive* (Midland Park, N.J.: Mahler Publishing, 1986), p. 1.

6. "Long-Term Business Success Can Hinge on Succession Planning," *Training Directors' Forum Newsletter* 5:4 (1989), p. 1.

7. Wilbur Moore, *The Conduct of the Corporation* (New York: Random House, 1962), p. 109.

8. Rosabeth Moss Kanter, *The Men and Women of the Corporation* (New York: Basic Books, 1977), p. 48.

9. Norman H. Carter, "Guaranteeing Management's Future Through Succession Planning," *Journal of Information Systems Management* 3:3 (1986), pp. 13–14.

10. Thomas Gilmore, *Making a Leadership Change: How Organizations and Leaders Can Handle Leadership Transitions Successfully* (San Francisco: Jossey-Bass, 1988), p. 19.

11. William J. Rothwell and H. C. Kazanas, *Human Resource Development: A Strategic Approach*, rev. ed. (Amherst, Mass.: Human Resource Development Press, 1994), p. 48.

12. Lynda Gratton and Michel Syrett, "Heirs Apparent: Succession Strategies for the Future," *Personnel Management* 22:1 (1990), p. 34.

13. A. Walker, "The Newest Job in Personnel: Human Resource Data Administrator," *Personnel Journal* 61:12 (1982), p. 5.

14. William J. Rothwell and H. C. Kazanas, *Planning and Managing Hu-*

man Resources: Strategic Planning for Personnel Management, rev. ed. (Amherst, Mass.: Human Resource Development Press, 1994).

15. Andrew O. Manzini and John D. Gridley, *Integrating Human Resources and Strategic Business Planning* (New York: AMACOM, 1986), p. 3.

16. Patricia McLagan, *The Models* (Alexandria, Va.: American Society for Training and Development, 1989), p. 7.

17. Rothwell and Kazanas, *Human Resource Development,* p. 16.

18. Meg Kerr, *Succession Planning in America's Corporations* (Palatine, Ill.: Anthony J. Fresina and Associates and Executive Knowledgeworks, 1987).

19. "The Numbers Game," *Time* 142:21 (1993), pp. 14–15.

20. Ibid.

21. Ibid.

22. Ibid.

23. Ann Morrison, *The New Leaders: Guidelines on Leadership Diversity in America* (San Francisco: Jossey-Bass, 1992), p. 1.

24. Ibid., p. 7.

25. Thomas Gilmore, *Making a Leadership Change: How Organizations and Leaders Can Handle Leadership Transitions Successfully* (San Francisco: Jossey-Bass, 1988), p. 10.

26. Arthur Sherman, George Bohlander, and Herbert Chruden, *Managing Human Resources,* 8th ed. (Cincinnati: South-Western Publishing Co., 1988), p. 226.

27. Warren Boroson and Linda Burgess, "Survivors' Syndrome," *Across the Board* 29:11 (1992), pp. 41–45.

28. Morrison, *The New Leaders,* p. 1.

29. M. Haire, "Approach to an Integrated Personnel Policy," *Industrial Relations* (1968), pp. 107–117.

30. Joan C. Szabo, "Finding the Right Workers," *Nation's Business* 79:2 (1991), p. 22.

31. D. Brown, "Race for the Corporate Throne," *Management Review* 78:11 (1989), pp. 26–27.

32. Lester Bittel and John Newstrom, *What Every Supervisor Should Know,* 6th ed. (New York: McGraw-Hill, 1990), p. 7.

33. Michelle Martinez, "Glass Walls Must Tumble Before Ceiling Breaks," *HR News* 11:4 (1992), p. A3.

34. Allen Kraut, Patricia Pedigo, Douglas McKenna, and Marvin Dunnette, "The Role of the Manager: What's Really Important in Different Management Jobs," *Academy of Management Executive* 3:4 (1989), p. 287.

35. J. Stuller, "Why Not 'Inplacement?'" *Training* 30:6 (1993), pp. 37–44.

36. William J. Rothwell, H. C. Kazanas, and Darla Haines, "Issues and Practices in Management Job Rotation Programs as Perceived by HRD Professionals," *Performance Improvement Quarterly* 5:1 (1992), pp. 49–69.

37. M. Lombardo and R. Eichinger, *Eighty-Eight Assignments for Development in Place: Enhancing the Developmental Challenge of Existing Jobs* (Greensboro, N.C.: The Center for Creative Leadership, 1989).

38. For a complete bibliography related to innovative career planning issues, see Paul M. Connolly, *Promotional Practices and Policies: Career Building in the '80s* (Highlights of the literature #41) (New York: Pergamon Press, 1985). While dated, it still provides an excellent overview of career planning issues.

39. See, for instance, William J. Rothwell, "Ten Strategies for Rethinking How Work Is Performed After Downsizing," *Performance and Instruction,* January 1993, pp. 1–4.

40. "Talent Pool In, Succession Plan Out," *HR Reporter* 9:10 (1992), pp. 3–6.

41. Matt Hennecke, "Toward the Change-Sensitive Organization," *Training* (May 1991), p. 58.

42. D. Ancona and D. Nadler, "Top Hats and Executive Tales: Designing the Senior Team," *Sloan Management Review* 3:1 (1989), pp. 19–28.

43. Richard Beckhard and Wendy Pritchard, *Changing the Essence: The Art of Creating and Leading Fundamental Change in Organizations* (San Francisco: Jossey-Bass, 1992); Warren Bennis, *Why Leaders Can't Lead* (San Francisco: Jossey-Bass, 1989); J. A. Conger, "The Dark Side of Leadership," *Organizational Dynamics* 19:2 (1990), pp. 44–55; Christopher Conte, "Leaders Are Born, But Many Companies Believe They Can Be Nurtured, Too," *The Wall Street Journal* (May 21, 1991), A1, col. 5; Ray J. Friant, "Leadership Training for Long-Term Results," *Management Review* 80:7 (1991), pp. 50–53; James G. Hunt, *Leadership: A New Synthesis* (Newbury Park, Calif: Sage, 1991); Jerry King, "Learning to Lead," *Personnel Management* 22:9 (1990), pp. 65–67; Peter Koestenbaum, *Leadership: The Inner Side of Greatness* (San Francisco: Jossey-Bass, 1991); John P. Kotter, *A Force for Change: How Leadership Differs from Management* (New York: Free Press, 1991); James M. Kouzes and Barry Z. Posner, *The Leadership Challenge* (San Francisco: Jossey-Bass, 1987); C. C. Many and H. P. Sims, Jr., "SuperLeadership: Beyond the Myth of Heroic Leadership," *Organizational Dynamics* 19:4 (1991), pp. 18–35; Peter Senge, "The Leader's New Work: Building Learning Organizations," *Sloan Management Review* 32:1 (1990), pp. 7–23; Benjamin Tregoe and Peter M. Tobia, "Greening Tomorrow's Leaders," *Across the Board* 28:10 (1991), pp. 12–14; Marshall Whitmire and Phillip R. Nienstedt, "Lead Leaders into the 90s," *Personnel Journal* 70:5 (1991), pp. 80–85.

Chapter 2

1. This paragraph is based on information in C. Derr, C. Jones, and E. Toomey, "Managing High-Potential Employees: Current Practices in

Thirty-Three U.S. Corporations," *Human Resource Management* 27:3 (1988), p. 278.

2. See S. Cunningham, "Coaching Today's Executive," *Public Utilities Fortnightly,* 128:2 (1991), pp. 22–25; Steven J. Stowell and Matt Starcevich, *The Coach: Creating Partnerships for a Competitive Edge* (Salt Lake City, Utah: Center for Management and Organization Effectiveness, 1987).

3. Charles E. Watson, *Management Development Through Training* (Reading, Mass.: Addison-Wesley, 1979).

4. Manuel London and Stephen A. Stumpf, *Managing Careers* (Reading, Mass.: Addison-Wesley, 1982), p. 274.

5. James E. McElwain, "Succession Plans Designed to Manage Change," *HR Magazine* 36:2 (1991), p. 67.

6. James Fraze, "Succession Planning Should Be a Priority for HR Professionals," *Resource,* June 1988, p. 4.

7. William J. Rothwell and H. C. Kazanas, *The Complete AMA Guide to Management Development: Training, Education, Development* (New York: AMACOM, 1993).

8. Fraze, "Succession Planning," p. 4.

9. Ibid.

10. Thomas North Gilmore, *Making a Leadership Change: How Organizations Can Handle Leadership Transitions Successfully* (San Francisco: Jossey-Bass, 1988), p. 10.

11. Fraze, "Succession Planning," p. 4.

12. David W. Rhodes, "Succession Planning—Overweight and Underperforming," *Journal of Business Strategy* 9:6 (1988), p. 62.

13. Ibid.

14. "AME Survey Identifies Priority Issues" *Industry Week,* 242:2 (1993), p. 26.

15. From William J. Rothwell and H. C. Kazanas, "Developing Management Employees to Cope with the Moving Target Effect," *Performance and Instruction* 32:8 (1993), pp. 1–5.

16. Ruy A. Teixeira and Lawrence Mishel, "Whose Skills Shortage— Workers or Management?" *Issues in Science and Technology* Summer 1993, p. 71.

17. Joe Pasqualetto, "New Competencies Define the HRIS Manager's Future Role," *Personnel Journal,* January 1993, p. 91.

18. Jeffrey E. Myers, "Downsizing Blues: How to Keep Up Morale," *Management Review* 82:4 (1993), p. 28.

19. Charlene Marmer Solomon, "The Loyalty Factor," *Personnel Journal,* September 1992, p. 54.

20. Ibid.

21. Randall S. Schuler, "Scanning the Environment: Planning for Human Resource Management and Organizational Change," *Human Resource Planning* 12:4 (1992), p. 258.

22. Ibid., p. 259.

23. See A. Morrison, *The New Leaders: Guidelines on Leadership Diversity in America* (San Francisco: Jossey-Bass, 1992), and A. Morrison, R. White, E. Van Velsor, and the Center for Creative Leadership, *Breaking the Glass Ceiling: Can Women Reach the Top of America's Largest Corporations?* (Reading, Mass.: Addison-Wesley, 1987).

24. Rose Mary Wentling, "Women in Middle Management: Their Career Development and Aspirations," *Business Horizons,* January-February 1992, p. 47.

25. Schuler, "Scanning the Environment," p. 260.

26. Ibid.

27. Peter F. Drucker, *The New Realities: In Government and Politics/In Economics and Business/In Society and World View* (New York: Harper & Row, 1989), p. 116.

28. Matt Hennecke, "Toward the Change-Sensitive Organization," *Training,* May 1991, p. 58.

Chapter 3

1. Jac Fitz-Enz, *How to Measure Human Resources Management* (New York: McGraw-Hill, 1984), p. 48.

2. Ibid.

3. Particularly good articles on this topic include: Paul Brauchle, "Costing Out the Value of Training" *Technical and Skills Training* 3:4 (1992), pp. 35–40; J. Hassett, "Simplifying ROI," *Training,* September 1992; J. Phillips, "Measuring the Return on HRD," *Employment Relations Today,* August 1991.

4. For example, see especially C. Derr, C. Jones, and E. Toomey, "Managing High-Potential Employees: Current Practices in Thirty-Three U.S. Corporations," *Human Resource Management* 27:3 (1988), pp. 273–290; O. Esman, "Succession Planning in Small and Medium-Sized Corporations," *HR Horizons* 91:103 (1991), pp. 15–19; *The Identification and Development of High Potential Managers* (Palatine, Ill.: Executive Knowledgeworks, 1987); Meg Kerr, *Succession Planning in America's Corporations* (Palatine, Ill.: Anthony J. Fresina and Associates and Executive Knowledgeworks, 1987); and E. Zajac, "CEO Selection, Succession, Compensation and Firm Performance: A Theoretical Integration and Empirical Analysis," *Strategic Management Journal* 11:3 (1990), pp. 217–230.

5. P. Linkow, "HRD at the Roots of Corporate Strategy," *Training and Development Journal* 39:5 (1985), pp. 85–87.

6. Karen A. Golden and Vasudevan Ramanujam, "Between a Dream and a Nightmare: On the Integration of the Human Resource Management and Strategic Business Planning Processes," *Human Resource Management* 24:4 (1985), p. 429.

7. William J. Rothwell and H. C. Kazanas, *Human Resource Development:*

A Strategic Approach, rev. ed. (Amherst, Mass.: Human Resource Development Press, 1994).

8. For research evidence, see William J. Rothwell and H. C. Kazanas, "Training: Key to Strategic Management," *Performance Improvement Quarterly* 3:1 (1990), pp. 42–56.

9. Robert C. Camp, *Benchmarking: The Search for Industry Best Practices That Lead to Superior Performance* (Milwaukee: Quality Press/American Society for Quality Control; White Plains, N.Y.: Quality Resources, 1989), p. 3. See also Michael J. Spendolini, *The Benchmarking Book* (New York: AMACOM, 1992).

10. Camp, *Benchmarking,* p. 17.

11. Burn Nanus, *Visionary Leadership: Creating a Compelling Sense of Direction for Your Organization* (San Francisco: Jossey-Bass, 1992).

12. Dave Francis and Mike Woodcock, *Unblocking Organizational Values* (Glenview, Ill.: Scott, Foresman, 1990), p. vii.

13. Diane Dormant, "The ABCDs of Managing Change," in M. Smith, ed., *Introduction to Performance Technology* (Washington, D.C.: National Society for Performance and Instruction, 1986), pp. 238–256, 239.

14. Ibid., p. 241.

15. Meg Kerr, *Succession Planning,* p. 53.

Chapter 4

1. James L. Gibson, John M. Ivancevich and James H. Donnelly, Jr., *Organizations: Behavior, Structure, Processes,* 5th ed. (Plano, Tex.: Business Publications, 1985), p. 280.

2. Walter R. Mahler and Stephen J. Drotter, *The Succession Planning Handbook for the Chief Executive.* (Midland Park, N.J.: Mahler Publishing, 1986), p. 8.

3. Meg Kerr, *Succession Planning in America's Corporations* (Palatine, Ill.: Anthony J. Fresina and Associates and Executive Knowledgeworks, 1987), p. 11.

4. "Choosing Your Successor," *Chief Executive Magazine,* May-June 1988, pp. 48–63; Jeffrey Sonnenfeld, *The Hero's Farewell: What Happens When CEOs Retire* (New York: Oxford University Press, 1988); Richard F. Vancil, *Passing the Baton: Managing the Process of CEO Succession* (Boston: Harvard Business School Press, 1987); E. Zajac, "CEO Selection, Succession, Compensation and Firm Performance: A Theoretical Integration and Empirical Analysis," *Strategic Management Journal* 11:3 (1990), pp. 217–230.

5. Joan C. Szabo, "Finding the Right Workers," *Nation's Business* 79:2 (1991), pp. 16–22.

Chapter 5

1. Allen Kraut, Patricia Pedigo, Douglas McKenna and Marvin Dunnette, "The Role of the Manager: What's Really Important in Dif-

ferent Management Jobs," *Academy of Management Executive* 3:4 (1989), p. 287.

2. See, for instance, R. Smither, "The Return of the Authoritarian Manager," *Training* 28:11 (1991), pp. 40–44.

Chapter 6

1. M. Pastin, "The Fallacy of Long-Range Thinking," *Training,* 23:5 (1986), pp. 47–53.

2. B. Staw, "Knee-Deep in the Big Muddy," *Organizational Behavior and Human Performance* 16:1 (1976), pp. 27–44.

3. Karen Stephenson and Valdis Krebs, "A More Accurate Way to Measure Diversity," *Personnel Journal* 72:10 (1993), pp. 66–72, 74.

4. Wilbur Moore, *The Conduct of the Corporation* (New York: Random House, 1962), p. 109.

5. Glenn E. Baker, A. Grubbs, and Thomas Ahern, "Triangulation: Strengthening Your Best Guess," *Performance Improvement Quarterly* 3:3 (1990), pp. 27–35.

6. Arthur W. Sherman, Jr., George W. Bohlander, and Herbert Chruden, *Managing Human Resources,* 8th ed. (Cincinnati: South-Western Publishing, 1988), pp. 95–96.

7. For one excellent approach, see Roger J. Plachy and Sandra J. Plachy, *Results-Oriented Job Descriptions* (New York: AMACOM, 1993).

8. W. Barlow and E. Hane, "A Practical Guide to the Americans with Disabilities Act," *Personnel Journal* 71:6 (1992), p. 54.

9. Kenneth E. Carlisle, *Analyzing Jobs and Tasks* (Englewood Cliffs, N.J.: Educational Technology Publications, 1986), p. 5.

10. For writings on the Americans with Disabilities Act, see W. Barlow and E. Hane, "A Practical Guide to the Americans with Disabilities Act," *Personnel Journal* 71:6 (1992), pp. 53–60; M. Chalker, "Tooling Up for ADA," *HRMagazine* (December 1991), pp. 61–63; 65; and J. Kohl and P. Greenlaw, "The Americans with Disabilities Act of 1990: Implications for Managers," *Sloan Management Review* 33:3 (1992), pp. 87–90. For information about management job descriptions, see, for instance, Max Wortman, Jr., and JoAnn Sperling, *Defining The Manager's Job,* 2nd ed. (New York: AMACOM, 1975).

11. William J. Rothwell, "HRD and the Americans with Disabilities Act," *Training and Development* 45:8 (1991), pp. 45–47.

12. Richard Boyatzis, *The Competent Manager: A Model for Effective Performance* (New York: Wiley 1982).

13. David Dubois, *Competency-Based Performance Improvement: A Strategy for Organizational Change* (Amherst, Mass.: Human Resource Development Press, 1993), p. 9.

14. See, for instance, David McClelland, "Testing for Competence Rather Than for "Intelligence," *American Psychologist,* 28:1 (1973), pp. 1–14;

David McClelland, *A Guide to Job Competency Assessment* (Boston: McBer and Co., 1976).

15. J. Wanous, *Organizational Entry: Recruitment, Selection, and Socialization of Newcomers* (Reading, Mass.: Addison-Wesley, 1980).

16. See, for instance, D. Feldman, "A Practical Program for Employee Socialization," *Organizational Dynamics,* Autumn 1976, pp. 64–80; Feldman, "The Multiple Socialization of Organization Members," *Academy of Management Review,* June 1983, pp. 258–272; Feldman and J. Brett, "Coping with New Jobs: A Comparative Study of New Hires and Job Changes," *Academy of Management Journal,* June 1983, pp. 258–272.

17. Ron Zemke, "Job Competencies: Can They Help You Design Better Training?" *Training* 19:5 (1982), p. 28.

18. Other excellent treatments of the subject may be found in Richard E. Boyatzis, *The Competent Manager: A Model for Effective Performance* (New York: Wiley, 1982); Lyle M. Spencer, Jr., and Signe M. Spencer, *Competence at Work: Models for Superior Performance* (New York: Wiley, 1993); Paul Sandwith, "A Hierarchy of Management Training Requirements: The Competency Domain Model," *Public Personnel Management* 22:1 (1993), pp. 43–62.

19. R. Norton, *DACUM Handbook* (Columbus, Ohio: The National Center for Research in Vocational Education, Ohio State University, 1985). See also D. Faber, E. Fangman, and J. Low, "DACUM: A Collaborative Tool for Workforce Development," *Journal of Studies in Technical Careers* 13:2 (1991), pp. 145–159.

20. Norton, *DACUM Handbook,* pp. 1–2.

21. See A. Osborn, *Applied Imagination,* 3rd ed. (New York: Scribner, 1963), and A. Van Gundy, *Techniques of Structured Problem Solving* (New York: Van Nostrand Reinhold, 1981).

22. Van Gundy, *Structured Problem Solving.*

23. See, for example, Gary McLean, Susan R. Damme, and Richard A. Swanson, eds., *Performance Approaisal: Perspectives on a Quality Management Approach* (Alexandria, Va.: American Society for Training and Development, 1990); Richard Martell and Mae R. Borg, "A Comparison of the Behavioral Rating Accuracy of Groups and Individual," *Journal of Applied Psychology* 78:1 (1993), pp. 43–50; Linda Thornburg, "How Do You Cut the Cake?" *HRMagazine* 37:10 (1992), pp. 66–72; Dave Zielinski, "Outdated Performance Appraisals Drag Down Quality Efforts," *Total Quality Newsletter* 4:4 (1993), pp. 1–3.

24. See, for instance, *Performance Appraisals: The Ongoing Legal Nightmare* (Ramsey, N.J.: Alexander Hamilton Institute, 1993).

25. Mary Walton, *The Deming Management Method* (New York: Perigee Books, 1986), p. 91.

26. See, for instance, S. Cunningham, "Coaching Today's Executive," *Public Utilities Fortnightly* 128:2 (1991), pp. 22–25; Steven J. Stowell and Matt Starcevich, *The Coach: Creating Partnerships for a Competitive*

Edge (Salt Lake City: Center for Management and Organization Effectiveness, 1987).

27. *BLR Encyclopedia of Performance Appraisal* (Madison, Conn.: Business and Legal Reports, 1985).

28. For assistance in conceptualizing a skill inventory and/or a record-keeping system for that purpose, see D. Gould, *Personnel Skills Inventory Skill Study* (Madison, Conn.: Business and Legal Reports, 1986).

Chapter 7

1. See William J. Rothwell and H. C. Kazanas, *Planning and Managing Human Resources: Strategic Planning for Personnel Management*, rev. ed. (Amherst, Mass.: Human Resource Development Press, 1994).

2. William J. Rothwell and H. C. Kazanas, "Developing Management Employees to Cope with the Moving Target Effect," *Performance and Instruction* 32:8 (1993), pp. 1–5.

3. See, for instance, Newman S. Peery, Jr., and Mahmoud Salem, "Strategic Management of Emerging Human Resource Issues," *Human Resource Development Quarterly* 4:1 (1993), pp. 81–95, and Raynold A. Svenson and Monica J. Rinderer, *The Training and Development Strategic Plan Workbook* (Englewood Cliffs, N.J.: Prentice-Hall, 1992). For works specifically on environmental scanning, see F. Aguilar, *Scanning the Business Environment* (New York: Macmillan, 1967); Patrick Callan, ed., *Environmental Scanning for Strategic Leadership* (San Francisco: Jossey-Bass, 1986); Gerald Celente, *Trend Tracking: The System to Profit from Today's Trends* (New York: Times Warner, 1990); L. Fahey, W. King, and V. Narayanan, "Environmental Scanning and Forecasting in Strategic Planning—The State of the Art," *Long Range Planning*, 14:1 (1981), pp. 32–39; R. Heath and Associates, *Strategic Issues Management: How Organizations Influence and Respond to Public Interests and Policies* (San Francisco: Jossey-Bass, 1988).

4. Harry Levinson, *Organizational Diagnosis* (Cambridge, Mass.: Harvard University Press, 1972); A. O. Manzini, *Organizational Diagnosis* (New York: AMACOM, 1988); Marvin Weisbord, *Organizational Diagnosis: A Workbook of Theory and Practice* (Reading, Mass.: Addison-Wesley, 1978).

5. This is an issue of classic debate: Does structure affect strategy or does strategy affect structure? The first discussion appears in A. Chandler, *Strategy and Structure: Chapters in the History of American Industrial Enterprise* (Cambridge, Mass.: Massachusetts Institute of Technology, 1962). Other authors are not sure that strategy always affects structure. See, for instance, J. Galbraith and D. Nathanson, "The Role of Organizational Structure and Process in Strategy Implementation," in D. Schendel and C. Hofer, Eds., *Strategic Management* (Boston: Little, Brown and Co., 1979).

6. See William J. Rothwell and H. C. Kazanas, *Human Resource Development: A Strategic Approach,* rev. ed. (Amherst, Mass.: Human Resource Development Press, 1994).

7. See, for instance, J. Wissema, A. Brand, and H. Van Der Pol, "The Incorporation of Management Development in Strategic Management," *Strategic Management Journal* 2 (1981), pp. 361–377.

8. See remarks in Larry Davis and E. McCallon, *Planning, Conducting, Evaluating Workshops* (Austin, Tex.: Learning Concepts, 1974).

9. William J. Rothwell and H. C. Kazanas, "Developing Management Employees to Cope with the Moving Target Effect," *Performance and Instruction,* 32:8 (1993), pp. 1–5.

10. Melvin Sorcher, *Predicting Executive Success: What It Takes to Make It Into Senior Management* (New York: Wiley, 1985), p. 2.

11. William J. Rothwell and H. C. Kazanas, *The Complete AMA Guide to Management Development: Training, Education, Development* (New York: AMACOM, 1993).

12. Ibid.

13. E. Lindsey, V. Homes, and M. McCall, *Key Events in Executives' Lives* (Greensboro, N.C.: The Center for Creative Leadership, 1987).

14. A similar approach is described at length in George S. Odiorne, *Strategic Management of Human Resources: A Portfolio Approach* (San Francisco: Jossey-Bass, 1984).

15. Rose Mary Wentling, "Women in Middle Management: Their Career Development and Aspirations," *Business Horizons,* January-February 1992, pp. 47–54.

16. Debra Cohen, "360 Degree Feedback Offers Varied Ways to Create Feedback Surveys," *HRMagazine* 38:11 (1993), pp. 32–38; Marvin Dunnette, "My Hammer or Your Hammer," *Human Resource Management* 32:2/3 (1993), pp. 373–384; Joy Fisher Hazucha, Sarah A. Hezlett, and Robert J. Schneider, "The Impact of 360-Degree Feedback on Management Skills Development," *Human Resource Management* 32:2/3 (1993), pp. 325–351; Robert E. Kaplan, "360-Degree Feedback PLUS: Boosting the Power of Co-worker Ratings for Executives," *Human Resource Management* 32:2/3 (1993), pp. 299–314; Manuel London and Richard W. Beatty, "360-Degree Feedback as a Competitive Advantage," *Human Resource Management* 32:2/3 (1993), pp. 353–372; Joel Moses, George P. Hollenbeck, and Melvin Sorcher, "Other People's Expectations," *Human Resource Management* 32:2/3 (1993), pp. 283–297; Dianne Nilsen and David P. Campbell, "Self-Observer Rating Discrepancies: Once an Overrater, Always an Overrater?" *Human Resource Management* 32:2/3 (1993), pp. 265–281; Kenneth M. Nowack, "360 Degree Feedback: The Whole Story," *Training and Development* 47:1 (1993), pp. 69–72; Catherine Romano, "Fear of Feedback," *Management Review* 82:12 (1993), pp. 38–41.

Chapter 8

1. Walter R. Mahler and Stephen J. Drotter, *The Succession Planning Handbook for the Chief Executive* (Midland Park, N.J.: Mahler Publishing, 1986).

2. Peter F. Drucker, "How to Make People Decisions," *Harvard Business Review* 63:4 (1985), pp. 22–26.

3. Stephen L. Mangum, "Recruitment and Job Search: The Recruitment Tactics of Employers," *Personnel Administrator* 27:6 (1982), pp. 90–102.

4. Lawrence S. Kleiman and Kimberly J. Clark, "User's Satisfaction with Job Posting," *Personnel Administrator* 29:9 (1984), pp. 104–108.

5. Lawrence S. Kleiman and Kimberly J. Clark, "An Effective Job Posting System," *Personnel Journal* 63:2 (1984), pp. 20–25.

6. Malcolm Knowles, *Using Learning Contracts: Practical Approaches to Individualizing and Structuring Learning* (San Francisco: Jossey-Bass, 1986), pp. 28–32.

7. R. Fritz, *Personal Performance Contracts: The Key to Job Success* (Los Altos, Calif.: Crisp, 1987).

8. Arthur X. Deegan II, *Succession Planning: Key to Corporate Excellence* (New York: Wiley-Interscience, 1986), p. 167.

9. Robert F. Mager, *Preparing Instructional Objectives*, 2nd ed. (Belmont, Calif.: Lear-Siegler, 1975).

10. M. Lombardo and R. Eichinger, *Eighty-Eight Assignments for Development in Place: Enhancing the Developmental Challenge of Existing Jobs* (Greensboro, N.C.: The Center for Creative Leadership, 1989).

11. A. Huczynski, *Encyclopedia of Management Development Methods* (London: Gower, 1983).

12. Gregory Chowanec, Charles Newstrom, and RHR International Company, "The Strategic Management of International Human Resources," *Business Quarterly* 56:1 (1991), pp. 65–70.

13. Merrick L. Jones, "Action Learning as a New Idea," *Journal of Management Development* 9:5 (1990), pp. 29–34; Victoria Marsick, "Experience-Based Learning: Executive Learning Outside the Classroon," *Journal of Management Development* 9:4 (1990), pp. 50–60; Hugh McLaughlin and Richard Thorpe, "Action Learning—A Paradigm in Emergence: The Problems Facing a Challenge to Traditional Management Education and Development," *British Journal of Management* 4 (1993), pp. 19–27; Alan Mumford, "Learning in Action," *Personnel Management* 23:7 (1991), pp. 34–37; Mike Pedler, ed., *Action Learning in Practice* (Aldershot, Hants, England: Gower, 1983); Reginald Revans, "Action Learning: Its Origins and Nature," in Mike Pedler, *Action Learning in Practice* (Aldershot, Hants, England: Gower, 1983); Reginald W. Revans, *Developing Effective Managers: A New Approach to Business Education* (New York: Praeger, 1971); Russ Vince and Linda Martin, "Inside Action Learning: An Exploration of the Psychology

and Politics of the Action Learning Model," *Management Education and Development* 24:3 (1993), pp. 205–215; Mike Wallace, "Can Action Learning Live Up to Its Reputation?" *Management Education and Development* 21:2 (1990), pp. 89–103; Forest Wortham, "An Examination of Program Planning in Management Career Development Programs in Corporations: The Theory-Practice Dimension," unpublished doctoral dissertation (University Park, Pa.: The Pennsylvania State University, 1992).

Chapter 9

1. James L. Adams, *Conceptual Blockbusting: A Guide to Better Ideas,* 3rd ed. (Reading, Mass.: Addison-Wesley, 1986), p. 7.
2. Michael Hammer and James Champy, *Reengineering the Corporation: A Manifesto for Business Revolution* (New York: HarperBusiness, 1993), p. 32.
3. G. Rummler and A. Brache, "Managing the White Space," *Training* 28:1 (1991), pp. 55–70.

Chapter 10

1. William J. Rothwell and Henry J. Sredl, *The American Society for Training and Development Reference Guide to Professional Human Resource Development Roles and Competencies,* rev. ed. (Amherst, Mass.: Human Resource Development Press, 1992), II, p. 411.
2. Most recently, see Nancy Dixon, *Evaluation: A Tool for Improving HRD Quality* (Alexandria, Va: The American Society for Training and Development, 1990); Jack Phillips, *Handbook of Training Evaluation and Measurement Methods,* 2nd ed. (Houston: Gulf Publishing, 1991); and Leslie Rae, *How to Measure Training Effectiveness* (Brookfield, Vt.: Gower Publishing, 1991).
3. Paul Brauchle, "Costing Out The Value of Training," *Technical and Skills Training* 3:4 (1992), pp. 35–40; W. Cascio, *Costing Human Resources: The Financial Impact of Behavior in Organizations,* 2nd ed. (Boston: PWS-Kent Publishing, 1987); C. Fauber, "Use of Improvement (Learning) Curves to Predict Learning Costs," *Production and Inventory Management* 30:3 (1989), pp. 57–60; T. Jackson, *Evaluation: Relating Training to Business Performance* (San Diego: Pfeiffer and Company, 1989); L. Spencer, *Calculating Human Resource Costs and Benefits* (Somerset, N.J.: Wiley, 1986); Richard Swanson and Deane Gradous, *Forecasting Financial Benefits of Human Resource Development* (San Francisco: Jossey-Bass, 1988).
4. See, for instance, Jack Gordon, "Training Budgets: Recession Takes a Bite 1991," *Training,* 28:10 (1991), p. 38.
5. See Donald Kirkpatrick, "Techniques for Evaluating Training Pro-

grams," *Journal of the American Society for Training and Development* [now called *Training and Development*] 14:1 (1960), pp. 13–18.

6. R. Brinkerhoff, "The Success Case: A Low-Cost High-Yield Evaluation," *Training and Development Journal* 37:8 (1983), pp. 58–61.

7. See William J. Rothwell and H. C. Kazanas, *Planning and Managing Human Resources: Strategic Planning for Personnel Management*, rev. ed. (Amherst, Mass.: Human Resource Development Press, 1994).

Epilogue

1. For example, see especially C. Derr, C. Jones, and E. Toomey, "Managing High-Potential Employees: Current Practices in Thirty-Three U.S. Corporations," *Human Resource Management* 27:3 (1988), pp. 273–290; and *The Identification and Development of High Potential Managers* (Palatine, Ill.: Executive Knowledgeworks, 1987).

2. William J. Rothwell, H. C. Kazanas, and Darla Haines, "Issues and Practices in Management Job Rotation Programs as Perceived by HRD Professionals," *Performance Improvement Quarterly* 5:1 (1992), pp. 49–69.

3. William J. Rothwell and H. C. Kazanas, *Improving On-the-Job Training* (San Francisco: Jossey-Bass, in press).

4. R. Bard and S. Elliott, *The National Directory of Corporate Training Programs: Get Yourself Recruited by the Companies That Can Launch Your Career*, 2nd rev. and updated ed. (New York: Doubleday, 1988); S. Gilbert, *The Career Training Sourcebook: Where to Get Free, Low-Cost, and Salaried Job Training* (New York: McGraw Hill, 1993); William J. Rothwell and H. C. Kazanas, *The Complete AMA Guide to Management Development* (New York: AMACOM, 1993).

5. E. Lindsey, V. Homes and M. McCall, *Key Events in Executives' Lives* (Greensboro, N.C.: Center for Creative Leadership, 1987); M. Lombardo and R. Eichinger, *Eighty-Eight Assignments for Development in Place: Enhancing the Developmental Challenge of Existing Jobs* (Greensboro, N.C.: Center for Creative Leadership, 1989).

6. Jack Kondrasuk, "The Best Method to Train Managers . . . ," *Training and Development Journal* 33:8 (1979), pp. 46–48.

7. Rothwell, Kazanas, and Haines, "Issues and Practices," pp. 49–69.

8. Robert M. Tomasko, *Downsizing: Reshaping the Corporation for the Future* (expanded and updated) (New York: AMACOM, 1990).

9. Ibid., p. xvi.

10. But see Warren Boroson and Linda Burgess, "Survivors' Syndrome," *Across the Board* 29:11 (1992), pp. 41–45.

11. D. Heenan, "The Downside of Downsizing," *Across The Board* 27:5 (1990), pp. 17–19.

12. See, for instance, William J. Rothwell, "Administering the Climate Survey: A Toolkit," *Journal of Technical Writing and Communication* 15:4 (1985), pp. 323–338.

13. Thomas J. Krajci, "Pay That Rewards Knowledge," *HRMagazine* 35:6 (1990), pp. 58–60.

14. W. Johnson, *Workforce 2000: Work and Workers for the 21st Century* (Alexandria, Va: The Hudson Institute, 1987).

15. Ibid., p. 81.

16. Ibid.

17. See, for instance, Ann Morrison, *The New Leaders: Guidelines on Leadership Diversity in America* (San Francisco: Jossey-Bass, 1992), p. 1; Morrison, R. White, E. Van Velsor, and the Center for Creative Leadership, *Breaking the Glass Ceiling: Can Women Reach the Top of America's Largest Corporations?* (Reading, Mass.: Addison-Wesley, 1987); Michelle Martinez, "Glass Walls Must Tumble Before Ceiling Breaks," *HR News* 11:4 (1992), p. A3.

18. Michael J. Marquardt and Dean W. Engel, "HRD Competencies for a Shrinking World," *Training and Development* 47:5 (1993), pp. 59–65.

Index